WELLSPRINGS OF THE FAITH

To
Mary
The Mother of God

WELLSPRINGS
OF THE FAITH

*" You shall draw waters with joy out of
the Saviour's fountains " —Isaias xii, 3*

by

THE MOST REVEREND

JOHN C. McQUAID, D.D., M.A., D.Litt.

*Archbishop of Dublin,
Primate of Ireland*

DUBLIN : CLONMORE AND REYNOLDS LTD.
LONDON : BURNS OATS & WASHBOURNE LTD.

First Published 1956

Contents

PART I—PASTORAL LETTERS

I—BASIC CHRISTIAN TRUTHS

II—THE GREAT MEANS OF GRACE

III—THE LAST THINGS

IV—OUR BLESSED MOTHER

PART II

ADDRESSES ON EDUCATIONAL SUBJECTS

ACKNOWLEDGEMENTS

The Literary Editor of the present work wishes to express his deep gratitude to both the Editor of the *Irish Messenger* and the Editor of the *Irish Catholic Truth Society Series* for permission to use certain pamphlets published by their respective firms containing some of His Grace's Pastorals and addresses.

Editor's Preface

THIS collection of Pastoral Letters and certain addresses of His Grace, Most Rev. Dr. McQuaid, Archbishop of Dublin, has been made, not without reluctance on the part of their author, to meet the desires of many persons in the English-speaking world.

The Pastorals of His Grace have appeared in pamphlet form. They are now made available in the more worthy setting of a book. At a time when the old sanctities, religion and the inviolate unity of family life are losing their hold on the public mind, when the foundations of Catholicism in faith and practice are threatened, His Grace frankly and consistently sets forth the great basic truths of our religion, the grand lines of Catholic teaching on all that is of paramount importance for life here and hereafter. The treatment is essentially constructive. There is no partial glance at an aspect of Catholic teaching : there is always a complete survey of the truth that is to be exposed, a scientific but sympathetic and wisely moderate presentation of all that its acceptance involves.

The doctrines treated cover so wide a field that within the narrow limits of a preface no fitting summary is possible. The Pastorals are marked by a rare combination of accurate theology, enlightened devotion and spiritual insight, while the attractive practical applications to everyday life give them a value all their own. They are indeed a sacred treasury of Catholic truth, stirring the soul to prayerful acceptance even while they delight the mind with the delicate artistry of their literary form.

The content of the addresses furnishes an admirable summary of what we might call Catholic education and ideals. Many of them have had not only nation-wide publicity in Catholic papers and magazines, but are read and eagerly sought for all over the globe. Hence, on the representation of the Earl of Wicklow, His Grace graciously gave permission to have the collection of these addresses made and published with the Pastorals by the firm of Clonmore and Reynolds.

LITERARY EDITOR.

FEAST OF THE MOST HOLY ROSARY,
October, 1956.

PART ONE
PASTORAL LETTERS

Basic Christian Truths

Chapter I

THE GIFT OF FAITH

It is opportune, in the confusion of which we are now the witnesses, to consider the privilege that God has given us in the gift of the True Faith. If as infants we have received the virtue of Faith in Baptism, the value of God's favour may have never been grasped by us. Normally we set small store by that which has cost us neither money nor pain. We may perhaps understand somewhat the goodness of God towards us and yet fail to appreciate the obligations that have their origin in His gift. For, we are usually conscious of what is advantageous, but prefer not to be reminded of what is a duty. Now gratitude to God, Who has restored us to the life of grace, requires at all times that we should try to estimate aright the privilege of the Faith. To-day the circumstances in which we are called to live demand a deeper understanding and a more constant loyalty in the children of the One, True Faith.

To study the gift of Faith is in fact to fix our gaze more closely on Our Divine Redeemer, Jesus Christ. For He is in His own words The Truth[1] : the final revelation of God to men. Of old God had spoken " at sundry times and in divers manners by the Prophets ; in these days, last of all, He hath spoken to us by His Son."[2] Jesus Christ is also the Way by which we go into the vision of God. " No man cometh to the Father, but by Me."[3] He is equally the Life, Who has come that we may have life and have it more abundantly.[4] Not only has He the words of eternal life, but He Himself is the Resurrection and the Life, in Whom, if a man believe, he will not die for ever.[5]

Jesus Christ : The Way, The Truth, The Life.

[1]John, xiv, 6. [2]Hebr. i, 1–2. [3]John, xiv, 6. [4]John, x, 10. [5]John, vi, 69 ; xi, 25, 26.

St. John assures us that to them that believe in Jesus Christ, Our Divine Saviour has given the power to become the sons of God.[1] Now this life, which, as it were, creates us again,[2] is Sanctifying Grace. In Jesus Christ it is found in all its fulness : we receive of His fulness in Baptism, which is our new birth to the life of God.[3] Our knowledge of such a gift is not discovered by our unaided reason. We have come to know of it only from the lips of God made Man. He has told us that He came from heaven to suffer and to die, that this life might be restored to us on earth and continued after death, in the Heaven, where He Himself now is, in the unity of the Father and the Holy Ghost.[4]

Our Divine Lord Jesus Christ has, then, shed His Precious Blood to give back to us no mere human gift. Our destiny is not a progress of our natural powers, nor a completion of our human nature. " We are called and we are the sons of God."[5] We are given a share in the nature of God,[6] and the gift which raises our human nature up to the level of God is itself most truly something properly divine. It is a grace, in that it is freely given, a thing in no sense owed to us as human beings. It is sanctifying, in that it changes and makes holy the very essence of our being, with an excellence that is genuinely divine. It is a life, in which, while our nature never ceases to be human, we are transferred to a sphere and an activity that belong to the nature of God alone.

Baptism and Faith.

It is the Will of God that we should not possess the direct vision of Himself on earth ; no man hath ever seen God.[7] God requires that we should do the works that He has commanded. He that hath His commandments and keepeth them, he it is that loveth Him.[8] In reward, God will give us the supernatural destiny that He has assigned to us. Jesus Christ wills that they whom the Father has given Him, may be with Him and may see the glory which is His since before creation.[9] The works which can merit a supernatural destiny must be themselves of the same

[1]John, i, 12. [2]2 Cor., v, 17. [3]John, i, 16 ; iii, 5. [4]John, vi, 40 ; viii, 58 ; x, 28–30 ; xvii, 24. [5]1 John, iii, 1. [6]2 Peter, i 4. [7]John vi, 46. [8]John xiv, 21. [9]John vi, 40.

order : they must be divine. Hence the different powers of man by which he works must be raised to the supernatural sphere, and this is done in Baptism, when the supernatural virtues are infused into the faculties of our being. The first of these virtues is that of Faith ; for the first necessity of a man is to know with certainty the supernatural end for which God has made him. Into the intelligence of man, reborn by Sanctifying Grace, God pours the quality which disposes the intelligence permanently to accept as true all that God reveals. By means of it, we are enabled to give assent to all that God has revealed to man, for the reason that God is Truth and can neither deceive us nor be Himself deceived. The mysteries revealed by God cannot be known by merely human reason : they cannot be seen to bear within themselves the evidence of their own truth. They can be believed only by assenting to the word of God as true, and man can give that assent of his mind only through the grace of God. Under the action of grace,[1] the will disposes the intelligence to believe without doubting all that God has revealed.

Thus, Faith, by which we first come into relation with God Himself, is a pure gift of God.[2] We know of its existence only because God has revealed it. We receive it only because God infuses it. We cannot directly increase it : God of His bounty deepens it in our minds in gratuitous reward for the good acts that we perform. In this life, by reason of our state as wayfarers,[3] Faith remains dark. We see, indeed, but in a dark manner.[4] We have not yet the unclouded vision which belongs to heaven. Not that Faith is uncertain, for its motive is God Himself, the Primary Truth, than Whom nothing can be conceived more truthful. That which we know by human reason is better proportioned to our human strength of knowing. That which we know by Faith is not indeed God as human reason can search out His nature, but God as He is in Himself, God as He utterly surpasses human reason, God as He reveals Himself, and as only He can reveal

A Pure Gift of God.

[1] Hebr., x, 38 ; John xv, 5 ; Cor., iii, 5.   [2] Philipp., i, 29 ; Hebr., x, 38 ; John vi, 44.   [3] 2 Cor., v, 6.   [4] 1 Cor. xiii, 12.

Himself in His inner life. No greater certainty can be possessed by man than that of Faith which rests upon the changeless nature of God, essential Truth.

Faith the Beginning of Eternal Life.

Faith, then, in the words of Sacred Scripture, is the beginning of eternal life : for Our Divine Redeemer has declared : " This is eternal life that they may know Thee the only true God and Jesus Christ Whom Thou hast sent."[1] And again, St. Paul, explaining that we are the children of Faith, calls Faith the quality by which the things that we hope to possess in Heaven are, as it were, made present to us here below, the gift which shows those things to be true and certain which reason and sense can of themselves never know.[2] And the Council of Trent teaches that Faith is " The beginning of salvation, the foundation and root of all justification."[3]

It is easy then to understand the word of God the Holy Ghost : " Without Faith it is impossible to please God."[4] For where Faith does not yet exist, there is not even the beginning of knowledge and certainty concerning our supernatural end : there is no foundation of a temple in which the Holy Trinity can consent to dwell ; there is no root of supernatural life from which the sap of grace can flow into all the activities of man.

It is also easy to understand the terrible words of Our Divine Lord Jesus Christ : " He who believeth not, shall be condemned."[5]   God, the Creator of the human soul and Supreme Master of human life, has the right to command the subjection of our mind.   If He speaks, it is Eternal Truth that speaks ; and He has spoken by Jesus Christ, His only Son.   We are obliged to believe all that Jesus Christ has taught.

The Catholic Church, Infallible Teacher of the Faith.

That it might be possible for each and every man, in all succeeding ages, to know with certainty all that God has revealed, Our Divine Lord Jesus Christ has established the Church which can be known by all to be exclusively His own.[6]   That Church we know is the Catholic Church. To her He has entrusted all His doctrine, with the injunc-

---

[1]John, xvii, 3. [2]Hebr., xi, 1. [3]Sess., vi, cap. 8. [4]Hebr., xi, 6. [5]Mark, xvi, 16. [6]Mark, i, 17 ; Luke, 1, 2 ; John, xv, 16 ; Matt., xviii, 17 ; Luke, ix, 6 ; Matt., xviii, 18 and John, xx, 23 ; John, xvii, 20–32.

tion to teach all men to observe all things whatsoever He has commanded.[1] Within the Church He has established one source of teaching, to which He has promised His constant and efficacious guidance until the end of time. To Peter and to his successors He has guaranteed the power infallibly to preserve, set forth and guard, the whole deposit of the Faith confided to the Church.[2] To Peter are given the keys which open the Kingdom of Heaven[3] : the keys of Faith in doctrine and of Faith in morals. For, as the Kingdom of Heaven can be revealed to us only in the doctrine of the Faith, so the Kingdom of Heaven can be entered only through sanctity of life which is based on the teaching of Jesus Christ.[4]

When therefore on the teaching authority of the Church we accept the doctrine of Faith and morals, we bend our minds and wills to the authority of Jesus Christ Himself. To young and old, ignorant and learned, the same unvarying truth is given for acceptance, and each assents with a faith that is supernatural, certain and complete. There cannot be in the Church's teaching an inner body of doctrine which only the few can grasp. There is no Saint, however holy, whose knowledge passes beyond the boundary of the Faith, for God Whom we love in Charity is known to us only by the virtue of supernatural Faith. There can be but one code of morals from which no class, however gifted, is exempt. Every member of the Church must give to God in Faith the homage of the total subjection of his being. In turn, he receives the full and uncorrupted heritage of the children of the Church, which is none other than the possession of God in Faith and Charity.

" Let that mind be in you which was in Christ Jesus."[5] *Docility to* It may be truly said that all our duty consists in hearkening *Teaching of* to the Church which declares to us the mind of Jesus Christ. *the Church.* Since we have been reborn to God by Sanctifying Grace, we are obliged to live habitually by that divine life. We are equally bound to bring all the activity of life under the control of the teaching of the Church. All things

[1]Matt., xxviii, 18–20. [2]Matt., xxviii, 20 ; John, i, 42 ; Mark, iii, 16 ; Matt., xviii, 17–18 ; John. xiv, 16–17 ; John, xxi, 15–17 ; Acts, xx, 28. [3]Matt., xvi, 19. [4]John, xvii, 17, 19. [5]Philip., ii, 5.

must be brought beneath the headship of Christ.[1] Every sphere of human knowledge, every object of human effort must, in a Catholic, be marked with the seal of Faith. In Baptism we have been set aside for ever in the true religion of Christ for the worship of God. The Sovereign God claims our full acknowledgement, without distinction of what is called religious or profane. Christ must be all in all.[2] And other foundation no man can lay save only that which God Himself has laid : Christ Jesus.[3]

Catholic Upbringing of Children.

Those Catholics then gravely err who consider that they may accept from the Church what in their view pertains to religious duty and for the rest, follow the teaching or caprice of human beings in what concerns their social or political or civic life. In particular, we draw attention to the most grave obligation binding on every Catholic to accept the legislation of the Church in everything that concerns the Catholic upbringing of children. Faith is the most precious because the most fundamental gift of God. It is therefore a crime for parents to expose their children to a weakening or a loss of Faith. No consideration of mere wealth or social exclusiveness or pretended culture can justify the sending of a child to a school which the Church does not sanction as approved and safe. And may we warn the Faithful that the atmosphere of a school may be more pernicious for a Catholic, because more subtly hostile, than the instruction given or the culture practised. The Church is gentle, after the manner of her Divine Founder, but, in regard to those who knowingly refuse to God His rights in Catholic education and scandalize the children and the immature, her deliberate severity is not different from that of Jesus Christ Himself.

Catholic Law on Marriage.

In the question too, of marriage, the Church most severely forbids marriage with non-Catholics. Her purpose is to safeguard fully the gift of Faith. It is to no purpose to point to marriages for which a dispensation has been obtained and of which the children have been honourably reared as Catholics. The danger to the Faith,

---

[1]Ephes., i, 10 ; 1 Cor., x, 31 ; Col., iii, 17. [2]Col., iii, 11. [3]1 Cor., iii, 11.

arising from the absence of unity in that which is most intimate to a human being, the supernatural knowledge and love of God, must always be regarded as present. The practice of Faith can be abandoned, and the gift of Faith frequently has been lost, as a result of marriage with a non-Catholic.

Further, it must be taken by Catholics to be an indisputable principle that the Church has the innate right to found properly Catholic associations for purposes of social charity. She is the Mother and exemplar of every form of charity. She has indeed founded her institutions in a supernatural love of the afflicted, that is evident on every page of history, but it must be clearly borne in mind that her charity has no other basis than the Faith of Jesus Christ. She will always demand for her members that, in illness or in health, they be treated with reverence for their sacred character of children reborn in Baptism to the life of God. She will spare no sacrifice, more especially in regard to children and the aged, solely because She has the vision of a supernatural destiny and must treat this world as a pilgrimage and probation. Purely human works and human welfare associations may be naturally good or even noble ; but since Jesus Christ has come on earth and revealed to us the obligation to accept His teaching, Catholics have the right and duty to group themselves in associations of social welfare that unequivocally base their aims and methods on the supernatural doctrine and practice of the Church.

Spiritual Charity based on Faith.

There is a danger to the Faith against which we would warn all Catholics, most particularly parents and teachers. We refer to the attitude of mind which forms the background of very much that is portrayed in literature and drama and especially the films. It is a spirit which acts as if God did not exist. It exalts mere man and worships human progress. It assumes that there is no hereafter. It does not reckon with a judgment by God after death.[1] It takes for granted that only this life is given us and that therefore the aim of life is the acquisition of wealth, with

Danger of Modern Attitude towards God's Teaching

[1] Rom., xiv., 10.

the power that wealth brings of satisfying lust. In such a scheme, happiness is more or less the grossness of sensuality. If such a doctrine were openly preached, it would be energetically resisted. But the teaching is conveyed by assumption ; it educates through emotion ; its appeal is conveyed to the senses by every device of human genius. The teaching is pagan. Our ideal of life is to be meek and humble of heart like our Divine Teacher. Our Divine Lord Jesus Christ has declared that any man who claims to love Him, must, unless he be a liar, keep His commandments. He has taught that no man can be His disciple, if he take not up his cross daily and follow in the path traced out by Him.

Duty of Parents and Teachers.

It is the sacred duty of parents and teachers to guard the young from the infection of corrupt ideas and by firm control to exercise vigilance over their reading and companions. In particular, they ought to take care to prevent the young from attending cinemas and theatres where paganism is subtly insinuated. And we would ask parents and teachers to ward off the insensitive vulgarity of mind and dress and gesture which now tends to manifest itself even in Catholic homes and schools. The nobility and graciousness of the culture which is Catholic is a heritage within the grasp of every member of the Church. There is no remedy for the current paganism and its consequent vulgarity except reverence for the things of God which is taught us by the Faith.

Love of Jesus Christ Crucified.

That we may the more constantly remember how great a gift is given us in the One, True Faith, we would urge all the Faithful to take the habit of frequently reading the Gospel narrative of the Sacred Passion and of cultivating a deep and contrite love of Jesus Christ Crucified. No one can look upon the Crucifix without seeing in it the proof that it was for us men and our salvation that God came down on earth. It is now easy to know that God is infinitely good when we see the torture and death that He most lovingly endured to win for us salvation. His Passion and Death are the permanent rebuke to human sensuality. Every manner of sin conspired to bring about His death, but in death He conquered the power of evil. There is no temptation or habit of sin that can resist His grace. His death is our peace for it opened heaven to us, and now we can look forward to the tranquillity of death in His grace and the possession of His own happiness for eternity.

He who has learned to know and love the Crucifix will the more fully understand the Mass. It is within our power, day after day, in a manner to assist at Calvary in the Holy Sacrifice of the Mass, where Jesus Christ renews the offering of Himself as Man to God, upon the Altar, in an unbloody manner, by the ministry of His priests. Only they who have meditated much, in a spirit of loving Faith, upon the Crucifix, can properly, in their little measure, enter into the perfect dispositions of Jesus Christ, Victim of infinite worth and Principal Offerer, Who as man acknowledges the sovereign dominion of God and returns Him adequate thanks for all His benefits.

It is not possible for a Catholic, who by the aid of grace has come to know and love the gift of Faith, to separate in thought and reverence Jesus Christ Crucified from His Blessed Mother. She stands beside the Cross, sharing His martyrdom. On the Cross He gave Her to us that she might distribute all the grace which by His death He has won for us. Of His fulness in truth we have all received, grace upon grace.[1] And first among graces, which Our Blessed Lady is empowered by Him to give, is the grace of Faith by which Christ her divine Son dwells in our hearts.[2] *Love of Our Blessed Lady.*

[1]John, i, 16. [2]Eph., iii, 17.

Chapter II

THE FALL AND OUR REDEMPTION

Forgetfulness of God. THE suffering that in our days has touched the lives of unnumbered people forces us to think upon the mystery of God's dealings with His creatures. In times of peace we are inclined to take for granted the Providence of God. Our plans for living with the success that we ambition absorb our daily thought and energy. When we pray to Almighty God, it is too often with the desire, to bend, if we may, the power of God in our direction. We would say, were we asked, that of course we were submissive to God's Providence, that our plans were meant to work in full accord with God's intentions, that we desired, in fact, only the accomplishment of God's will. Too frequently we are only set upon doing our own will.

It requires the touch of God's hand upon us in suffering to prove to us how deep-rooted is our self-sufficient attitude before God. In grievous pain, in the loss of goods, in the death of those dear to us, we are suddenly reminded that we cannot rule our own lives as we would wish. God uses such moments to teach us that we are only creatures, and the knowledge is bitterly chastening to our pride. God has seemed to us so distant that we have forgotten His Sovereignty. He has been invisible and therefore we have not reckoned with His presence. But, in the pain of others, and more especially in the suffering of our own souls, we are compelled to realise that we are only the servants of an absolute Master.

Beauty of God the Creator. It is a very great grace to know that we are not necessary to God ; that, in truth, we might never have existed at all. God is the only Being Who must exist. From all eternity, He exists, Three Divine Persons, in unity of nature. He alone has no beginning and cannot have an end. He alone owes His existence to no other being. He is existence ; and all things else that are, can exist only in utter dependence

20

upon Him. In Him exists the infinity of all that is perfection.
He cannot be subject to any change. He cannot be measured
in any way by time. He cannot be limited by space. To all
creatures He is ever present, inasmuch as all are subject
to His power, are open to His gaze and are held in being by
His hand. What could such a Being gain from the creation
of any one of us ?

God could have created or not created. He could have
called this world or another world into existence. With
absolute freedom He chose to call this universe out of
nothingness. But when His eternal plan was executed, no
change appeared, or could appear, in the unruffled peace
of the inner life of God. Almighty Wisdom, Power and
Love were not increased by the order and perfection of
the Universe. Rather, the only purpose of the creature could
be to serve the glory of Almighty God by showing forth
His Truth, His Goodness and His Beauty.

Man, who should be in God's design the Master of the
earth, was formed that he might more intimately reveal
the richness of the Creator's nature. " Let us make man
to our image and likeness,"[1] a being capable of knowing
God from the things that God had made and of loving
God from the sight of the goodness that he saw diffused
throughout creation. From the slime of the earth God
made man's body, but the soul of man God Himself breathed
into him : a masterpiece of God's wisdom and creative
love, intelligent and free, but as much a creature as the tiniest
ant or the smallest pebble. Our pride, then, in presence
of the Creator is an utter failure to acknowledge the fact
that we are merely creatures.

But our indebtedness to God is deeper still : man was *The*
created not a mere human being, but from the first instant *Goodness of God Our*
was given a share in the nature of God Himself. Can any *Father.*
fact give us a wider or deeper insight into the goodness
of our Creator than the mystery of the love that created man
in the state of grace ? At the first instant of his origin, by the
freest bounty of God, man was given a gift which completely
surpassed his created nature, and all that his created nature

[1]Gen. i, 26.

could require for its perfection or could by merely human power attain. On earth to share already in the life of God and, earth's sojourn completed, to be given at once the unclouded Vision of the Blessed Trinity was the creative design of God in man's regard. " What is man," cries out the Psalmist, " that Thou art mindful of him, or the son of man that Thou visitest him ? " [1] It is good to humble ourselves by recounting our limitless debts to God.

The story of God the Creator's goodness is not ended. That man might live more perfectly as a child of God, another bounty was added to his nature. His sensitive nature was made completely subject to his reason in such wise that he was not hindered in the accomplishment of God's will, nor urged to evil. His body, which of its nature was corruptible, was rendered free from the necessity of death. His state on earth was one of unbroken happiness, for no bodily ills assailed him nor grief of mind oppressed him : man's life was an untroubled harmony of order. And all this endowment of grace and of grace's accompanying ornaments was held by our First Parents in trust for all the human race that was to spring from them. One precept was enjoined, in proof and acknowledgement of God's absolute Sovereignty. Surely an easy precept, in view of man's deepest intimacy with God, his surpassing knowledge of the Creator and his burning love of God Whom he saw to be so good.

Ingratitude of God's Children.

And yet, man rejected God. " Who," says the Sacred Scripture, " understandeth sin ? " [2] The " mystery of wickedness " [3] is the name by which God the Holy Ghost describes it. To us who are now so self-sufficient it is a most salutary rebuke to our pride to know that at one stroke we shattered the creative plan of God. On the first occasion on which we sought to plan our life apart from God, we broke the order of His All-seeing Wisdom and His Almighty Love. Over against the order of the changeless God we set our puny effort to reach our end, apart from the Creator and by our unaided efforts. The goal that we reached has been the forfeit of our supernatural life, revolt

[1]Ps. viii, 5.   [2]Ps. xviii. 13.   [3]Thess. ii. 7.

of the senses, illness, pain, death and the wretchedness of
life. We chose, instead of the sweet friendship of a child of
God, the captivity of hell and unending exile from the
bosom of our Creator. " Know thou," says God, " and
see, that it is an evil and a bitter thing for thee to have
left the Lord thy God."[1]

The sin which we have committed, and of which we *Restoration*
are still capable, is truly a mystery. The insistent love *of Fallen*
of God, we may reverently say, is a more humiliating *World.*
mystery still. But the aspect of man's fall which terrifies
one most is that, of himself, he was radically incapable of
repairing his own ruin. We read that man hid himself
from God.[2] But the infinite mercy of God sought us out,
not indeed to overwhelm the creature of His hands by a
revelation of His power, but only to rebuke, with unchanging calm. And then, to man, who could not in the
least avail to restore himself, God promised redemption
by His Son made Man, to be born of the Immaculate
Virgin.[3] Of a truth, we shall need eternity to reach some
understanding of the mystery of God's love.

Even if we had lived in the days before the Incarnation, when man was still bowed to earth in mind and
heart, and only with pain could lift himself up to see the
things of God, none the less our pride could not have
justified itself, had we but remembered the proofs of the
surpassing goodness of the Creator. How shall we explain
our forgetfulness of our true position as merest creatures
and as sinners redeemed, now that Our Divine Redeemer
has lived with us on earth ? The more we reflect upon the
bounty of God to us, the deeper ought we to sink in lowliness before Him. For now we know with certainty that
God Himself in human flesh has wiped away and adequately
repaired [4] our infinite offence against the Creator. God
Incarnate is become our Teacher.[5] Looking on Him Who
has united our poor nature with the divine in His own
Person, now we can hope to be united eternally with the
Divinity. Hearing the words of life [6] from the lips of

---

[1]Jer. ii, 19.   [2]Gen. iii, 8.   [3]Gen. iii, 15.   [4]John i, 29 ; I Cor. xv, 3 ;
Hebr. ii, 17.   [5]Matt. ii, 29–30.   [6]John vi, 64 and 69.

Absolute Truth, we can trust Him and follow Him in the path wherein He Himself has walked before us.[1] In particular, it is easy for us, who are weak and sinful, to look on Jesus Christ Who is like to us in all things, sin excepted,[2] and cling to God in the loving friendship of divine charity.[3]

True, He is no longer seen on earth in human form ; but He is found in countless Tabernacles, as truly present as He is in Heaven. His word is not heard as formerly in Palestine, but for almost two thousand years His Church has spoken with the certitude of His voice. We cannot claim ignorance of the duty, not merely to think according to the teaching of the Church, but also and more especially, to live according to the dictates of the Faith, in our homes, in our avocations and in our social life. The excuse does not exist for us that we do not know the difference between right and wrong, for the Faith has shown us in the Church the one supreme Arbiter on earth of moral law, established by God and sustained by His efficacious power.[4] We have, besides, the unfailing series of eminently holy persons whom the grace of Jesus Christ has given as models to the world,[5] within the fold of His one true Church. Our privileged position as members of that Church makes still more grave our heedlessness, in face of the absolute rights of our Creator.

Man's Stubborn Resistance. There is, in addition, the individual Providence of God in regard to every soul. Each man, if he reflects, can recall a history of God's mercy as special to him as if he alone existed in the universe. Baptism, by which the life of grace is first given and the soul is set aside for the service of God in the true religion of Christ, is only the birth to a life that is penetrated with the bounties of our Divine Redeemer. Not the least is the grace of a careful education in a Catholic home, wherein the most holy image of Mary guards the purity of the children. The Sacrament of Penance renews, one might say unceasingly, the forgiveness of God. The Blessed Eucharist received, if one wishes daily, unites the soul most intimately with Jesus Christ. The Sacrament of Confirmation imparts the character or power to live

[1] John xiii, 15 ; xiv, 6.   [2] Hebr. iv, 15.   [3] John xiv, 21 and 23.   [4] Matt, xvi, 18–19 ; xxviii, 18–20.   [5] Acts xiii, 47 ; Matt. v, 14–16 ; Ephes, v, 8.

manfully in the Faith of Jesus Christ. There is no state of
life which is not sanctified by the special grace of the
Redeemer. And at the end there is the Last Anointing to
wipe away the trace of sin and comfort the soul in its final
struggle. In truth, the secret history of each soul is the
story of God's unending patience, as He repairs and purifies
and sanctifies the creature of His choice.

These are the truths of God's dealing with mankind.
Over against these facts we are obliged to set the truth
that man accepts with deep reluctance the sovereignty
of God, and too often, only in the instantaneous judgment after death, fully admits his arrogance and disordered
love of self. It is not then a matter for wonder that the
Church so frequently in her prayers and ceremonies calls
us to penance for our wrongful pride. And God Himself
does not cease to remind us by sufferings of every sort that
we are only pilgrims. While yet there is time to pray, the
most fitting attitude for man is to kneel abased at the thought
of God, Changeless, Almighty, everlastingly Good. And
nowhere can each of us more adequately find his proper
place before God than when, united with Our Saviour, we
kneel assisting at the Holy Sacrifice. From the first words
of Holy Mass we are obliged to bow down, admitting that
we are sinners. At the Offertory, we crave forgiveness for
our numberless sins and stumblings and negligences.
Throughout the Canon, we entreat Almighty God to
accept us, not for our merits, but because of the infinite
worth of the Victim and the Principal Offerer, Jesus Christ.
The Holy Sacrifice itself, which truly represents and
commemorates the Sacrifice of the Cross, reminds us,
while it applies to our souls the virtue of the Cross, that
our wickedness has cost Jesus Christ the shedding
of His Precious Blood. " In union chiefly," says the Canon,
" with the glorious Virgin Mary, Mother of God, with
the Apostles and the Martyrs," even we can enter into
the dispositions of Jesus Christ,[1] Who as man most fully
acknowledges the absolute sovereignty of God the Father
and offers Him completely adequate thanks for all His

[1]John viii, 29 ; Heb. x, 9–10.

benefits to mankind. Thus we, who of ourselves are nothing, can, while assisting at the Holy Sacrifice, already imitate the action of the Saints in heaven, whom Sacred Scripture shows us casting their crowns of merit before God in ceaseless adoration.

Childlike Submission with Mary.

That attitude is very contrary to the normal arrogance of man's daily life. We may well ask how is it possible for us to attain the purity of understanding and humility of heart that will enable us to acknowledge in great things and in small the Mastership of God. The Canon of the Mass has answered our question : " in union chiefly with the glorious Virgin Mary, Mother of God, by whose merits and prayers grant that in all things we may be guarded by Thy protecting aid : and therefore, we entreat Thee, accept this Offering of us Thy servants." The heart of man has every need of God's surrounding grace that it may be pure and lowly and reflective. To Mary the Mother of Our Divine Redeemer it has been granted to obtain for us and distribute every grace. For the sake of Her Divine Son at the first instant of her conception Mary was preserved from even the trace of sin. She can avail to win for us purity, freedom from the disorder of passion that blinds us to God [1] while it delivers us up to senseless pride. In the first moment of the Incarnation, Mary abased herself before God as the slave of the Lord,[2] and in the Canticle exulted only in the triumph of God Who had done great things to her.[3] She can now impetrate for us the grace to subject our minds and hearts and wills in every phase of life, to the mind of Jesus Christ which is revealed to us by His One True Church. Mary kept in her heart the memory of all that God had done for her.[4] She can obtain for us the saving grace of a recollected heart, which, whatever our daily occupation and whatever the trials that assail us, turns from the deceptive emptiness of everything created,[5] and serenely fixes its will on God.[6]

[1]I Cor. ii, 14. [2]Luke i, 38. [3]Luke i, 49. [4]Luke ii, 19. [5]Wisd. iv, 12. [6]*Cf.* I John iii, 1–2 ; I Cor. xiii, 12.

Chapter III

ATONEMENT

THE season of Lent has been established by the Church *The Message of Lent.*
to remind us of our true position before God. The obligation
of fasting for forty days painfully checks our inclination
to make the end of life our comfort and our pleasures. The
duty of almsgiving subtracts the means by which we can
satisfy our selfishness and turns our eyes upon the suffering
of our neighbour. The penance of prayer submits our mind
and will to God in the lowliness of contrition for our sins.
Meditation on the Passion of Our Divine Redeemer teaches
us the malice of sin which required the death on the Cross
of God made man.

During Lent we suffer, but it is not, for the most part, *The Malice of Sin.*
because of sin. Easily we admit that sin is the root of all
our sorrow. Yet that most keenly hurts us which touches
us ourselves in body or in soul : pain of body, contempt
for our qualities, the injustice of ingratitude. The evil
of our own sin and of the sin of others as an offence against
God is, we shall admit, hidden from us. " Who can understand sins ? "[1] asks the Psalmist. Only God, and they, in
part, who, by the light of Faith, know God. Because of the
weakness of our faith we do not suffer at the thought of
God being outraged. We have grave need of faith to appreciate the malice of sin ; we have need of love for God
Whom sin offends, and love for our neighbour, whom sin
can destroy in Hell. Only from Faith and Charity is born
the sorrowful desire to repair our own sin and the sin of
others.

The teaching of our holy Faith upon the necessity of *The Need of Divine Atonement.*
a divine Redeemer brings home most clearly the limitless
wickedness of sin.[2] Our sin is indeed but the act of a limited

[1]Ps. xviii, 13. [2]St. Thomas, *Summa Theologiae*, Ia. IIae. qq. 86, 87 ;
III. q. 1, a. 2, 3 ; *cf.* III q. 46, a. 1 ; *cf.* III *Sent. dist.* 20, q. 1 ad 2 ; *De Verit.*
q. 28 ad 2 ; Opusc. 3, c. 7 ; *cf.* Pius XI, *Miserentissimus Redemptor.*

creature, yet in that act of a finite mind and will there is a certain infinity of malice. For the offence of our sin is measured by the infinite holiness of God, Who is disobeyed and dishonoured. No creature, no matter what his holiness, could offer to God an atonement that would be anything but limited. Were one to heap on such a creature the pain of all the world or lend him the sorrow of all human hearts, his reparation would still be merely human : it would not be adequate to satisfy the infinite sanctity of God. Only one remedy for the limitless malice of our sin has been found : the love of God Who sent us His only-begotten Son to die upon the Cross, Jesus Christ, Our Divine Redeemer.

The Divine Redeemer, Jesus Christ.

Because Jesus Christ is God, His actions are those of a Divine Person. Because Jesus Christ is Man, His actions are properly human, but they are of infinite avail, by reason of the Divine Person of the Word Incarnate. Thus, at length, was it possible for human nature, which had offended God, to offer to God, through Jesus Christ, a satisfaction that is infinite in value. The homage thus offered to God in the human nature assumed by Jesus Christ is more than equal to the outrage of human sin. The atonement to the infinite majesty of God at last is accepted as adequate and even superabundant. The burnt-offerings of the Old Law had reminded man that, because of sin, he was worthy of death : they had not availed to take away his sin or atone for sin to God.[1] " Sacrifice and oblation Thou wouldst not ; but a body Thou hast fitted to me," wrote the Psalmist of the future Redeemer. " Then said I, Behold I come. In the head of the book it is written of Me that I should do Thy will, O God." [2] And the will of God required that Jesus Christ, the Divine Redeemer and the only Mediator, should die for our redemption. " Thus it is written and thus it behoved Christ to suffer." [3] " Therefore doth the Father love Me," said Our Divine Lord, " because I lay down my life." [4]

The Lamb of God.

It is a mystery hidden from eternity that God should become man to atone for our sins, and that His atonement

---

[1]*Summa Theol.*, Ia. IIae. q. 102, a. 3, ad. 5.   [2]Hebr. x, 5–7.   [3]Luke xxiv, 46.   [4]John x, 17.

should have been decreed in suffering and death.[1] Our
Divine Lord explained to the disciples on the road to
Emmaus that already Moses and the Prophets had spoken
of a Messias Who should suffer.[2] The knowledge was
hidden even from the chosen Apostles. Isaias had written
of the innocent Victim who should bear our sins. New
things God would declare, and before they should spring
forth He would make men to hear them. Little had men
hearkened to the declaration that the Saviour should
be " despised and the most abject of men, a man of sorrows
and acquainted with infirmity, on whom the Lord hath
laid the iniquity of us all." [3] The Angel had said that He
should save His people from their sins.[4] Our Divine
Redeemer had applied to Himself the Prophecy of Isaias.[5]
Very clearly He had foretold His impending Passion and
Death. He spoke the word openly. " Lay you up in your
hearts these words," he had warned, " for it shall come
to pass that the Son of Man shall be delivered into the hands
of men." [6] He had asserted that He would give His life as a
ransom for men.[7] He had described Himself at the Last
Supper, just before His death, as a consecrated Victim
offered in sacrifice for those whom He loved.[8] He had
died before the eyes of His Apostles, and yet even they had
not understood that God demanded the redemption of the
Cross.[9] Only when He had risen from the dead and sent
the Holy Ghost to bring back all things to their memory
did the Apostles and Disciples understand the suffering
Redeemer.[10]

Jesus Christ in delivering Himself up to the Divine
Justice satisfied for our sins.[11] He was offered because
He willed it.[12] In the Sacred Scriptures when there is
mention of Christ's satisfaction, the emphasis is placed
on His obedience to the Father and on His love for men,
wherewith He undertook the Cross. " God commendeth

The Satisfaction of the Precious Blood.

[1]Eph. iii, 9 ; Col. i, 26 ; 1 Tim. iii, 16. [2]Luke xxiv, 27. [3]Is. xlii, 9 ;
liii, 3, 6 ; Matt. viii, 17. [4]Matt, i, 21. [5]Luke iv. 18–21. [6]Luke ix, 44 ;
22 ; xvii, 25 ; Matt. xx, 17–19 ; Mark x, 32–34. [7]Matt. xx, 28 ; Mark x,
45. [8]John xvii, 19. [9]John xx, 9. [10]John xiv, 26 ; Acts ii, 36 ; iv, 10–12 ;
v. 30–31 ; vii, 52 ; viii, 32–35 ; x, 42–43. [11]Council of Trent, Sess. vi,
c. 7 ; cf. *Summa Theol.*, iii, q. 48, a. 2. [12]Is. liii, 7 ; 1 Peter ii, 23 ;
John x, 17–18 ; xviii, 11 ; Hebr. ix, 14.

His charity to us," writes St. Paul, " because, when as
yet we were sinners according to the time, Christ died
for us. Much more therefore being now justified by His
blood shall we be saved from wrath through Him, by
whom we have now received reconciliation." [1] " Surely,"
the Prophet had written, " He hath borne our infirmities
and carried our sorrows : He was wounded for our iniquities ; He was bruised for our sins," [2] " because
God hath first loved us and sent His Son to be a propitiation
for our sins." [3] " Christ died once for our sins, the just for
the unjust that He might offer us to God." [4] " The Son of
God," urges St. Paul, " loved me and delivered Himself
for me." [5] " He gave Himself for us that He might redeem
us from all iniquity." [6] How complete that satisfaction
of Jesus Christ, nay rather, how limitless the ransom paid
for us must be, is seen when we consider that, by the union
of the divine and human nature in the Word, the Passion
and Death of Jesus Christ take on the divine dignity of the
Incarnate Son of God.

*The Merit
of the
Precious
Blood.*

By shedding His Precious Blood as the price of our
Redemption, Our Divine Redeemer has truly satisfied
Divine Justice and has freed us from the slavery of sin
and the Demon.[7] " Now is the judgment of the world,
now shall the prince of this world be cast out." [8] " God
hath delivered us from the power of darkness." [9] But
the Redemption has meant infinitely more than the mere
removal of our sin. By the merit of the Life and Passion
and Death of Jesus Christ,[10] we have been " translated
by God into the Kingdom of the Son of His love, in Whom
we have redemption through His blood." [11] " He bore
our sins in His body on the Cross, that we being dead to
sin should live to justice." [12] He came to do the will of
God, " in the which will, we are sanctified, by the oblation
of the body of Jesus Christ once." [13] " He became
obedient unto death," writes St. Paul, " even the death

[1]Rom. v. 8. *Cf.* John viii, 28–29. [2]Is. liii, 4–5. [3]1 John iv, 10. [4]1 Pet. iii,
18. [5]Gal. ii, 20. [6]Tit. ii, 14. [7]Col. i, 14, 20 ; Eph. i, 7 ; 1 Cor. vi, 20 ;
Gal. iii, 13 ; Hebr. ix, 12, 28. *Summa Theol.*, iii. q. 49, a. 1–4. [8]John
xii, 31 ; *cf.* John xv, 30 ; xvi, 11. [9]Col. i, 13 ; *cf.* Gal. i, 4. [10]Council of
Trent, Sess. VI. 7. *Summa Theol.*, iii. q. 48, a. 1 ; *Quodlib.* 2. a. 2.
[11]Col. i, 13, 22 ; Rom. vi, 6. [12]1 Petr. ii, 24. [13]Hebr. x, 10.

of the Cross, for which cause God hath exalted Him and given Him a name which is above all names." [1] Thus is He become " to all that obey Him a cause of eternal salvation." [2]

"As in Adam all die, so in Christ all shall be made alive." [3] The grace which Adam had lost for us has been restored by Our Divine Redeemer. Not only are we become the people of God, [4] who have achieved His mercy, we are also His friends, even His children, by sanctifying grace. "Now we know the grace of Our Lord Jesus Christ, that being rich, He became poor for our sakes, in the lowliness of His death, that through His poverty we might be rich." [5] "Most great and precious promises," writes St. Peter, "hath He given us that by these you may be made partakers of the divine nature." [6] "We have not received the spirit of bondage in fear, but the spirit of adoption of sons whereby we cry Abba, Father, and if sons, heirs also, heirs indeed of God and joint heirs with Christ." [7] "This now is the will of God your sanctification;" [8] and our holiness in Christ makes of us, both body and soul, the temple of God. "Know you not that you are the temple of God and that the Spirit of God dwelleth in you." [9] "The Spirit of Truth shall abide with you and shall be in you." [10]

The Fruits of the Precious Blood.

When we look at the Crucifix we scarcely think of all that the satisfaction and merit of our Divine Redeemer has won for men. It is the sign of salvation for the whole human race. "Christ Jesus has come into this world to save sinners, the propitiation for our sins, and not for our sins only, but also for those of all the world." [11] He himself had promised that, if He were lifted up in sacrifice on the Cross, He would draw all things to Himself. [12] We have been drawn to Him by the grace imparted in the Sacraments. To those who are willing to receive Him in faith and love, He has given the power to become the sons of God. [13] The Redemption is not

The Lesson of the Crucifix.

[1] Philipp. ii, 8–9. [2] Hebr. v, 9. [3] 1 Cor. xv, 22. [4] 1 Petr. ii, 9. [5] 2 Cor. viii, 9; cf. Rom. viii, 32. [6] 2 Pet. i, 4. [7] Rom. viii, 15, 17. [8] 1 Thess. iv, 3. [9] 1 Cor. iii, 16–17; vi. 19; Rom. v. 5; viii, 11. [10] John xiv, 17. [11] 1 Tim. i, 15; 1 John ii, 2. [12] John xii, 32. [13] John i, 12.

forced on us ; it is made effective only by our co-operation with the grace of Jesus Christ.[1] " Unless a man be born again of water and the Holy Ghost, he cannot enter into the kingdom of God," merited by Jesus Christ.[2] By the Sacrament of Baptism we are incorporated into the life of our Divine Redeemer. He Himself has described to us the intimacy of that grace as the sap which vivifies the Vine and all its tiny branches. " I am the Vine," said Jesus Christ, " you are the branches. Remain in Me. As the branch cannot bear fruit of itself unless it remains in the Vine, so neither you, unless you remain in Me."[3] So close is that mysterious union that St. Paul can speak of Christ as life : " To me to live is Christ."[4] And in the last discourse before His death, Our Divine Redeemer teaches us that this union by grace is the reason for which God the Father loves us even as He loves His Son : " that they all may be one as Thou, Father, in Me, and I in Thee ; that they also may be one in Us. I in them, and Thou in Me : that they may be made perfect in one : and the world may know that Thou hast sent Me and hast loved them as Thou hast loved Me."[5]

Our Union with Christ Crucified.

To remain in Christ by grace there is an essential requisite: that we keep His Commandments. Not only must we accept Him by faith, but with our heart and will we must follow Him in charity. We must bear fruit, and the fruit of the branch cannot be different from the fruit of the Vine. " Remain in My love. If ye shall have kept My command-ments, you shall remain in My love."[6] What the pattern of that life in Christ must be is shown to us by Jesus Christ Himself. Immediately after He had begun to teach His Apostles that the Son of Man must suffer many things and be rejected and be killed, our Divine Lord laid down the only way in which any man can follow Him : " If any man will come after Me, let him deny himself and take up his cross daily and follow Me."[7] In the pain of penance we must follow the Man of Sorrows, for we have sinned and it is our

---

[1]Council of Trent, Sess. VI, c. 3 ; *Summa Theol.*, iii, q. 49, a. 1 ; *Summa contra Gent.*, iv, 55 ; 2 Cor. vii, 1, 10. [2]John iii, 5. [3]John xv, 4–5. [4]Philipp. i, 21. [5]John xvii, 21–23. [6]John xv, 9–10, 16. [7]Luke ix, 22–23.

sins that once He bore in His body. In a sense, we must
share His passion and death : " we are buried together
with Him by baptism unto death, that as Christ is risen
from the dead by the glory of the Father, so we also may
walk in newness of life." [1] In the measure in which we
shall have crucified the flesh and its lusts,[2] we shall merit
the peace of His resurrection in the serenity of love. " Come
to Me," He has promised, "all you that labour and are
heavy burdened and I will refresh you, for My yoke is sweet
and My burden light." [3]

The Crucifix has still a wider meaning : not alone is
each of us drawn to Christ by the merits of His death,
but all men are incorporated into one body of which Jesus
Christ is Head.[4] " You are the Body of Christ and
members of member." [5] The mysterious union of
grace between Christ and the faithful makes of the Church
one thing with Jesus Christ. " As the body is one and
hath many members ; and all the members, whereas they
are many, yet are one body ; so also is Christ." [6] Under
the influence of the Holy Ghost, whom Jesus Christ communicates to the Church, the faithful increase in likeness
to their Head. Walking in the Spirit, " doing the truth in
charity, they grow in Him Who is the Head, even Christ,
unto the measure of the age of the fulness of Christ." [7]

It is the law of God's decree that we cannot reach the *Like to the*
fulness of the grace of Christ which shall be ours, unless *Image of the*
we become like to the image of the Crucified.[8] " The *Crucified.*
servant is not greater than his Master." [9] The way of the
Beatitudes is none other than the path trodden by our
Divine Redeemer.[10] He has promised us sadness in this
world ; He has assured us of the hatred that was His own
lot on earth, for the sole reason that we are not of this
world, that He dwells in us and we in Him.[11] " Ought not
Christ to have suffered these things," He asked of the
disciples, " and so to enter His glory ? " [12] " For unto this

[1]Rom. vi, 4. [2]Gal. v, 16–24 ; vi, 14. [3]Matt. xi, 29–30. [4]*Summa
Theol.* iii, q. 8 ; *cf.* Pius XII, *Mystici Corporis,* 29th June, 1943. [5]1 Cor.
xii, 27. [6]1 Cor. xii, 12. [7]Eph. ii, 22 ; Gal. v, 25 ; Eph. iv, 15–16, 13 ;
1 Thess. ii, 12 ; iv. 8 ; 2 Tim. i, 14. [8]Rom. viii, 29. [9]John xv, 20.
[10]Matt. v, 5–12 ; *cf. Summa Theol.,* Ia. IIae. q. 108. [11]John xvi. 22 ; xv.
18–19. [12]Luke xxiv, 26,

are you called," adds St. Peter, "because Christ also suffered for us, leaving you an example that you should follow His steps."[1] There is no escape from the absolute words of Jesus Christ : " he that taketh not up his cross and followeth Me is not worthy of Me."[2]

Our Union with Christ in Suffering. It may seem strange that God should ask for the atonement of our pain, yet such is His undoubted will. God has required that every soul should expiate his guilt in union with the one Redeemer, Jesus Christ. It is not our suffering, however bitter, that can avail to satisfy for sin. It is our suffering with Christ in union of grace that God is pleased to accept as reparation of our sins. It cannot be that there is anything wanting to the Passion of Jesus Christ. What is wanting is our measure of personal pain according to the decree of God. Therefore St. Paul mysteriously declares : " I fill up in my flesh what is wanting of the sufferings of Christ, for His Body, which is the Church" :[3] that personal suffering from which the superabundant Passion of Christ has not exempted any member of the Church. Till the number of the elect shall have been complete this Passion of the Church must give its meed of satisfaction and of merit, in union with the death of Jesus Christ.

And as "none of us liveth to himself," [4] so no man's suffering in union of grace with Christ is permitted by God to be without salutary influence within the Church. "And if one member suffer anything, all the members suffer with it, and if one member glory, all the members rejoice with it." [5] It is not merely that, as the Apostle urges, we are called upon to carry each others' burdens.[6] It is rather that we should have in us " the mind that is in Christ Jesus," [7] that " we should walk in love, as Christ also hath loved us and delivered Himself up for us an oblation and a sacrifice to God." [8] By reason of our union in grace with Jesus Christ, each one of us can become,

---

[1] I Pet. ii, 21. [2] Matt. x, 38 ; *cf.* Gal. v, 22–26. [3] Col. i, 24 ; *cf.* Council of Trent, Sess. XIV, c. 8 ; St. Thomas Aquinas. *Comm. in Ep. ad Coloss.* [4] Rom. xiv, 7–8. [5] I Cor. xii, 26 ; *cf.* Eph. iv, 2–6 ; Col. iii, 12–15. [6] Gal. vi, 2 ; *cf.* St. Thomas Aquinas, *Comm. in Ep. ad Gal ; Summa Theol.*, Suppl. q. 13, a. 2 ; Ia. IIae. q. 114, a. 6 ; *Summa contra Gent.* IIIc. 158 in fine. [7] Phil. ii, 5 ; I Cor. ii, 16. [8] Eph. v. 2 ; *cf.* John xv, 12 ; Rom. xii, 9–21 ; xiii, 10, xv, 1–7.

In his tiny way, as one who expiates with the Divine Redeemer. "And Christ died for all, that they who live, may not live to themselves, but unto Him Who died for them and rose again."[1]

It may well seem that the call to expiate for others is *The Apostolate of Suffering.* the exclusive gift of some privileged souls. Such a thought can only prove to us that we have not understood our union in grace with Our Divine Redeemer. Certain it is that there have always been men and women called by God to share, mysteriously and more intimately, in the redemptive suffering of His Divine Son. It is not a vocation which one can give oneself. It is a burden laid on the soul by God, after years of purification from deliberate faults and from attachment to things created. It is a special calling found in a soul whom suffering has detached from self and perfected in the patience of humility.[2] It cannot live except on the deepest reverence for God Whose infinite sanctity is offended by our sins. To immolate oneself for the sins of men is to be called upon to share in the desire of Christ Who loved us to the point of delivering Himself up for us in death.[3] The charity of Christ constrains such souls,[4] and to live in that desire is to be consumed in a progressive immolation, because, to give all to God, one must incessantly give more.

It is indeed an error to think that such souls are only cloistered : they are found in every walk of life. They are the grains of wheat, of which Our Divine Lord spoke, which fall into earth and in obscurity die to self, that they may produce great fruit of holiness.[5] It is equally an error to believe that each, in his measure, may not atone for the offences of the world. We do not realise that we cannot say the *Our Father* without, in Our Divine Lord's very words, praying for the widest extension of God's kingdom and entreating God for pardon of all men : forgive, not, "me my trespasses," but, "us, our trespasses."

[1] 2 Cor. v. 15 ; 1 Cor. xv, 3 ; *cf.* Eph. i, 4 ; Rom. xii, 5 ; 1 Cor. i, 26–31 ; *cf.* Leo XIII, *Mirae Caritatis* and Pius XI, *Miserentissimus Redemptor.* [2] John xv, 2 ; Luke viii, 15 ; Rom. v. 3 ; Col. i, 11 ; James i, 3–4 ; 1 Pet. v, 10 ; *cf.* 1 Cor. xi, 32 ; Hebr. xii, 11 ; Ps. lxvi, 10 ; Prov. iii, 11–12 ; Tob. iii, 21 ; xii, 13 ; *cf. Summa Theol.* Ia. IIae. q. 61, a. 5, corp. ; q. 68, a. 2, 5, 8. [3] Luke xxii, 15. [4] 2 Cor. v. 14. [5] John xii, 24 ; *cf.* 1 Cor. vi, 19–20.

Lead, not " me," we pray, but " us." Deliver, not " me," but " us," from evil. And we ask that the will of God be done in all the earth as it is done in Heaven. We cannot say the *Hail Mary* without asking Our Lady to intercede for *us* sinners, now and at the hour of *our* death. The prayers of the Church, especially within the Mass, are for the most part couched in the plural, that we may link ourselves with all the members of the Body of Christ which is the Church.

Sharing in the Atonement of Christ.

1. Eucharist.

To each of us are offered the same means of grace as God has given His most chosen souls. There is first the most holy Eucharist, of which Our Divine Lord has said : " he that eateth Me, the same shall live by Me." [1] To be transformed into Christ is the effect of the Blessed Eucharist. As easily approach a furnace without feeling fire as receive Jesus Christ, in genuine Faith and love, without experiencing His horror of sin and His desire for atonement.

2. Blessed Sacrament.

We have the Blessed Sacrament in the tabernacles of the world. The silence and obscurity of His thirty years at Nazareth are not more striking than His abandonment on earth by those for whom He shed His Precious Blood. It is no wonder that the Hidden Victim of the Tabernacle attracts the generosity of every soul who would comfort the Saviour for the negligence of His friends.

3. Sacrifice of the Mass.

We have the holy Sacrifice of the Mass of which the soul is the undying dispositions of Jesus Christ towards God the Father : adoration, in the absolute acknowledgement of the sovereignty of God Whom sin rejects ; atonement and reparation, in the total immolation of the Cross ; petition for sinners " who have been redeemed, not with corruptible things, but with the Precious Blood of Christ " ; thanksgiving, for the acceptance of the reparation made by Jesus Christ. It would seem that we must grow old in assistance at the Holy Sacrifice before the mystery of the burning thirst of Christ upon the Cross is understood.[2]

4. Passion.

We have the consideration of the Passion and the Death of Jesus Christ in the Sorrowful Mysteries and in

[1] John vi, 58.   [2] John xix, 28 ; 1 Pet. i, 18–19.

the Stations of the Cross. No manner of suffering, no intensity of agony was spared Him, but a lifetime is not long enough to appreciate the details of His Passion. No more will eternity be long enough to understand the infinite love of God for us sinners whom He has ransomed.

We have the devotion to the Sacred Heart of Jesus. To our times the Church has reserved this manifestation of the redemptive love of Jesus Christ which showed itself most vehemently in the Passion and which is commemorated incessantly in the Mass. The Sacred Heart sums up the teaching of St. John : " God is Charity." [1] " The kindliness of God," explains St. Paul, " hath appeared in Jesus Christ, Who loved me and delivered Himself for me." [2]

5. Sacred Heart of Jesus.

We have the knowledge and the love of Mary, Mother of God made man. She who was closest to the Divine Redeemer was chosen to stand beneath the Cross on Calvary. In the martyrdom of that hour, she was given by Him to sinners to be their Mother and thus to dispense the graces which the reparation of the Cross had won.[3]

6. Mary.

These are the treasures of our Christian heritage, the use of which has formed the souls whom God has called to share in the redemption of mankind.

It may be asked with what actions can we make reparation for our sins and for the sins of others. With the actions of our daily life. What is more ordinary than water ? Yet the tiny drop of water is added to the wine which becomes the Precious Blood. Our little actions, transformed by grace, in union with the sufferings of Our Divine Redeemer, are accepted by God as atonement for our sins. To Our Divine Lord alone we owe the description of our daily life as a carrying of the Cross. What word more aptly depicts the chafing of our experience day by day ? There is no stage of life from childhood to the grave in which we cannot unite our Cross with the Passion and Death of Our Divine Lord Jesus Christ.

Our Reparation.

1. The Burden of daily Life.

At a time when persistent attempts are being made to

2. The Prayer of Children.

[1] I John iv, 16. [2] Tit. iii, 4–5 ; Gal. ii, 20. [3] John xix, 25–27.

eliminate Jesus Christ from the life of children, it is well
to recall how powerful is the intercession of a child. Their
innocence had a special appeal to our Divine Redeemer.[1]
It is easy to teach them the meaning of the Crucifix and
the Tabernacle. They do not know the malice of our sins,
but they can understand the hurt of sin to Jesus Christ.
And they can be taught to plead for grace for the sinners
of the world.

*3. The
Sanctifica-
tion of
Sickness.*

To the sick, if they but knew it, is given the vocation
to share in the redemption of the world. One wonders
if there is, in the universe of men, a greater strength than
the weakness of the sick, when, in union with the sacrifice
of the Cross, they accept their pain and offer it to God
for the salvation of the world. " When I am weak," says
St. Paul, " then am I powerful."[2] The isolation of the
sick and their loneliness of heart, their humiliating incapa-
city and dependence on the charity of others are the link
which binds them invisibly to countless fellow-sufferers,
but chiefly to our suffering Redeemer in His Passion
and His death. In their apparent inactivity the sick lie,
as it were, upon the Cross. They make visible the mystery
of our atonement in union with Jesus Christ, Head of
the Body which is His Church. In God's design, the Cross
was the proof of the love wherewith God loved all sinful
men, and the suffering of the members of His Church
is at once the proof of God's personal love and the instrument of atonement for themselves and for others. Conscious
of the silent sacrifice they offer, the sick can look less on
the Cross they endure than on the love of Him who sends
the Cross, less on the pain than on the submissive love
with which they can suffer, in union with the atonement
of the Divine Redeemer. Thus is the power of God made
effective in our weakness,[3] for the redemption of the world.

*4. The
loving
Acceptance
of Death.*

It may be that the sick take long to understand the
privilege of the love which God is showing them. In truth,
our sicknesses are given us to prepare the total offering
of ourselves in death. We may wait for the darkening

---

[1]Matt. xi, 25 ; Luke x, 21 ; Matt. xviii, 2–5 ; Mark. x, 13–15.   [2]2 Cor.
xii, 10 ; *cf.* 2 Cor. xiii, 4.   [3]2 Cor. xii, 9.

hours to believe in the boundless mercy of God, Whom
we have perhaps neglected. None the less, by His grace,
we can yet surrender our life into the hands of God, in
a supreme and final act of love.[1] To die is a penalty which
we can accept in loving atonement for all sins. At the
dread moment when this earth is slipping from our grasp
and no sight of the other world is given us, we may experience a desolating void which, in its little way, resembles
the abandonment of Christ upon the Cross.[2] It is the
moment to unite our heart with the Divine Redeemer,
in the complete donation of His obedience and love. And
then, we trust, all will be consummated,[3] in the serenity
of the peace which the Precious Blood has won.

[1]Luke xxiii, 46. [2]Matt. xxvii, 46 ; Mark xv, 34 ; [3]John xvii, 4 ; xix, 30.

Chapter IV

ON SUFFERING IN THE CHRISTIAN LIFE

The Jubilee Year.

DURING the present year[1] we shall again have an opportunity of gaining the Indulgence of the Holy Year. In his eagerness to afford us the occasion of making satisfaction for our sins, the Holy Father has graciously extended the Jubilee to all the countries of the world. Last year it was necessary to make the pilgrimage to Rome. Now it is required merely to visit the churches designated for each parish. The long journey to Rome, however made, involved suffering. The gentle conditions prescribed for the Indulgence of this year cannot compare with the severity of a pilgrimage. Yet one feels that the spirit of a Jubilee calls for expiation in penance.

The correct disposition.

We should do well to remember that it is not the work of penance that avails with God, but the disposition of him who suffers. This year provides us with an occasion for examining our attitude towards the pain and sorrow of our life. With great profit, we can recall our trials that we may convince ourselves, in the light of riper wisdom, how little we have understood the role of suffering in the Christian life. Not one of us can say that he has reaped the harvest of grace that the contradictions of his life have offered. Each of us must admit in sorrow that he has failed to use the crosses he has met as an expiation to God for sin. At least we can now look back and accept the kind Providence of God, so many times rejected by us in the past.

Christian attitude towards pain and sorrow.

We can equally prepare our hearts for the suffering that is yet to come. Even if we were not daily promised another crisis in which the agony of the universe will be renewed, we have the certainty that the shadow of the Cross must lie upon us each day. Since we began to be conscious, we have been acquainted with pain. As the years advanced, the conviction grew in us that there cannot be on earth a joy

[1] 1951.

unmixed with sorrow. Our measure of future grief we cannot know. Whether the great waters of tribulation shall pass over us, or whether we shall be called to bear a lesser burden of daily pain, is the secret of God Himself. Certain it is that we shall suffer. And it is well to make ready, in understanding and desire, that we may patiently endure the Cross. In faith and in love, we can go forward now to meet the will of God.

It is only our holy Faith that can give us the key to the mystery of evil. The pagan writers, ancient and modern, have written beautifully of the sorrow of the world. It is as if the discipline of grief had tamed their pride, and a delicate light of God had for a moment shone upon their darkness. But their gentle melancholy has not healed mankind. For the most part, outside the influence of the Faith, the attitude towards suffering has been either harsh or reckless : men have withdrawn into obstinate endurance or flung themselves into a whirl of sensuality. Occasionally we glimpse a fortitude that is noble in so far as it is patient. Generally, however, in every answer given by the pagans to the problem of evil, there is found an attempt to solve the difficulty by taking refuge in escape. The Christian attitude to evil cannot be indifferent ; no more can it be contemptuous or cowardly.

For the Faith teaches us that the origin of evil is original sin.[1] Adam, by his disobedience to God, lost the state of sanctifying grace and, with it, the virtues infused by God into his soul and the gifts of the Holy Ghost. Any grave offence against God is a profound contempt for the Sovereign Creator. Adam's sin was, in our regard, the most disastrous of human crimes. For Adam had received in trust, for all that would be born from him, his state of original holiness. By his single sin he forfeited, not only for himself, but for all mankind, the free gift of the most bountiful Creator.[2]

Origin of Evil is Original Sin.

Henceforth each man is born outside the realm of grace : his soul is deprived of sanctifying grace, by which he would be so raised above the level of mere human nature as to

[1]Gen. ii–iii. ; Wisd., ii, 24 ; Rom. v, 12–21 ; *Summa Theol.* 1 a, q. 95 ; Conc. Trid., sess. v. [2]Ps. 1, 7 ; Eph. ii, 3 ; Conc. Trid., sess. v., can. 2, 3 ; *Summa Theol.* 1a, 2ae, q. 81, 2a, 2ae, q. 163.

share in the nature of God Himself. He is no longer holy.
He comes into this world shorn of the virtues and the gifts
of the Holy Ghost. He is not only stripped of the inheritance
which he owed to the overflowing mercy of the Creator, but
he is wounded in body and in soul. He must mourn the
loss of the special gifts of Adam which would have rendered
him free from death, immune from ignorance, untouched by
suffering and disorder of desires. He is reduced to a state
of slavery, in the kingdom where Satan, God's enemy, is
Chief of all who refuse to acknowledge the sovereignty of
God.   Man is born thus turned away from God, Whom he
would have known in the clear faith of God's revelation and
loved in unbroken charity. With difficulty will he now
discover what is true, especially where God Himself and
His law are concerned. With ease will he turn to what is
vicious. With reluctance will he stir himself to overcome the
obstacles to virtue. With alacrity will he seek what the senses
urge as good, against the light and precept of right reason.
Moral evil of sin with all the distress of human life ; physical
evil of pain with its necessary goal of death : this is the grim
heritage of the sons of Adam.[1] This, each one must feel,
in the touching phrase of God the Holy Ghost, is indeed
" the wound of his own heart."[2]

The super-
abundance
of Grace.
We cannot fully grasp the meaning of original sin, but
we can understand that this evil is not an argument against
the justice of God. We have but lost that which has been
given to Adam in trust for all his children, on the simple
condition of obedience to an easy precept. We are deprived
of gifts that were not owed to human nature as such, but
only to human nature as God was pleased to raise it to the
supernatural state of Adam, the head of all the human race.
Neither can original sin and its train of bitter consequences
be rightly called repugnant to the wisdom and goodness of
God. The Creator cannot permit an evil to exist, unless in
view of a greater good.[3] What that good might be in the
plan of God we could never tell beforehand. Now that the
Incarnation has taken place, we can at once understand that
God has allowed the vast flow of evil to abound in His

[1] *Summa Theol.* 2a, 2ae, q. 164.   [2] 3 Kings, viii, 38.   [3] *Summa Theol.* 3a,
q. 1, ad 1, ad 3 ; a. 3, ad 3 ; 1a, q. 49, a. 1, a. 2.

universe, only that the grace of the Divine Redeemer might overflow our world, as the covering waters of the sea. What we have lost in Adam, we have regained, in fuller measure and in more marvellous manner, in the person of God Himself, made man for our redemption.[1]

It is a very touching proof of the loving mercy of God that, immediately after the sin of Adam, He should have promised the Redeemer, Who would restore mankind to the state of sanctifying grace and free him from the slavery of sin.[2] For us and for our salvation God would not spare even His own Son, but would deliver Him up for us all.[3] God made man would be " the propitiation for our sins, and not for ours only, but also for those of the whole world."[4] So full would be the grace of the Redemption that we should be able to say that, with Jesus Christ, God " had given us all things."[5] So complete would be the repairing love of the redemptive death of Jesus Christ that we, who are weighed down by the ever-present sight of evil in ourselves and others, could exclaim at the magnificence of the grace of Christ : " the sufferings of this time are not worthy to be compared with the glory to come, that shall be revealed in us."[6]

And firstly, we have in the life of Jesus Christ a perfect example of obedience to God. Adam had sinned by disobedience. The new Adam would live on earth only in full subjection to the will of His Heavenly Father. At His entrance into the world, this obedience is emphasised : " Sacrifice and oblation Thou wouldst not, but a body Thou hast fitted for me. . . . Behold I come. In the head of the book it is written of me that I should do Thy will, O God."[7] The first utterance of Jesus Christ reminds us that He must be about His Father's business.[8] His life was spent for the most part in subjection to the Guardian whom God had chosen and to the human Mother who had given Him birth at Bethlehem.[9] His first public act was to purge His Father's house of the traders, whose trafficking was

The Obedience of Jesus unto Death.

[1]Rom. v. 20 ; *Summa Theol.* 3a, qq. 48–49. [2]Gen. iii, 15 ; Hebr. ii, 14. [3]Rom. viii, 32 ; *cf.* St. Thomas, In Rom. viii. [4]1 John ii, 2. [5]Rom. viii, 32 ; 2 Pet. i, 4. [6]Rom. viii, 18. [7]Hebr. x, 5. [8]Luke ii, 49. [9]Luke ii, 51.

unlawful.[1] " My meat," He declared, " is to do the will
of Him that sent me, that I may perfect His work."[2] The
sum of His life on earth He revealed when He said : " I do
always the things that please Him."[3] Therefore God the
Father, in the voice from Heaven, made manifest His good-
pleasure : " This is my beloved Son, in whom I am well
pleased. Hear ye Him."[4]

But the docility of Jesus Christ led Him to the Cross :
" Therefore doth the Father love Me, because I lay down
My life. No man taketh it from Me, but I lay it down of
Myself. This commandment have I received of My
Father."[5] The justice of God had decreed that the redemption of humanity should be accomplished only by the
shedding of the blood of God made man.[6] Our Divine
Master knew the goal to which His human life was tending.
Serene in His unity with the Father, He passed through
all the dangers prepared by His crafty enemies. At a given
moment, they wished to assail Him violently and cast Him
from the hill of Nazareth ; unperturbed He passed through
their midst. " No man laid hands on Him because His hour
was not yet come."[7] Up to the moment chosen by God,
Our Divine Redeemer would drink to the full the cup of
human suffering : hunger and thirst, the heat of the roads,
the cold of the night, the toil of the apostolate. He would
meet the wiles of the envious, the open ignorance of the
crowd, the insult of hostile speech. As He permitted the
toils to close in on Him, in the last week, He spoke of the
parable of the husbandmen. Casting the beloved Son out
of the vineyard, they killed Him.[8] Eight days before the
Transfiguration, He had foretold His passion and death and
resurrection.[9] Shortly after, He repeated the prophecy of
His being handed over to the Gentiles, that He might be
mocked and spat upon, scourged and put to death.[10] Yet,
only at the end, at the entry to Jerusalem, did He allow
His soul to feel the terror of the coming Passion. Should

---

[1]Matt. xxi, 12 ; Mark xi, 15–17 ; Luke xix, 45–46.   [2]John iv, 34.
[3]John viii, 29. [4]Matt. xvii, 5 ; Mark ix, 6 ; Luke ix, 35 ; cf. Matt. iii, 17.
[5]John x, 17–18. [6]John i, 7 ; Apoc. i, 5 ; vi, 6–12 ; Hebr. ix, 14 ; xiii,
20. [7]Luke iv, 30 ; John viii, 20. [8]Luke xx, 9–18. [9]Matt. xvi, 21 ; Mark
viii, 31 ; Luke ix, 22. [10]Matt. xvii, 22–23 ; Mark ix, 31 ; Luke ix, 44.

He pray : " Father, save Me from this hour " ? And at once
He Himself answered : " But, for this cause I came unto
this hour."[1] Later in the garden at Gethsemane, He permitted the flood of fear and bitterness to flow across His
soul at the approach of His death. " Not My will, but Thine
be done," were His final words, as He rose to meet betrayal
at the hands of His chosen friend and elect Apostle.[2] And
lastly, on the Cross, in the mystery of the abandonment in
which He expiated the iniquity of mankind, He expired
with the cry : " Father, into Thy hands I commend My
spirit. It is consummated."[3] The urgency of His love for
the Father, Who had decreed the redemption of men
through the shedding of blood, had found its supreme
expression in the sacrifice of the Cross.

" Ought not the Christ to have suffered these things and
so to enter into His glory ? " asked the Risen Saviour on the
evening of His resurrection.[4] Long before, He had declared
with a plainness that was not understood : " If any man will
come after Me, let him deny himself, take up his cross daily
and follow Me."[5] Must we then follow Him in pain and
sorrow even to the death ? There is no other road, according
to the Divine Redeemer, Who is for us " the Way, the Truth
and the Life. No man cometh to the Father," He asserted,
" but by Me."[6] " For unto this," wrote St. Peter, " are you
called : because Christ suffered for you, leaving you an
example that you should follow His steps."[7] What those
steps must be, the emphatic and repeated assertions of God
made man have made completely clear : suffering has now a
redemptive value when united with the sufferings of Jesus
Christ.[8] There is not the possibility of illusion for one who
reads the Sacred Text sincerely. There is one test of the
faithful following of Christ : "he that hath My commandments and keepeth them, he it is that loveth Me."[9] The son
who is moved with repentance and afterwards goes to the
vineyard, is he who does the Father's will.[10] The man who

*The
Redemptive
value of
Suffering.*

[1]John xii, 27.   [2]Matt. xxvi, 37–46 ; Mark xiv, 32–45 ; Luke xxii, 39–
48 ; John xviii, 4–11 ; *cf.* St. Thomas, In Matt. xxvi. [3]Luke xxiii,
46 ; John xix, 30. [4]Luke xxiv, 26. [5]Luke ix, 23. [6]John xiv, 6 ; Rom.
viii, 29. [7]1 Pet. ii, 20–21. [8]John xii, 24–25 ; Matt. v, 1–12 ; *Contra
Gent.*, iv, 55 ; *Summa Theol.* 3a, q. 48, a. 1. [9]John xiv, 21. [10]Matt. xxi,
28–31.

builds the house of his life on the rock of the commandments alone survives the storm.[1] The heart which receives the seed of the word of God and keeps it, brings forth fruit in the measure of its dispositions. All others believe for a time, and fall away in a period of temptation, or else, being choked with the cares and riches and pleasures of this life, yield no fruit of salvation.[2] It is easy to rejoice, like the disciples of John, for a time, in the light of Jesus Christ.[3] But any man who loveth Him, will keep His word.[4] We cannot be worthy of Him unless we take up our cross and follow Him.[5] He that shall lose his life of disordered self-will by the crucifixion of himself shall find his life, regenerated in the grace of Jesus Christ.[6]

The loving acceptance of our pain. Thus does our docility to the teaching of Our Divine Redeemer lead us also to the Cross. In the light of Faith we see that the problem of suffering is not solved, except by the loving acceptance of our pain. And in suffering we are not alone : we are most intimately united to Jesus Christ by grace. He it is Who has called us : " Come to Me all you that labour and are burdened and I will refresh you. Take up *My* yoke " ; not, be it noted, our own yoke of rebellion against God and flight from suffering, but the yoke of the patient following of Jesus Christ, Who is meek to endure and humble of heart. " My yoke," says the Divine Redeemer, Who for love of us suffered in all His earthly life, " is sweet and my burden light."[7] To us that yoke is sweet and that burden light, only because our most loving Lord has shed His precious Blood, in the redemption of the Cross.

Purification by suffering. St. Paul teaches us that " we are heirs indeed of God and joint heirs with Christ." He adds, however, at once : " Yet so, if we suffer with Him, that we may be also glorified with Him."[8] Our Divine Redeemer entered into the heritage of His glory through His passion and death. We may not attain the inheritance He has won for us, by a different or by an easier path. Therefore it is written : " through many

---

[1]Matt. vii, 24–27 ; Luke vi, 47–49. [2]Matt. xiii, 3–8 ; 18–23 ; Mark, iv, 2–8 ; 13–20 ; Luke viii, 4–15. [3]John v, 35. [4]John xiv, 23. [5]Matt. x. 38 ; *cf.* Luke xiv, 27. [6]Matt. x, 39 ; xvi, 25 ; Mark viii, 35 ; Luke ix, 24 ; Rom. viii, 6. [7]Matt. xi, 28–30. [8]Rom. viii, 17 ; Gal. iv, 7.

tribulations we must enter into the Kingdom of God."[1] And Our Divine Lord Himself revealed the plan of God in permitting the pain and sorrow of our life : " I am the true vine and My Father is the husbandman. Every branch in Me that beareth not fruit He will take away, and every one that beareth fruit, He will purge it, that it may bring forth more fruit."[2] Even those who are in vital union with Christ by sanctifying grace are stated to require a purification. God Himself will prune their soul, by cutting away the objects to which they turn for an undue support. He will send trials and suffering which will convince them of their incessant need of God and the depth of their lurking self-love. No one can say on this earth that he needs no further purification : " If," said St. John, " we say that we have no sin, we deceive ourselves."[3] And, he adds, " he that is holy, let him be sanctified still more."[4] The purification thus promised by the kind Providence of God has one purpose only : that we bear more fruit of virtue. " This," says the Holy Ghost,"is the will of God, your sanctification."[5]

They whom God most sanctified were made, in suffering, most like to Jesus Christ. St. Joseph is a lowly and hidden figure in the story of our Redemption. Yet, because of his exceptional mission as the spouse of Mary and the protector of Jesus Christ, God must have endowed him with unique gifts of character and holiness. Next to the Mother of God, he is the holiest of God's saints. Yet, when we are allowed to glimpse his features in the pages of the Gospels, he is shown us laden with the burden of most acute anxiety, fleeing from the savage envy of Herod, responsible in Egypt for the support of Mary and her infant Child.[6] Apart from the mention of the Child's subjection to him, St. Joseph is seen only in the poignant days when the Child was lost Whom God had chosen him to guard.[7] Of the royal house of David, he earned his bread and sustained the Holy Family, by working as a carpenter in the hillside village of Nazareth. This is the Protector of the Universal Church of God.

Sanctification by suffering : St. Joseph and Our Lady.

[1]Acts xiv, 21. [2]John xv, 1–8. [3]1 John i, 8. [4]Apoc. xx, 11. [5]1 Thess. iv, 3. [6]Matt. i, 18–24 ; ii, 13–23. [7]Luke ii, 41–51.

If we consider the life of the holiest of God's children, the Immaculate Mother of God, who was preserved from the shadow of Adam's sin and by grace made sinless in all her life, we witness a martyrdom which is the closest image possible of the sorrowful life and cruel Passion of Jesus Christ. Mary's surpassing knowledge of the Sacred Scriptures had shown her that the Messiah would be the Man of Sorrows. When, therefore, she consented to become His Mother, she knew with marvellous intelligence that she must share the sorrow of His life and death. And every incident of His life did but thrust the sword of Simeon's prophecy more deeply into her remembering heart.[1] At each access of further grief, her holiness rose in a surge of vaster grace. The three days' loss, the constant vision of the Passion during the hidden life, the separation of the years of His apostolate, the knowledge of the persecution that in the end would kill her Son : these are the steps by which her soul was made capable of the holiness that " stood beneath the Cross."[2] There is no sorrow like the sorrow of the Mother whom God had chosen for Himself. And ever her sorrow God has used to help us, for, by the merit of her compassionate union with the one Redeemer Jesus Christ, Mary is become the Consoler of the afflicted and the Mediatrix of the grace of Christ.

Atonement by suffering. We may not then complain who strive to follow, at an almost infinite distance, in the footsteps of our Saviour crucified. We shall be less acutely conscious of our pain of soul and body, if we think of how He dealt with those who were closest to His heart on earth. They were privileged to share most intensely in the sorrowful atonement of the Divine Redeemer. It is not possible—because it is against our nature—to love suffering for itself. Evil, physical and moral, is a defect, the absence of a goodness which ought to be present. But, by the light of the Faith we are enabled to appreciate the redemptive power of suffering, when it is united with the passion and death of Jesus Christ. Through grace we can take up our cross with courage, even with serenity. If the purification of our self-

[1]Luke ii, 34–35.   [2]John xix, 25.

ON SUFFERING IN THE CHRISTIAN LIFE   49

love progresses through life, and if God, through the
increasing action of the gifts of the Holy Ghost, enlightens
us and draws us, we can find even joy in the effects of
suffering. " For to me to live is Christ," exclaimed St.
Paul.[1] " I reckon that I know nothing unless Jesus Christ,
and Him crucified."[2]

We forget that Our Divine Master has given us a *A*
Sacrament for suffering. On the night before He died, Our *Sacrament*
Divine Lord uttered the strange saying : " it is expedient *for daily*
suffering :
to you that I go." His Apostles, who had grown accustomed *Confirmation.*
to lean upon Him in every need, could not understand how
the absence of His physical presence could lend them
comfort. He explained : " For, if I go not, the Paraclete
will not come to you, but if I go, I will send Him to you."[3]
He has sent the Holy Ghost and we have received Him, in
the Sacrament of Confirmation, unto strength.

By the Sacrament of Baptism we are born again to the
life of sanctifying grace. By the Sacrament of Confirmation
that grace is increased, as befits one who is no longer an
infant in the spiritual life, but who now is an adult and shares
more perfectly in the fulness of the grace of Christ.[4] In
addition, the special grace of this Sacrament fits us to act
for God with the constancy of men, by the bold and public
profession of the Faith. This increase of fortitude and of all
the gifts of God the Holy Ghost is the source of the supernatural courage, which rises up to overcome temptation
and the obstacles to a virtuous life. Nor is this grace a
momentary strength : it gives a firmer title to the actual
graces that we shall need until the end of life. We are
sealed with the character which gives a deeper likeness to
Jesus Christ, our Head, and a more noble post within His
Kingdom : for, by Confirmation we are made soldiers of
Christ, that we may endure the trials of the Christian life
and, when the need demands, share in the apostolate of our
holy Faith.[5]

The Sacrament of Confirmation equips us for the trials
of every phase of life : for youth, when temptation is open

[1]Phil. i, 21. [2]1 Cor. ii, 2. [3]John xvi, 7. [4]Acts viii, 15–17 ; xix, 1–8 ;
Hebr. vi, 1–4 ; *cf.* Eph. iv, 13. [5]*Summa Theol.* 3a q. 72, a. 8 ; a. 9 ad
1 and 2 ; a. 11 ad 2.

and more vehement ; for middle-age, when disillusion tends to blunt the soul with a resignation of cynical maturity ; for old-age, when selfishness exacts a tyranny of service.

Super-natural help in suffering.

To help us to profit by our daily cross, we have in addition the Blessed Eucharist. Day after day we can sustain and increase our life of grace by receiving Jesus Christ Himself as the spiritual nourishment of our souls. As often as we choose, we can be purified from sin, by absolution, in the Sacrament of Penance. We enjoy the unceasing company and protection of the holy Angels.[1] We are sustained all day and night, by the tireless protection of our Blessed Mother. Surely it is easy to carry our cross, in so far as the cross means the pain of avoiding mortal sin and the increasing effort to remove deliberate faults. We who belong to Christ ought to have crucified our dis-ordered nature with its evil desires.[2] We ought equally to be crucified to the world, in that habitually we resist the influence of men, who will not subject themselves to God.[3] Distress has been promised to us in the world, but we have been bidden to have confidence, for Our Divine Redeemer has conquered the world.[4] His redemp-tion, we know, is perfect in its victory :[5] it is we who must fill up what is wanting on our part,[6] by taking up our cross and, in the strength of grace, following Him day by day.

A Sacrament for the suffering of death : Extreme Unction.

On the side of God, we ask, what more could He have done to assist us in the suffering of life ? There is yet another revelation of the loving clemency of God : He has given us a Sacrament for the suffering of death. Even the holiest of His servants must naturally shrink from death : it is the final penalty of original sin. They may have spent a life in the love of God that is born of our holy Faith. Their love will have pressed them each day more closely to imitate the docility of Jesus Christ, in embracing what-ever is the will of God. And thus they may be said to have lived habitually in the disposition which is the soul of the Mass. " He that loveth Me," said Our Divine Master, " shall be loved of My Father, and I will love him and will

[1]Ps. sc. 11 ; Hebr. i, 14 ; Matt. xviii, 10. [2]Gal. v, 24. [3]Gal. vi, 14. [4]John xvi, 33, 21–22 ; 1 John v, 4. [5]John xvii, 2 ; 1 Cor. xv, 54–57 ; John xvi, 33 ; Apoc. v, 9–14 ; vii, 14–17. [6]Coll. i, 24.

manifest Myself to him."[63] God may have turned the sorrow of His servants into joy, into the constant and intimate conviction of His loving presence. Yet, when it comes to death, we must all be penetrated with a sense of the sovereign holiness of God. Nothing unclean can come before Him; nothing unrequited can resist His justice.[2] The memory of sin, though long forgiven, may trouble us. The certainty of graces lost in trials unworthily accepted may be a heavy shadow on our peace. For such a moment has the Sacrament of Last Anointing been instituted.

With the gentleness of oil poured into wounds, the indulgence of God descends upon the dying. In this Sacrament, sanctifying grace is increased, and the soul is prepared to enter, even at once, into the glory of God. The spiritual languor that is a consequence of sin is removed, venial faults not yet forgiven are wiped away, the penalty due to sin is remitted.[3] In the soul that is more perfectly disposed, such a Sacrament restores the whiteness of baptismal innocence and opens the gates of Heaven.[4] It is the fulfilment of the promise of our loving Saviour: " You now indeed have sorrow, but I will see you again, and your heart will rejoice. I will come again and will take you to Myself, that, where I am, you also may be. And your joy no man shall take from you."[5] "For God shall wipe away all tears: and death shall be no more, nor mourning nor crying nor sorrow shall be any more, for the former things are passed away."[6]

" The glory to come that shall be revealed in us."

---

[1]John xiv, 21. [2]Apoc. xxi, 27 ; Eph. v, 5 ; John i, 18 ; vi, 46. [3]James v, 14–16 ; Conc. Trid. sess. xiv, cap. 1, 2 ; *Summa Theol. Suppl.*, qq. 29–30. [4]*Summa Theol. Suppl.*, q. 29, a. 1, ad 2. [5]John xvi, 22 ; xiv, 3. [6]Apoc. xxi, 4.

Chapter V

THE LAW OF SELF-DENIAL *

DURING the past year we have all suffered to some extent from the prevailing circumstances of the world-war. On several occasions it has been our duty to ask the Faithful of the Diocese to thank God for His mercy in preserving us from actual warfare. The reason for our humble gratitude continues at the present moment. Once or twice, too, we have seized the opportunity to urge on everyone the duty of showing charity, in the measure that is possible, to all who were experiencing distress. That call has been met by the Faithful of this Diocese, and indeed by many who are not of our flock, with a generosity that has been quite exceptional.

Self-denial a Universal Law.

If, then, at the season of Lent, we bring to your notice the duty of Christian self-denial and Christian patience, it is not because we are ignorant or unmindful of the suffering in our midst, particularly among the poor of this City and Diocese, but rather because the obligation of self-restraint and patience exists for every follower of Jesus Christ, in youth as in advancing years, in health as in illness, in riches and in poverty, in gladness and in affliction. The poor of Christ are favoured, in that, by reason of their penury, they are less liable to the pride and cruelty and unchastity that are begotten of wealth. They are blessed alike in that the Creator Himself deliberately chose their mode of life, when He came among us as the Redeemer of mankind. They are privileged because the model of all Christian families called the " Holy Family " was poor, both in the goods of earth and in the eyes of men. It is indeed true that the poor, by their Christian virtue, are a rebuke to the insolence of wealth and an example of tranquil dignity to the covetousness which has no peace. Yet, the same Divine Teacher,

*Pastoral Letter of Lent, 1942.

" who had not where to lay His head " [1] on earth, has declared that they only who, in spirit, are poor, have a right to count upon His blessing.[2] They who, in fact, are poor, have their own temptations, because they share in the common danger of our human weakness.

To every human being, then, Our Divine Lord has issued His warning, in terms that admit of no denial, in words that no honest man can claim to be obscure. St. Luke emphasises the truth that Christ spoke, not merely to the few who were Apostles, but to all. " And He said to all : If any man will come after Me, let him deny himself and take up his cross daily and follow Me." [3]

Our Lord makes it clear that to follow Him is a free choice made with the help of grace, not a slavish compulsion nor an unthinking impulse. But among those who do follow, not one man is free to choose his own method. There is a single path : there is one law : " to deny himself and take up his cross daily." Few facts of life are a more pathetic proof of our fallen human nature than our blindness in seeing, not to mention our slowness in accepting, this plain statement of God Himself.

It is vain to put forward in argument against the seeming harshness of this statement of Our Divine Master the unfailing tenderness of God made Man. The Gospel pages indeed declare the charm of His infancy and the gentle subjection of His youth.[4] We read that His hand was put forth to heal every manner of illness.[5] The broken of soul and body were His especial care. To the poor above all was He sent to preach.[6] No portrait of dignity and courtesy can adequately reveal His graciousness. St. Mary Magdalene and St. John are equally the evidence of His divine condescension. His own Mother, given to us on Calvary to be our Mother also,[7] is an unending proof of His most considerate affection. And greater love, He himself has said, no man can have than that he lay down his life for his friends.[8] With what intensity of agony He has shown that greatest love we dimly understand, when we have spent a

Reconciliation with Mercy of God.

---

[1]Matt. viii, 20. [2]Matt. v, 2. [3]Luke ix, 23. [4]Luke ii, 51. [5]Matt. iv, 23. [6]Luke iv, 18. [7]John xix, 26. [8]John xv, 13.

lifetime looking at the Crucifix. And yet, Our Divine Lord never once withdrew a syllable of the final law He had Himself declared : "If any man will come after Me, let him deny himself and take up his cross daily and follow Me."

Example of Jesus Christ. Even if Our Divine Lord had not spoken so plainly, the example of His own life could have left no sincere inquirer in doubt as to the Christian way of life. The Creator Who had said : " If I should be hungry, I would not tell thee : for the world is mine and the fulness thereof," [1] when He came into His own creation as an infant, was born in a stable at Bethlehem. And Bethlehem finds its explanation only at the end in Calvary. As the Father had given Him commandment, so did He, becoming obedient unto the death of the Cross. [2] For, from the first moment of the Incarnation, Our Divine Redeemer was a victim, vowed to sacrifice, because of sin. " A body Thou hast fitted to me. Holocausts for sin did not please Thee. Then said I : Behold I come. In the head of the book it is written of me that I should do Thy will, O God." [3] That will mean a life of suffering, in every sense of human weariness and pain and persecution, at the hands of every type of human sinner. He was " a sign which should be contradicted " and already the jealousy of a human tyrant sought to quench His infant life. [4] He was poor and in labours from His youth. [5] He did not contend nor cry out. [6] He was meek and humble of heart. [7] He did not consider that He should sternly exact from men the respect due outwardly to His divinity : rather did He divest Himself of His external glory and assume the form of a slave. [8] Fixing His soul upon the joy that would result from His redeeming sacrifice, He endured the Cross. [9] To sum up His life in the words of God the Holy Ghost : " He went about doing good." [10] And for reward from us He received what He had Himself so clearly and so often foretold : " The Son of Man must suffer many things and be rejected and be killed. And they shall mock Him and spit on Him and scourge Him and kill Him." [11] And the disciples,

[1]Ps. xlix, 12. [2]John xiv, 31 ; Phil. ii, 8. [3]Heb. x, 5. [4]Luke ii, 34 ; Matt. ii, 3—22. [5]Ps. lxxxvii, 16. [6]Matt. xii, 19. [7]Matt. xi, 29. [8]Phil. ii, 6—7. [9]Heb. xii, 2. [10]Acts x, 38. [11]Mark viii, 31 ; x, 34. Acts iii, 18.

we read, "were astonished" at His words, and "were afraid." [1] They had not yet understood the nature or the depth of human sinfulness.

We too may well be astonished and afraid, for we are *Ultimate* in presence of the mystery of human sin, which demanded *reason for* the sacrifice of the Cross. Only when we attempt to fathom *Self-denial.* the iniquity of offence against God, do we begin to understand the reason for Our Divine Lord's stark command "If any man will come after Me, let him deny himself." For there is in each man's being the double wound of original and personal sin. No doubt the grace of our Redeemer has restored us in Baptism to the divine state in which we share in the nature of God. And the grace of Christ in the Sacrament of Penance gives back that state, should we have ever lost it by our personal fault. Yet, the elevating and the healing grace of Jesus Christ does not fully efface the lamentable effects of original and personal sins. To each one of us is left the heritage of woe which our First Parents have transmitted to us and which we ourselves have deliberately made more heavy and more galling.

The necessity, then, for Christian self-denial is rooted in the discord of our fallen nature. Our senses are no longer subject to our reason, nor is reason submissive to the light of Faith. Revolt can make itself felt within the soul, before reason can intervene or, what is more painful, even after reason has issued its command. In our intelligence there is a darkness, in which imprudence thrives ; in our will there is a selfishness that disregards the supremacy of God, and in our sense-nature, there is not only a weakness that shrinks from the effort of doing good, but also a lust that urges to every form of bodily excess. These wounds of our being, which the grace of Baptism would slowly heal, have been made deeper in all men by deliberate, personal sins. And the repetition of sin is responsible for a greater dulness in regard to the truths of our Divine Master's teaching, a more heavy sluggishness in the exercise of virtue, a keener incitement to the sins of sense. Of a truth, we may reverently exclaim

[1] Mark x, 32.

that Jesus Christ " knew what was in man," [1] when He
issued the absolute law of Christian self-denial.

Our need of the grace of Jesus Christ is not less absolute
if we are to follow Him in the Christian way of living.
Each man must impose upon himself that self-restraint
which is the avoidance of every sin that would extinguish
the life of God in him : to that degree of divine charity
every living soul is bound. Nor will he succeed in any
but a mean and halting measure, unless by firm vigilance,
he studies his personal weaknesses and by the grace of
Jesus Christ generously attempts to lessen the number of
deliberate, venial sins. Mortal sin is indeed complete
aversion from God, our supernatural end ; an utter
destruction of the life of grace. Venial sin is not full death,
but it is that little malady which, often experienced, disposes
one for the onset of a fatal illness. No Christian who is at all
earnest in fidelity to the law of God, will easily admit the
inconsiderate treachery of habitual, venial faults. On the
contrary, his love of God will urge Him to the self-denial of
charity which, in the words of St. Paul, crucifies, for the
sake of Jesus Christ, the disorder of his nature, with all its
evil inclinations.[2]

*Natural
Scope.*

This crucifixion, in union with Jesus Christ, is that
daily carrying of the Cross, of which Our Divine Lord
spoke so definitely. By the Cross He meant all the pain
of life, arising from oneself, one's neighbour and one's
circumstances. For each it is different ; for each it is
sufficient ; for all it is the way of life, first trodden and
marked out by our sinless Redeemer. " Tribulation and
anguish upon every soul of man that worketh evil." [3]
Yet, by the mercy of God, this tribulation, which is an
effect of sin, when borne with patience, is accepted as
a satisfaction due to God : it helps to efface the results
of sin and to guard us against the surprise or violence
of temptation. Further, if one examines his daily Cross,
he will see in it precisely the suffering that he himself
would never have willingly chosen. God, our most loving
Father, sees, with unfailing insight, our particular need of

[1]John ii, 25.   [2]Gal. v, 24.   [3]Rom. ii, 9.

spiritual purification. The trial He sends, as distinct from the mortification we ourselves would choose, unerringly searches out and cleanses our hidden selfishness, our lurking rebellion and our secret distaste of virtue.

It might be thought that the law of Jesus Christ con- *Salutary* cerning self-restraint and daily bearing of one's Cross *Effects.* is a grim enactment carrying but desolation into human life. It is the healing law of Him who made and redeemed our human nature. They have not learned the sweetness of the yoke of Christ who think in terms of bitterness concerning Christian self-denial. " Learn of Me," said Jesus Christ. " I have given you an example, that as I have done to you, so you do also. Take up My yoke upon you, and you shall find rest to your souls, for My yoke is sweet and My burden light." [1] Who that knows his own soul even a little, will think that he can find in himself, much less in his disordered nature, sweetness or ease or rest ? At times we complain that the hand of God has touched us ; we forget that His hand itself was pierced. He Who, in prayer and penance, has taken upon him Christ's yoke of the daily cross, must soon bear witness to the truth that he does not carry it alone, but that Jesus Christ, in him and with him, carries the heaviest share. " Amen, amen, I say to you, unless the grain of wheat," which is the Christian soul, " falling into the ground, die," to its life of self-love, " itself remaineth alone," apart from the healing peace of the Divine Redeemer. " But if it die," in the death to self which is the daily carrying of the Cross, " it bringeth forth much fruit." [2]

The fruit of the Redemption is supernatural holiness. As by the mercy of God, the patient endurance of our trials merits to be a satisfaction for our sins, so is this Christian fortitude allowed to be an association with the work of the Redeemer. He Who, being sinless, alone merited our justification by His life and death, now accepts our pain as an intercession for the souls of men. The life of every member of that vast multitude, which is the conquest of the Precious Blood, to the degree in which it is united with the Divine Redeemer, produces much fruit of holiness and

[1]John xiii, 15 ; Matt. xi, 29–30. [2]John xii, 24–25.

fills up, in its tiny way, that which is wanting in redemptive suffering for the Church.[1] We are not alone ; we are all members of one Body, of which Christ is Head.[2] And when in the ceaseless renewal of Calvary, Jesus Christ offers Himself to God, He offers also every soul in the state of grace and those souls, in particular, who, in supernatural union with Himself, patiently accept their daily Cross of satisfaction and reparation.

" To me," says St. Paul, " to live is Christ." [3] Every Christian can repeat his sentiment. It is very possible for every man, by the grace of God, to live in the self-same spirit of His Divine Teacher and Redeemer. " Behold I come to do Thy will. I do always the things that please Him." [4] That submission of Christ as man rose like a fountain of unending waters in every act of His human life, nor does it cease to well up at this moment in the sacrifice of the Mass and in the possession of the Beatific Vision. To imitate that utter subjection and oblation of all our being to God, through Jesus Christ, is our bounden duty, is, in fact, all our life. No human being has ever imitated Christ's submission with such perfection as did His most holy Mother. Sinless herself, she offered her Divine Son to God and offered herself in union with Him, on Calvary, nor has she ever ceased to offer to God with Christ the souls of all the just. To her has God committed the loving task of obtaining for us the grace that will not only conquer evil, but also mould in our lives the image of Jesus Christ to which we must be conformed.[5]

Mary our Model.

At this sacred season, then, we exhort each member of our flock to put away all sin and to offer himself to God, as a victim living by grace, holy and pleasing to God. There is, the Holy Ghost tells us, one will of God in respect of us : " This is the will of God your sanctification." [6] And holiness is the following of Jesus Christ. But in that following, one way alone has been prescribed by Jesus Christ, true God, true man : " If any man will come after Me, let him deny himself and take up his cross daily and follow Me."

[1]Col. i, 24. [2]Eph. i, 22 ; Col. i, 18. [3]Phil. i, 21. [4]Heb. x, 9 ; John viii, 29.
[5]Rom. viii, 29. [6]Thess. iv, 3.

Chapter VI

THE CHRISTIAN FAMILY*

ON the first occasion that we address the Clergy and Faithful of this Diocese in a Lenten Pastoral, we wish to draw attention to the life of Faith, which a Catholic is called upon to practise in virtue of his Baptism.

There is a danger that the admonitions of a Pastoral may be understood as meaning that grave abuses exist in regard to those matters which a Bishop chooses to explain. It may also be forgotten that, for the few persons who are unfaithful to their Catholic duties, there must be reckoned all the vast multitude of souls, whose daily lives are a permanent proof of supernatural goodness.

Therefore, we may be allowed to say at once, that since God in His own designs chose us, through His Vicar on earth, to rule this See, nothing has so strongly impressed us as the wholehearted obedience of the Clergy and the unstinted loyalty of the Faithful. Such obedience and loyalty can have no other explanation than the deep-rooted practice of divine Faith. *Living to Faith in Daily Life.*

For this singular manifestation of Catholic life, we wish once again to express our deep gratitude. Nor can we fail to voice the belief that the flourishing condition of religion in our Diocese has been largely merited by the prayerful life and patient suffering of our saintly predecessor the late Archbishop Byrne. We feel that, given this spirit of devotedness, we have but to ask and the practice of Faith will be carried more intensely into the most ordinary actions of everyday life. *The Holy Family Our Model.*

Hence we entreat all, both Clergy and people, to fix their eyes more frequently on the Holy Home of Nazareth, as the model of our lives, both private and public. Therein was found a treasure, than which no greater can be

*Pastoral Letter of Lent, 1941.

imagined : God Himself made man, His Blessed Mother and His Foster-Father, Saint Joseph. Yet, obscurity and suffering marked those sacred lives, which were of priceless value to God. Such a choice by God of the painful things that we naturally reject, teaches us to see in the daily round of duty, however hidden and apparently unmeaning, the certain Will of God. There can be no other means of union with God than the due acceptance, in Faith and Charity, of all that each day may bring us from His hand. Only the Faith, which sees God thus in daily life, can give us, in every circumstance, the peace and the endurance for which every man thirsts in his inmost being.

To parents especially we direct our words, when we ask that all should first study and then practise the lessons of the Home of Nazareth. For parents ought to see in their children, before all else, souls whom God has given them to mould for Himself. They must, therefore, consider that they have a sacred duty to prepare their children, from earliest childhood, to carry the Cross in daily life. For, the vocation and the happiness of a Christian is to follow Our Divine Master in loving self-denial. But it will be impossible to train youth to the maturity of Christian virtue, unless from infancy the habit of obedience has become, so to speak, an instinct. It is not always understood that the whole attitude of parents, spoken and unspoken, towards the things of the Faith is a most powerful influence for virtue or vice in the lives of children. Likewise it is the sacred privilege of parents to give to their children the first knowledge of God, of Our Divine Master and of Our Blessed Lady, through the prayers recited with the little ones morning and evening and through the Catechism lessons, heard and explained.

Catholic Home Life —Essentials.
If to this teaching and example of parents, there be added the practice of the Family Rosary, whereby the household is gathered each night at the feet of Our Divine Redeemer, beneath the loving guidance of His Mother, very surely the discipline and peace and goodness of Nazareth must once again be found in all our homes.

It is a grave error to believe that a School can ever hope to supplant the essential work of parents or can succeed in fully correcting the indiscipline that a parent's neglect has permitted to develop. If to-day, in the case of youth, a want of Christian self-restraint is sometimes to be deplored, there is abundant reason to believe that the absence of virtue in the young can too often be traced to the lack of vigilance in the parents.

Nor may Schools be altogether exempted from blame. A Christian education, worthy of the name, will aim first of all at instruction and training in Christian living. Teachers, then, who fail to give proper training in reasonable self-denial and who neglect to mould their pupils in the Way of the Cross, must share the responsibility for the subsequent lapses of the children. And it may well be asked if Schools for Girls are sufficiently aware of their obligation to inculcate, with prudence, a Christian reverence for the divine vocation of motherhood, to which most of the pupils will certainly be called.

Training given in Catholic Schools.

It is not, we regret to say, among the past pupils of Primary Schools that one may look for the exceptional and graver infidelity to Christian duties. Rather often those persons whose social position and higher education befit them to be examples of a life of Faith are precisely those who prove to be a scandal to the poor. They forget that the more abundant gifts of God are a serious responsibility, demanding the exercise of deeper Faith and more generous devotedness to the less fortunate. We would gravely warn all such, without exception, that the law of God which commands modesty of dress, temperance in drink, chastity of conduct and avoidance of all that is dangerous to Faith, has the same binding force in every station of life, whether lowly or exalted.

Happily, the Christian life that is so faithfully practised by the vast multitude of the Faithful is, by its vigour, the most consoling guarantee of the future. The trials of our times have helped to strengthen our belief that " we have not here a lasting City, but seek one that is to come." [1] Our sufferings—very much less painful indeed than those of other lands—have not separated us from the thought and

Our Support in Trials.

[1] Heb. xiii, 14.

love of the Home of Nazareth. In a spirit of supernatural obedience, we shall continue to accept the measures which the Supreme Civil Authority may find it necessary to ordain. Much may be asked that will cause us suffering. Yet it is, to the eyes of Faith, a pain that will help us to do penance for our sins and draw us closer to the expiation of Our Divine Redeemer and His Sorrowing Mother. It is equally a bond of charity with the suffering people of every land, whose entreaty for lasting peace is poured out, day and night, before the Throne of God.

Faith the Foundation of Social Peace.
The very widespread yearning for social peace is itself a proof of the grave need of social reform. That peace and order we can now prepare, only if each of us by the help of Faith, sets peace and order in his own life. Too often our eyes are set on distant things, to the neglect of the daily task which God requires of us just now. And yet, is not the future made secure only by the right use of present time and circumstances ? The social regeneration, for which so many are now earnestly seeking, is a futile aim, unless by Faith we realise that the actual Will of God in daily life is the chief concern of every individual man and woman. Whatever shape the detailed reform of the social structure ultimately may take, the only lasting basis of reconstruction can be the True Faith that we profess. For God Himself, Eternal Truth, has said : " Other foundation no man can lay but that which is laid, which is Christ Jesus." [1] Hence any merely human approach to a solution, in the present or the future, of our social problems, especially in what concerns the entire life of the poor, the sick and the children, may indeed bring a certain momentary relief : it must, however, fail in regard to that which alone is permanent and divine, the supernatural aspect of our people's life.

Therefore we would appeal to all who, by reason of duty or charitable interest or higher education, are engaged in social work or studies to make it their first concern to appreciate the vast riches of the treasury of our Faith, with its divinely-given remedies for all our social life. A deep esteem of Catholic doctrine must lead in generous souls to

[1] I Cor. iii, 11.

practical fruits of supernatural social activity, instead of merely human benefaction.

And in this context, we would point out that the emphasis now being laid on Civics may easily be erroneous. No activity of life may be withdrawn from the guidance of Faith and the control of Charity. For a Catholic people, the only Civics that may lawfully be taught and practised is that, which, because it is deliberately based on the teaching of our Faith, is treated as the exercise in social life of supernatural virtues, chiefly the virtues of Justice and Charity.

Earnestly, then, we ask all—more especially the poor, the suffering and the obscure, whose lives so closely resemble the all-holy life of God made Man on earth, to rouse their Faith to see in daily duties, in monotony and pain, the sacred instruments by which God makes holy those whom He has called by Baptism to supernatural union with Himself. Thus can each person, doing the will of God in charity, prepare for the peace which God in His mercy will one day grant.

Lastly, as a sacred duty and a loving task, we would urge *Virgin* every member of our flock to turn more insistently, in these *Most* days of anxiety, to Our Blessed Lady, Our Protectress. She *Faithful.* is indeed our very tender Mother. She is also the Mother of Sorrows, of whom we read that she " *stood* by the Cross of Jesus." [1] She is likewise the Virgin most powerful, to whom alone God promised a strength, such that she would crush whatever, in man or demon, can oppose the sovereignty of God. To her, then, as Mediatrix of all graces, with fullest confidence, strongly we entrust the protection of our country, the guardianship of peace and the salvation of every soul within our Diocese.

[1] St. John xix, 25.

II—The Great Means of Grace

Chapter I

THE WORSHIP OF THE CHURCH

IT is natural to man to worship God. By the mere light of his reason, he can reflect upon the marvellous universe of which he is a part and thereby reach the certain knowledge of a personal Creator.[1] He can look into his own being and grasp the truth that God has made him, that he has not made himself.[2] He can see that creatures lower than himself give praise to the Creator by their very existence and by the instinct with which they follow the law of their being.[3] For himself, however, man will understand that he must glorify God by the tribute of the powers of his soul.[4] Realising his complete dependence as a creature, he will be urged to adore the Supreme Being by the subjection of his mind. He will express to God the thanksgiving of his heart for the benefits of life. He will be moved, in his will, to love the Being Whose goodness is the source of all that is perfect. He will read imprinted by God on his conscience a law of right and wrong and will feel the imperative claim of that law to be obeyed.[5] He will fear the Divine Lawgiver Who, in a life to come, must vindicate His own enactments if they have been disobeyed, and reward the faithful fulfilment of His commands.[6]

Religion is natural to man.

Religion is natural to man ; but human history is the sad recital of the gradual corruption of man's natural inclination to worship the Supreme Being. The worship which ought to have been given to the Creator was, by a perversion of man's intelligence, given to many gods, even to brutish

[1]Vatican Council, Session III, cc. 1–3 ; Rom. i, 20 ; Wisd. xiii, 1–9. *Summa Theologica*, 2a, 2ae, qq. 81–85. Leo XIII, Encyclical Letter, *Libertas.* [2]Ps. xcix, 3 ; cxviii, 73 ; Job x, 8–9 ; xxvi, 4 ; xxxiii, 4 ; Is. xlv, 12, 18. [3]Ps. xcvi, 6 ; xcii, 5 ; ciii ; cxlviii, 3–10. [4]Is. xliii, 7 ; Ecclus. xliii, 29–37 ; Dan. iii, 57–81. [5]Rom. ii, 14–15. [6]Cf. Gen. xv, 1 ; Deut. xxxii, 35 ; Wisd. xvi, 15–16 ; Prov. xxviii, 18 ; Hebr, xi, 6 ; cf. *Summ. Theol.* 1a, 2ae, q. 90, a. 1, ad 1 ; q. 91, a. 2.

animals.[1] Of necessity, this impiety was followed by the degradation of man's moral life. In ancient times the peoples, of whom we have preserved an accurate historical picture, are known to have been given over to idolatry and most sensual superstition. In our own day, the primitive peoples have been proved to believe in One Supreme Being, but they too worship many gods and hold perverted views of moral conduct. Of old, even the noblest pagans have been defiled by notions that are opposed to true religion and right human conduct. To-day the philosophers, who would teach mankind, are themselves uncertain about the most fundamental truths that concern God and human life.

Original Sin and False Worship.

One cannot understand how human nature could ever err so gravely about God and about man's duties towards God, unless man had suffered in mind and will and heart a profound disturbance. His nature, were it unimpaired, could not so pervert his natural inclination to worship God as to change the virtue of religion into a way of sensual corruption. The primitive traditions hint obscurely at such a fall from right reason and true religion. The revelation of God very definitely teaches that such a disturbance occurred in Original Sin.[2]

Man's responsibility.

It must not be thought that human kind is to be excused from the fault of its own degradation. God the Holy Ghost, through the Apostle St. Paul, in a passage of gravest warning,[3] teaches that man could know the invisible Creator from the visible things of the Creation, but that, instead of glorifying and thanking God, he changed the glory of the incorruptible God into the likeness of corruptible man and beasts. Man's wisdom became foolishness and his heart was darkened. In such a sin man was inexcusable, says the Apostle, and, therefore, God allowed man's wrongful conduct to become an instrument of punishment : he was delivered up to unclean and shameful excesses of bodily lusts. So close is the necessary link between man's

---

[1]Gen. vi, 5–6, 11–13 ; Exod. xx, 1–5 ; Ps. xiii, 1–3 ; Osee iv, 1–2 ; Wisd. xiv, 12–27 ; Is. xliv, 9–1 ; Gal. v, 19–21 ; Apoc. xx, 8. [2]Rom. v, 12 ; 14–19 ; 1 Cor, xv, 21–22 ; Eph. ii, 3 ; Conc. Araus. Can. 1–2 ; Conc. Trident. Sess. v. [3]Rom. i, 23–32. Cf. Eph. ii, 11–12 ; iv, 17–19 ; Col. iii, 5–7 ; Gal. v, 19–21. Cf. Wisd. xii, 25–27.

*Need of
Divine
Revelation.*

notion of God and man's service of God in human conduct !

It is clear from ancient history and from modern experience that the majority of men are so set about with difficulties, so torn by internal passions, that they cannot safely or easily attain all the truths that human reason can discover about God and rightful living. God must Himself intervene to teach mankind these natural truths with authority and definiteness. It is infinitely more necessary that God should Himself reveal those truths that are beyond the capability of the human mind ever to reach by natural reasoning.[1] These are the truths about the inner life of God and about the sharing by man in the divine nature through sanctifying grace. Only the infinite goodness of God can explain the revelation of Himself to man. Man's difficulty in reaching even a natural knowledge of the Creator is to be set down to the fault of Original Sin. God's justice, however, was not bound to heal that difficulty. But once that the goodness of God had mercifully allowed to man a destiny utterly exceeding his nature or power or due, then it was fitting, even necessary, for God to unveil the mystery of His own true nature and instruct mankind in the one true way of life.[2] To reach after death the intimate vision of God Himself, man's spiritual powers had to be raised in this life above their natural capacity, his intellect by supernatural faith, his will by supernatural hope and charity.

To this vision of God in the happiness of God Himself all the revelation of God to man has been from the very first directed. God, Whom we know in the temporary darkness of Faith, in Whose word we believe as the assertion of unfailing Truth, is God Whom we shall see in the eternal clarity of the Beatific Vision. God, to Whom we confidently reach out in the trust of Hope, is God Whom we shall possess in Heaven. God, Whom we choose with all the strength of mind and will and heart by charity, is God Whom we shall hold in the closest union of our soul as our eternal and unchanging love.[3]

[1]Conc. Vatic. Sess. 3, c. 2. Pius ix, Syllabus, 4.   [2]Cf. John xiv, 6 ; Gal. vi, 15. [3]Hebr. xi, 1 ; Rom. i, 17 ; 1 Cor. xiii, 12–13.

We shall never be able to thank God for His mercy in *True* allowing us to be the heirs of His revelation. Not so many *worship of* are so learned in ancient history as to have realised the *Chosen* depths of pagan ignorance and wickedness from which *People.* they have been delivered. Most Catholics, however, have learned the story of how God preserved His chosen people from the surrounding idolatry. It is the story of the unceasing care with which God kept alive among men both the true knowledge of Himself and the acceptable worship of the One, True God.

At all times there were faithful souls who rightly worshipped the Creator. Noe was a just man, who, amidst the corruption of his fellow-men, walked with God.[1] We read that, on being saved from the Deluge, he offered God holocausts upon an altar, and the odour of the sacrifice was sweet before the Lord.[2] From that time forward we are struck by the emphasis of the sacred narrative of the closeness of God to His people and by the detailed commands of God concerning the worship that must be given Him. One family is chosen, that of Abraham.[3] Abraham is saved from the destruction of the wicked cities of Sodom and Gomorrah.[4] The test of his acknowledgement of God's dominion is made by the order to sacrifice his own son Isaac.[5] And, because of his obedience, God promises that in the descendants of Abraham shall all the nations of the earth be blessed. To Jacob was renewed, in the vision of Angels, the same promise and he was made the father of the twelve tribes.[6] For four hundred years the Israelites lived in Egypt. They entered this pagan land a group of families and, by the extraordinary providence of God, they came out, under the leadership of Moses, a fully formed nation. To Moses was granted the declaration of the law of God and the minute prescriptions for true worship.[7] The Tabernacle, which contained the Ark of the Covenant and which prefigured the Temple, was given by God to be a central place of worship.[8] One tribe, of Levi,

[1]Gen. vi, 9 ; Ecclus. xliv, 17. [2]Gen. vi, 20–21. [3]Gen. xii, 1–4 ; Ecclus. xliv, 20–21. [4]Gen. xix, 27–28. [5]Gen. xxii, 1–12 ; 1 Mach. ii 52 ; Hebr. xi, 8–10, 17 ; Deut. iv, 8. [6]Gen. xxviii, 12–15 ; Ecclus. xliv, 26. [7]Num. xii, 5–8 ; Deut. v, 5 ; xxxiv, 10 ; Heb. iii, 5 ; xi, 24–28. [8]Exod. xxv.

was set apart to perform the ceremonies of the Law.[1]
After the sufferings in the desert, the chosen people entered
the land promised to Jacob.[2] Under the Kings, the Temple
was built as the centre of rightful worship, where all the
ceremonies required by God could be fulfilled with exactness
and magnificence.[3] None the less, lapses of God's people
into idolatry were very frequent, and for that cause they
were punished by the captivity in Babylon.[4] Purified at
length by their sufferings, the Israelites returned nor ever
after lapsed into the worship of false gods.[5] The Temple
was rebuilt and sacrifice renewed.[6] Later, however, the
Persians were allowed to dominate Jerusalem; the Greeks
in turn were permitted to defile the Temple,[7] and at last
the independence of God's people was lost in the conquest
of the Romans.[8]

*The Promise
of the Divine
Redeemer.*
It is a strange, sad story of human failure and of God's
faithful love. No treachery of man was able to defeat the
wisdom and the goodness of God, Who had willed to reveal
Himself to men. At the beginning, after the fall of Adam,
a Redeemer was clearly promised.[9] Amidst the darkness of
idolatry, the flame of the knowledge and the worship of
God was kept alive at first in faithful individuals, then in a
chosen family, later in an elected nation. Slowly the revelation of the promised Saviour is made more clear in prophecy
until the Israelites are taught that He will be born of the
house of Jacob, of the tribe of Juda and of the family of
David.[10] He will be born of a Virgin, in the city of Bethlehem.[11] He will suffer and by His pain shall all men be
redeemed and sanctified.[12] His death by crucifixion is
foretold by Zachary : " they shall look on Me Whom they
have pierced."[13] The sacrifice of His death is that clean
oblation foreseen by Malachy, by which, from the rising
to the setting of the sun, God shall be glorified among all
peoples.[14]

[1]Num. xvii, xviii. [2]Jos. xi, 23. [3]3 Kings, v-viii. [4]4 Kings xxii, 16-17 ;
xxiii, 22–24 ; xxv. [5]Esdr. i. [6]Esdr. vi, 15–17. [7]1 Mach. i. [8]1 Mach. viii ;
xiv, 40 ; xv, 15–23 ; Luke ii, 1–2 ; iii, i ; xxiii, 2 ; xx, 25 ; John, xix, 12,
15. [9]Gen. iii, 15. [10]Gen. xlix, 10 ; Num. xxiv, 17 ; Is. ix, 6–7 ; Mich.
v, 2 ; John vii, 42 ; Matt. i, 1 ; Luke i, 27, 32, 69 ; Mark x, 47 ; Rom. i,
3. [11]Is. vii, 14 ; Mich. v, 2. [12]Ps. xxi, 7–8 ; Is. i, 6 ; lii, 14 ; liii, 3–12 ; cf.
Philipp ii, 5–8 ; 1 Pet. ii, 24 ; Matt. viii, 17. [13]Zach. xii, 10. [14]Mal. i, 11.

Then, at length, God, Who had spoken by His Prophets, *The Redemption.* spoke to man by His own Son.[1] " And the Word was made flesh and dwelt among us."[2] At that moment all was changed ; the glory of Israel and the light of the pagans had at last appeared.[3] For the first time, Almighty God received from human nature an adequate adoration, a complete thanksgiving. To Jesus Christ all the prophecies had referred ; for Him the chosen people had been preserved. He was " the light of God's brightness that shone on the darkened eyes of men."[4] The Law of Moses would be perfected on his teaching.[5] The sacrifice of the Temple would be completed and replaced by the sacrifice of God made Man upon the Cross. Because Jesus Christ is God, He would offer in His human nature an infinite atonement for sin. Only in Jesus Christ, God made Man, could human kind be reconciled to God. And such is the satisfaction of Jesus Christ for the offence of sin that it is an adequate reparation of infinite value.

To that offering of Himself in sacrifice, foretold by *The Sacrifice of* Isaias and Zachary and Malachy, all the life of Jesus Christ *the Cross.* looked forward. Of His entrance into the world it is written : " Sacrifice and oblation Thou wouldst not : but a body Thou hast fitted to Me. Then said I : Behold I come. In the head of the book it is written of Me that I should do Thy will, O God."[6] " In which will," says the Sacred Scriptures, " we are sanctified by the oblation of the body of Jesus Christ once."[7] The Presentation of the Child in the Temple recalls the suffering that would be His, when His own people would offer Him upon a Cross.[8] When as a boy He is found in the Temple, He asserts that His only purpose is to do the will of God, His Father.[9] Later, in His public life, He declares that His very food is to do the will of Him who sent Him.[10] Again He adds : " I do always the things that please Him."[11] As His life of perfect subjection to God draws to a close, He takes occasion to warn His apostles that He must suffer and die at the hands

---

[1]Hebr. i, 1–2 ; Tit. ii, 11 ; iii, 4 ; Gal. iv, 4–5 ; Eph. iii, 2–5. [2]John i, 14. [3]Luke ii, 32. [4]Preface of Mass of the Nativity. [5]Matt. v, 17 ; Hebr. x, 9. [6]Hebr. x, 5–9. [7]Ib. x, 10. [8]Luke ii, 22–38. [9]Luke ii, 49. [10]John iv, 34. [11]John viii, 29 ; v, 30 ; vi, 38.

of men.[1] It was as if His chosen people, in spite of the most evident miracles, renewed the incessant apostacy of their ancestors.[2] And God made of their hatred the instrument of our salvation. If Jesus Christ was crucified, in obedience to the will of His Father, it was not that His enemies had triumphed. " Therefore doth the Father love Me : because I lay down my life that I may take it up again. No man taketh it away from Me : but I lay it down Myself. And I have power to lay it down : and I have power to take it up again. This commandment have I received of the Father."[3]

The night before He died, He promised that His precious Blood would be the ransom which as Victim He would pay.[4] Entering our world He had said : " I come to do Thy will."[5] In death, His final words sealed the obedience of His life— " it is consummated."[6] He gave Himself for us in sacrifice that " He might redeem us from all iniquity."[7]

The Sacrifice of the Cross is the perfect acknowledgment by Jesus Christ of man's subjection to God Almighty, the Creator. It is the full thanksgiving of Jesus Christ for all the benefits of God to man. It is adequate satisfaction for the sin of Adam and of all mankind, made by Him Who alone could offer a complete atonement to Almighty God. It is the most acceptable petition for the needs of men, presented to God by Him Whose filial obedience could never falter.[8]

The Sacrifice of the Mass.

It might well seem enough that God should have redeemed us by the sacrifice of Himself on Calvary. But His infinite love found a means of leaving a memorial and a true renewal of that sacrifice : at the Last Supper He instituted the Blessed Eucharist.[9] Thus, says the Council of Trent, He has left to His beloved Spouse, the Church, a visible sacrifice—such as human nature demands—by which the

---

[1]Luke ix, 44 ; xvii, 25 ; Mark x, 32–34 ; Matt. xx, 17–19 ; John iii, 14 ; Acts i, 16. [2]John xv, 24 ; x, 38. [3]John x, 17–18. [4]Matt. xxvi, 28 ; Mark xiv, 24 ; Luke xxii, 20. [5]Hebr. x, 9. [6]John xix, 20. [7]Tit. ii, 4 ; 1 John iv, 10 ; 1 Pet. iii, 18 ; Col. i, 14, 20 ; Hebr. ix, 12, 28 ; Gal. iii, 13 ; Cf. *Summ. Theol.* iii, q. 49, a. 1–4. [8]Conc. Trid. Sess. 22, c. 2 ; Eph. v, 2 ; Tit. ii, 13 ; Rom. v, 8–9, 19 ; viii, 32 ; Phil. ii, 6–11. Cf. *Summ. Theol.*, 2a. 2ae, qq. 84, 85. Pius IX, Encycl. *Amantissimi ;* Pius XII, Encycl. *Mediator Dei.* [9]John. xiii, 1.

sacrifice once offered in blood on the Cross may be renewed and its memory remain until the end of time.[1]

That Jesus Christ willed at the Last Supper to offer a true sacrifice is evidenced by the words of sacrifice He used : " This is My body that is *given* for you.[2] This is My blood of the New Testament that shall be *shed* for many unto remission of sins."[3] Only in this sacrifice can be found the oblation foretold by the Prophet which is both holy and universal ; which is clean and is offered to God from the rising of the sun to the going down thereof.[4] For, wherever Mass is offered, we have renewed, under the sign of the sacrament, the true offering and the real immolation of Jesus Christ Himself.

That Our Divine Redeemer willed to institute a sacrifice that shall be perpetual is shown by the command He gave to His Apostles and to their successors : " Do this in commemoration of Me."[5]

All the life of Jesus Christ was a preparation for the sacrifice of the Cross, the supreme act of our Redemption, by which due homage was offered to God and adequate satisfaction made for sin. So now, all the life of the Church of Christ is centred on the Blessed Eucharist. Under the appearances of bread and wine, this sacrament contains really, truly and substantially, the Body and Blood of Jesus Christ, which are offered to God as the Sacrifice of the New Law and distributed to the faithful as the spiritual food of their souls. It is true to say that the Blessed Eucharist then prolongs on earth the Incarnation. As the Second Person of the Blessed Trinity, being conceived of the Holy Ghost and born of the Virgin Mary,[6] came down on earth to redeem mankind, so now, the same Divine Redeemer makes Himself present in our midst, under the sacrament of the Blessed Eucharist, to renew perpetually the sacrifice of the Cross in Holy Mass and to distribute grace in Holy Communion.[7]

[1]Conc. Trid. Sess. xxii, c. 1. [2]Matt. xxvi, 26 ; Mark xiv, 22 ; Luke xxii, 19. [3]Matt. xxvi, 27–28 ; Mark, xiv, 23–24 ; Luke xxii, 20 ; 1 Cor. xi, 23–26 ; x, 16–17. [4]Mal. i, 11. [5]Luke xxii, 19 ; 1 Cor. xi, 26. [6]Matt. i, 20 ; Luke i, 26–38. [7]Conc. Trid. Sess. 22, c. 2 ; Sess. 21, c. 3. Leo XIII Encycl. *Mirae Caritatis.*

During His life, Jesus Christ had said that the Father seeks those who may adore Him in spirit and in truth.[1] That adoration is secured by the Church which Jesus Christ Himself established, to which He entrusted all the means of sanctity, the sacraments, and to which He gave the gift of the infallible guidance of the Holy Ghost. Thus it is that to enable us to adore God in union with Jesus Christ in the one true sacrifice of the New Law, He has instituted the sacrament of Baptism.[2] By this sacrament we are set aside in the one, true religion of Christ to worship God, as God Himself has willed that He must be worshipped.[3] For the first time, grace is poured into our soul; we are given to share in the nature of God Himself.[4] We become the brothers of Jesus Christ :[5] we are made the branches of the True Vine which imparts the sap and life of grace.[6] If later we should sin in human weakness, the sacrament of Penance will restore the penitent to the friendship of God. To make us firm in resisting whatever would imperil the life of grace, we are strengthened by the Holy Ghost in the sacrament of Confirmation. The unending succession of the true children of God is guaranteed the Church in the sacrament of Marriage. The unfailing line of those who will teach the truths of Jesus Christ and offer the sacrifice of the Mass is secured by the sacrament of Holy Order. Extreme Unction is the soothing vigour that helps us to reach more easily in eternal bliss the union that Holy Viaticum has begun on earth. One and all, these sacraments, by which the grace of Christ is first imparted or is restored or is increased, have for their end the Blessed Eucharist. Only when we have been made holy by the grace of Jesus Christ, can we fully unite with Him, as He offers to God the perfect homage of the Mass, and from Him receive in Holy Communion the fruits of the Redemption, in every benefit of grace.

All Christian life thus gravitates around the Divine Person of God made Man, Who redeemed us by the sacrifice of the Cross and renews that sacrifice in Holy Mass. The

---

[1]John iv, 23–24. [2]John iii, 3. [3]1 Cor. xii, 13 ; Gal. iii, 27 ; Matt. xxviii, 19 ; Eph. iv, 24. [4]2 Pet. i, 4 ; Eph. iv, 22–24 ; Col. ii, 12 ; iii, 9. [5]Rom. viii, 17 ; Tit. iii, 5–7 ; Eph. iv, 6. [6]John xv, 5 ; iii, 3–6.

worship paid to God must be perennial. The imparting
of grace to men, in the application of the infinite merits
of the Divine Redeemer, must equally have no cessation.

Therefore the Church, guided by God the Holy Ghost, *The
Church's*
had developed around the central act of sacrifice, the cycle *Year and*
of feasts which recall the mysteries of our Redemption. *the Life of
Our Divine*
Offertory and Consecration and Communion remain *Redeemer.*
unchanged within the Mass but varying prayers and
ceremonies and readings from Sacred Scripture explain
the mysteries of Jesus Christ. They also serve to renew
in us the dispositions of the soul of Our Divine Redeemer,
Who offers us with Himself to God in the Holy Sacrifice.

In Advent, we live again the weary years of waiting for the
promised Saviour. But the mind of the Church in that
season is brightened by continual reference to the Gospel
of the Annunciation. In penance, but with fullest confidence
we await the coming of Him, for Whom, since man's
creation, all things in human history have been but a
preparation.

At Christmas, we welcome the Infant with great joy, for
the new light of God at length has shone upon our darkened
world.[1] Yet, the birth in a stable during winter at once
forewarns us that here is the suffering Messiah, foretold by
the Prophets.[2] Only the humble are admitted to greet
Him, for His voice will not be heard abroad and He is
come to heal the broken heart.[3] Almost at once Herod
seeks to kill Him, a presage of the pursuit that will conclude
on Calvary.[4] Even as an Infant He sheds His blood in
the Circumcision.[5] In the Presentation, He is offered in the
Temple, a sign of sacrifice, and the prophecy of His rejection
by His own people is clearly made.[6]

In Septuagesima, we turn back to consider the Fall of
Adam and the consequent sinfulness of men. In Lent, we
are shown the sinless Redeemer fasting for forty days
before He enters on the way that ends in death.[7] In
penance for our sins, we make ready for the great week,

---

[1]John viii, 12 ; i, 4 ; xii, 36, 46 ; 1 Thess. v, 5 ; 2 Cor. iv, 4. [2]Luke
xxiv, 26-27 ; 44-47 ; Acts iii, 18 ; xxvi, 22-23. [3]Is. xlii, 1-4 ; xli, 9 ;
Matt. xii, 17-21 ; Luke iv, 18-21. [4]Matt. ii, 13-14. [5]Luke ii, 21. [6]Luke
ii, 34. [7]Luke iv, 1-14.

called the Holy Week, in which are recalled the dread Passion of Jesus Christ and His death by crucifixion on Mount Calvary.

Easter has little meaning for us, with its triumph of Jesus Christ, unless we have learned to see in the glory of the Resurrection the reward of the obedience unto death, even the death of the Cross, that alone achieved the Redemption of mankind.[1] Until the Ascension we glimpse Our Divine Lord in His glorious life, as He gives His last instructions to the Apostles on whom He has built His Church.[2] The Ascension we can at length understand from the words of Our Divine Lord before He died[3] to be necessary in the plan of God, " for now Jesus Christ seated at the right hand of the Father ever lives to intercede for us."[4] And the first fruit of that intercession is the sending of God the Holy Ghost, Who henceforth will dwell within the Church, guarding her from error in the teaching of Jesus Christ and sanctifying in the grace of Christ the members, who, by Baptism, are incorporated into His One true Church.[5]

The Church's Year and the Redemption.

Thereafter, the Church's year never permits us to forget for long the redemption of the Cross. The feast of the Most Holy Trinity sets before us the mystery of God's inner life. We have learned of that life only through Jesus Christ, and we share in it only in virtue of His death.[6] Corpus Christi and the feast of the Sacred Heart renew the memory of the infinite love that gave us the Blessed Eucharist, our sacrifice and our means of union with the Word made Flesh. The feast of the Precious Blood recalls soon after the infinite price that was required for our redemption.[7] The Transfiguration allows us to glimpse, in the face of Jesus Christ, the glory that the feast of the Blessed Trinity has revealed to us as the inner life of God and as the reward of our faithful love on earth.[8]

The Church's Year and Our Lady.

Woven into the cycle of the Church's year are all the feasts of the Mother of Jesus. As she never lived apart from Him,

[1]Philipp. ii, 8. [2]John xx-xxi ; Mark xvi, 14–20 ; Matt. xxviii. [3]John xvi, 7 ; xv, 16–18, 26 ; Luke xxiv, 49. [4]Hebr. vii, 25. [5]Acts ii, 1–4 ; Rom. v, 5 ; 1 Cor. vi, 19 ; Col. ii, 9–12, 17. [6]John xvii, 2–3 ; Col. ii, 14–15. [7]1 Cor. vi, 20 ; vii, 23 ; cf. Matt. xxvii, 9. [8]Matt. xvii, 2 ; Mark ix, 1 ; Col. i 12–13 : 2 Thess. ii, 12–13 ; 1 Pet. 3–4.

from the moment of His conception till His death, so now, in the worship of the Church, she is unfailingly linked with the life of Jesus Christ, her Son and our Redeemer. Surrounding her as their Mother and their Queen, stand all the saints, whose virtue in imitating Jesus Christ the Church incessantly recalls. With Mary, too, are grouped all those who, by special commission of the Church, and under solemn vows, recite the Divine Office, the sacrifice of praise, from morning until morning, from end to end of all the earth. With Mary are united in the bonds of charity and prayer, all the children of whom she is the spiritual Mother, to whom she has distributed the grace of Jesus Christ : the suffering souls in Purgatory, the Blessed in Heaven, the faithful here on earth.

Thus in the Church, by the communion of the saints, *Unity in* through Jesus Christ, our only Mediator,[1] as He offers *Jesus Christ.* Himself to God perpetually in the holy sacrifice of the Mass, there rises to God an unfailing fount of adoration and thanksgiving, of reparation and petition, which is none other than the prayer of Jesus Christ. " I have glorified Thee on earth. I have finished the work which Thou gavest Me to do. Holy Father, keep them in Thy name whom Thou hast given to Me, that they all may be one, as Thou Father in Me and I in Thee, that they also may be one in Us."[2]

[1] Tim. ii, 5. [2] John xvii, 4, 11, 21 ; cf. Eph. v, 1 ; iv, 15, 20–24 ; iii, 16–19.

Chapter II

PRAYER

Prayer is Universal. In the providence of God, prayer is found throughout the universe. There is an entreaty in the cry of the beasts, which is their plea to us for sympathy. In their instinctive way, they call on God, Who gives them food in opportune time.[1] He is, Our Divine Lord tells us, so mindful of the animals that not a sparrow can fall from the sky, without His intervention.[2] In human life, there is no man who does not pray to his superiors ; for life is so ordered that he cannot reach the goal of his numberless desires, without becoming a suppliant in a thousand ways. By gesture, by word of mouth, by letter, by interview, pleading must be made. And many a man, who will not bend the knee to God, is forced, if he but thought of it, to be a beggar to his fellow-man. If we could realise how much of life is spent in prayer to others, who have the power to do our will, we should more easily understand the obligation of man's prayer to God. " The Lord Thy God thou shalt adore, and Him only shalt thou serve." [3] Who that looks at our world, restless and darkened in the isolation it has made for itself by forgetfulness of God, does not feel it binding on him to pray to God for mercy and to learn, if he may, how to pray to God more perfectly ?

(a) Why we should pray. God is supreme. It is a law graven in our human nature to show reverence to a superior.[4] Now, God is *Supreme*, He has had no beginning ; He will have no end. In Himself, He is all perfection. We say that He is wisdom and power, goodness and love, but we cannot express in human words His being. We take refuge from our ignorance by applying to Him the title *infinite*, but the content of that word escapes us. It is a

---

[1]Ps. cxxiii, 27 ; cxliv, 15. [2]Matt., x, 29. [3]Matt., iv, 10 ; Deut., vi, 13 ; x, 12. [4]*Summ. Theol.*, 2a, 2ae, q. 102, art. 2. For Prayer, *vide* 2a, 2ae, q. 83, art. 1–17.

confession that we cannot measure Him Who is [1]. We fail
to understand even how much He must exceed our power of
understanding Him. " Great is the Lord and exceedingly to
be praised," cries out the Psalmist, " according to Thy name,
O God, so also is Thy praise. This is God, our God, unto
eternity." [2]

God has another title to our adoration : He is the sole
Creator. God, to Whom nothing can be added, chose to call
us out of nothingness. The universe, by its order and its
beauty, shows forth the perfection of the Creator. [3] Man,
because he resembles God more intimately in his mind and
will, can acknowledge the power and wisdom of God, and
can esteem the goodness which is alone the cause of his
existence. [4] The same Hand that created us holds us in
continuous existence. Truly, the Mastership of God extends
to every fibre of our being and every activity of our faculties.
The servant ought to reverence the Master from Whom he
holds the breath of life. *(b) God is the sole Creator.*

In addition, God is the *author* of all *good things*. Everything that sustains or solaces or charms is owed to the
Creator. The goods of earth and sea and sky, the elements
that serve us, the joys of mind, the support of friendship,
the love of families, all courtesies, all beauties, every harmony
of order ; " My hand," says God, " made all these things." [5]
For, " the earth is the Lord's and the fulness thereof : the
world and all that dwell therein." [6] Even if we were not of
the household of the Faith, we should be obliged to express
our thanks to God, the Author of all these gifts. " Thou are
worthy, O Lord, Our God, to receive glory and honour
and power, because Thou hast created all things, and for
Thy will they were, and have been created." [7] *(c) God is the Author of all good things.*

But the *adoration of a soul in sanctifying grace* is something very different from a merely natural reverence. In
God, we see now not only our Creator, but the Providence
of our lives, the Giver of endless benefits. We salute in
God the exceeding love, which has given us, without
any merit on our part, to share in His very life. [8] By grace *(d) God has given us His divine life.*

[1]Exod. iii, 14–15. [2]Ps. xlvii, 1, 2, 15. [3]Gen. 1, 31. [4]Gen. i, 27; ii, 7.
[5]Is. lxvi, 2. [6]Ps. xxiii, 1. [7]Apoc. iv, 11. [8]2 Pet. i, 4.

we are transformed in our being and in all our powers. We could have known God by the light of His Creation. We could have loved Him for the perfections that the creatures of His hand revealed.[1] But, given sanctifying grace, we are born again, we possess a new power of operation.[2] Finite though we are and ever must remain, we have now for object of our knowledge God as He knows Himself, for object of our love God as He loves Himself. This new nature will have its full fruition in the Beatific Vision, but already on earth it flowers in charity or in the love that causes us to esteem God and adhere to Him as known by Faith to be infinitely good and lovable. This gift of grace, or share in the divine life of God, we owe completely to the ransom of the Precious Blood of God made Man.[3] We have been redeemed; our fallen state has been repaired by the merits of the only Saviour, Jesus Christ.[4]

Prayer of the Blessed in Heaven. If the virtue of religion bids us to offer to God the reverence and honour that are His due, what shall that *new act of religion* be, by which the soul, redeemed and sanctified, shall declare its full dependence upon God the Perfect Being, its Creator, and its utter need of Him as the Author of all its good?[5] The Apocalypse makes answer, when it shows us the Blessed in Heaven offering to God the Son "the golden vials, full of odours, which are the prayers of the Saints" or of the Faithful on earth. "And they sang a new canticle saying: 'Thou are worthy, O Lord, to take the book and to open the seals thereof, because Thou wast slain and hast redeemed us to God, in Thy blood, out of every tribe and tongue and people and nation.'" The angelic hosts repeat the prayer of the redeemed: "And I heard the voice of many Angels round the throne and the living creatures and the ancients, and the number of them was thousands of thousands, saying with a loud voice: 'The Lamb that was slain is worthy to receive power and divinity, wisdom and strength and honour and glory and benediction'." Finally, all created

---

[1]Rom. i, 20; Eph. iv, 18. [2]2 Cor. v, 17; Gal. vi, 15; John iii, 5; i, 12; 2 Pet. i, 4; James i, 12. [3]Matt. xx, 28; Mark x, 45. [4]1 Pet. ii, 24; 1 John ii, 12; Luke xix, 10. [5]*Summ. Theol.*, loc. cit., q. 83, art. 2, art. 3.

things unite to venerate in similar terms the conquest
of the Precious Blood : " And every creature which is in
heaven and on earth and under the earth and such as are
in the sea, I heard all saying : To Him that sitteth on the
throne and to the Lamb, benediction and honour and
glory and power for ever and ever." To which prayer the
Blessed make reply, Amen. And falling down " they adored
Him that liveth for ever and ever."[1]

The *prayer of the Church* is not different in its adoring *Prayer of*
reverence from that of the Blessed in Heaven. During *the Church*
the offering of the Holy Sacrifice, the Church intones the *on earth.*
Gloria in excelsis Deo. The accents of that hymn and
the sentiments expressed recall at once the " new canticle "
revealed to us by God the Holy Ghost. " Glory to God
in the highest. We praise Thee ; we bless Thee ; we adore
Thee ; we glorify Thee." First, bending low, like the
ancients before the throne of God, we acclaim God as
supreme. We adore Him ; we rejoice that He is infinite ;
we offer Him the tribute of our joy in His perfection.
" We give Thee thanks for Thy great glory, O Lord God,
Heavenly King, God the Father Almighty." Turning to
the benefits which show forth His power and wisdom
and goodness, we thank Him for the glory that is in fact
our blessedness. The gifts of creation, the world of grace,
the life of Jesus Christ on earth, the intercession of His
Mother ; all things that are, exist for God. " O Lord Jesus
Christ, the Only-Begotten Son, O Lord God, Lamb of
God, Son of the Father, Who takest away the sins of the
world, receive our prayer." Mindful of the greatest blessing
of God's providence, our redemption in the Precious Blood,
at once we turn to salute the Saviour, Who is at once God
the Son and the Victim slain for our salvation.[2] Because
He has truly taken away the sins of men, we entreat Him
to hear our prayer. " Thou Who sittest at the right hand
of the Father, have mercy on us." Now risen from the
dead, our Divine Redeemer likes to make unending intercession for us.[3] "Mercy on us, who cost Him life itself,

[1]Apoc. v, 8–14.   [2]1 Tim. ii, 5–6 ; John iii, 14–17 ; x, 15 ; Acts v,
30–31 ; 1 John i, 7. [3]Heb. vii, 25.

is all we ask ; but in that word, mercy, are contained every grace for earth, even Heaven itself." " For Thou only art holy. Thou only art the Lord. Thou only, O Jesus Christ, with the Holy Ghost, art most high in the glory of God the Father. Amen." Our plea for mercy cannot fail, for it is made to the Redeemer, Who, with the Father and the Holy Ghost, is God.

Adoration of God ; thanksgiving for His glory ; and, as befits the redeemed who are pilgrims still, contrite entreaty to the one Redeemer, with confidence in the Blessed Trinity, our God : thus does the Church, under the influence of the Holy Ghost, instruct us in the mode of prayer that repeats the adoration of the Angels and the Blessed in Heaven.

When we make such prayer to God, *the whole of our being*, body and soul, is dedicated to His worship.[1] With our lips we speak, offering to God the power which marks us off from the merely animal creation. This vocal prayer is owed to God that the body may share in paying Him due reverence. By the repetition of our words, the soul is stimulated to rise above the senses and make that prayer " of mind and spirit,"[2] which is properly the act of the supernatural virtue of religion.

Our Prayer a raising of the soul to God.

For, if we reflect upon the prayer of the Church just quoted it must be evident that, in the first place, prayer is a *raising of the mind* to God, in Faith. The words we use do but affirm our belief in the existence of God and His perfections. The deeper our knowledge of the mysteries taught us by the Faith, the more readily shall we understand how lovable is God. On the wings of words which express the content of the Faith, the soul is lifted up to God to reach Him, as He is, in the understanding of Faith.[3] The heart and will then easily follow in acts of Hope and Charity, longing to possess God without fear of losing Him, adhering to God Whom we have grasped as limitlessly good and lovable to the utmost of our power. Thus to " pray in spirit and in truth "[4] is to bring to bear on God in adoration all the vast energy of the spiritual

[1] *Summ. Theol.*, loc. cit., art. 12—cf. 2a, 2ae, q. 84, art. 2, ad. 2. [2] 1 Cor. xiv. 15. [3] Cf. *Summ. Theol.*, loc. cit., art. 15. [4] John iv, 23-24.

being called the soul : its thoughts, its aims, its fears, its joys. God, " Who seeth in secret," [1] tells us that He searches out the heart,[2] as if it were the inmost being that He looks on in our prayer. And how He values the soul of man He has Himself made clear when He declared : what doth it profit a man if he gain the whole world and suffer the loss of his own soul ? Or what exchange shall a man give for his soul ?[3]

The *richness of the prayer* made by any soul in the state of sanctifying grace is seldom understood. Even a sinner's prayer, when made in Faith, is a raising of the mind and soul to God. It has no merit which could lay claim in justice to God's answer. In His mercy, God is pleased to regard its power of intercession.[4] But the prayer that springs from a soul in the state of grace has a power over the heart of God that, in a certain sense, is infallible. For God, looking on the soul redeemed by the Precious Blood of His only-begotten Son, beholds no longer a mere human creature of His own making. He sees instead the reflection of His own divine life, for the soul in grace is transformed in its being and its powers. Its prayer, then, partakes of that which is properly divine. By grace we have been enrolled in the family of God our Father and given a right to the eternal inheritance of the Beatific Vision : " we are the sons of God, and, if sons, heirs also, heirs indeed of God and joint heirs with Christ." [5] We are become, by grace, like to the image of Jesus Christ,[6] of Whom God the Father declared : " This is my beloved Son, in Whom I am well pleased."[7] Our prayer is therefore the cry of a child to God its Father. And if a human father cannot resist the call of his flesh and blood for bread, can God refuse the entreaty of His child ?[8]

Richness of our Prayers through Sanctifying Grace.

The prayer of a soul in grace has yet another claim on God : it is always made *in the name of Jesus Christ.* Not on our own wretchedness do we now presume to ask ; we speak in the name of Jesus, by His own com-

Our Prayer in the Name of Jesus Christ.

[1]Matt. vi, 6, 18. [2]1 Kings xvi, 7 ; Ps. vii, 10 ; Rom. viii, 27 ; Apoc. ii, 23. [3]Matt. xvi, 26 ; Mark viii, 36 ; Luke ix, 25. [4]*Summ. Theol.,* loc. cit., art. 16. [5]Rom. viii, 16–17 ; 21–23. [6]Rom. viii, 29 ; 1 Cor. xv, 47–49. [7]Matt. xvii, 5 ; Luke iii, 22 ; John iii, 36. [8]Matt. vii, 9–11 ; Luke xi, 11–13.

mand.[1] Before the power of that Name, every knee must bend.[2] No other Name under Heaven is given to men, whereby we must be saved.[3] It is Our Divine Lord Himself Who assures us : "Whatsoever you shall ask the Father in My name, that will I do."[4]

Our Prayer assisted by The Holy Ghost.

We rarely pause to think that the prayer of the soul in sanctifying grace is *assisted by God the Holy Ghost.* "The Promise of the Father" dwells in our heart.[5] "The Spirit helpeth our infirmity, for we know not what we should pray for as we ought. But the Spirit Himself asketh for us,"[6] in that the Third Divine Person teaches us how to pray. He inspires us to ask for what is right, He rouses within us desires, which, under His influence, can be only helpful to our salvation. He causes us, in particular, to long for eternal life. He is the author of the yearnings for the things of God that cannot be described in human speech, especially the union with God, which is the vision of Himself.

The Prayer of Jesus Christ.

If such, in the view of God, be the prayer of any soul in the state of grace, what, we may ask in wonder, was not the unspeakable value of the *prayer of Jesus Christ* ? We read that He used to spend the night in the prayer of God.[7] In the prayer in the Garden of Olives, on the night before he died, He has left us an example of prayer than which there is none more perfect. It is a testament setting forth all the qualities that should mark true prayer to God.[8]

(a) Its Confidence.

We have heard Our Divine Lord on several occasions during His earthly life call on God as " Father." In particular we remember the moment when His Apostles had asked Him to teach them how to pray.[9] So now His prayer commences with the address of tenderest *confidence*, " Father." A short time before, He had declared, " I have finished the work which Thou gavest me to do."[10] Now, as He faced His Passion, in the brief interval between the Last Supper and His betrayal, the sins of men, our

---

[1]Mark xvi, 18 ; Matt. xviii, 20 ; John xiv, 13 ; xvi, 26 ; Col. ii, 17. [2]Phil. ii, 10. [3]Acts iv, 12. [4]John xiv, 13. [5]John xiv, 16–26 ; Rom. v, 5 ; viii, 9–11. [6]Rom. viii, 26–27. [7]Luke vi, 12. [8]Matt. xxvi, 36–46 ; Mark xiv, 26–42 ; Luke xxii, 39–46. [9]Matt. vi, 9 ; Luke xi, 2. [10]John xvii, 4.

own included, flooded in over His soul.[1] The vision of
His Blood shed in vain for many, the sight of all His
torture crushed Him to the earth and pressed the blood
out through His veins, in agony of sadness and fear.
" Father," He prayed, "all things are possible to Thee.
Let this chalice pass from Me." We should never pray
if we had not trust in the goodness of Him Whom we
entreat and in His power to help. The confidence of Jesus
Christ in God knows no limits, for the Father on Whom
He calls is the God of infinite goodness. He had promised,
besides, so very many times to hearken to the prayer
of the lowly.[2] And the same Father can help, for He is
the God of infinite power : "All things are possible to
Thee." Is not this the Father of Whom Jesus Christ has
said : " Father, I give Thee thanks that Thou hast heard
Me. And I knew that Thou hearest Me always ? "[3] " All
things are possible to Thee," He prayed ; " if Thou wilt,
remove this chalice from Me."

Yet, on this occasion, God did not seem to hear. There-
upon Jesus repeated His prayer, with the *constancy* that
God has willed to require from us. God has felt obliged
to command us to ask and to knock.[4] With us it would
seem as if God insists that we should knock upon His
door that He may stir up our desires. Only when the
heart has been unlocked by strong desires, does it become
capacious of God's favours.[5] Jesus Christ is our example.
" Again the second time, He went and prayed saying :
My Father, if this chalice may not pass away, but I must
drink it, Thy will be done." For the third time He pleaded,
" And He prayed the third time, saying the same words."
More intensely still Christ entreated : " and being in an
agony, He prayed the longer."

*(b) Its
Constancy.*

The *humility* of the prayer of Christ in the Garden
is not less exemplary than its confidence and its constancy.
He Who had remained serene throughout the Last Supper,
in the presence of Judas and of the chosen Apostles, who
would abandon Him, now openly admits the sorrow that

*(c) Its
Humility.*

---

[1]Ps. xvii, 5–6—cf. *Summ. Theol.*, iii, q. 46, art. 5 and 6. [2]Ps. ix, 11 ;
xxxiii, 7 ; xc, 15 ; Jer. xxxiii, 3 ; Zach. x, 6. [3]John xi, 41–42. [4]Matt. vii,
7–8 ; Luke xi, 8, 9 ; James i, 6. [5]John xvi, 24.

of itself could slay Him : " My soul is sorrowful even unto death."

He, Who had been the mainstay of His disciples, asks, in His human desolation, for the comfort of the companionship that they would refuse : " Stay you here and watch with Me." The lowly posture of His body is itself an act of adoration : "kneeling down, He prayed. And He fell upon His face." " With a strong cry and tears, He offered up prayers and supplications to Him that was able to save Him from death."[1] Yet the accents of His prayer were not an insistence : "If it be possible," He asked : " if this chalice may not pass away, but I must drink it." " Let this chalice pass from Me," He pleaded, Who, in His human life, had strengthened the weary hands of unnumbered sufferers.

(d) Its Wisdom.

But in nothing is the humility of the prayer of Christ more evident than in the *wisdom* of His prayer : "If this chalice may not pass away, but I must drink it, Thy will be done." The Holy Ghost, we have learned, teaches us how to pray. Who can declare the unhindered efficacy of the Gifts of God the Holy Ghost in the human soul of Jesus Christ ? What Jesus asks, in fact, is not so much deliverance from the bodily torment and brutal disdain of His Passion and Death on the Cross, but more particularly the fullest obedience to the will of God, His Father. Our prayers, in the providence of God, must be made. Our prayers cannot change the will of God. Endowed with the qualities of the prayer of Christ, our prayers do not modify but rather fulfil the plan of God, for God has decreed that that shall come to pass which has been sought in prayer.[2] Hence that prayer alone is wise, with the wisdom given to it by the Holy Ghost, which is humble in its full acceptance of the will of God. So to submit oneself is to enter into and accomplish the design of God.[3] And the wise humility of such a prayer is always answered in the way that God, in unfailing wisdom and goodness, has decreed is best. The answer of God the Father to the prayer of Jesus was given straightway : " And there appeared

[1] Hebr. v, 7—cf. *Summ. Theol.*, iii, q. 47, art. 3. [2] *Summ. Theol.*, loc. cit., art. 2. [3] Matt. vii, 21.

to Him an Angel from Heaven, strengthening Him." In that strength, He arose. "Rise up," He cried to His Apostles, "let us go." In the power that came to Him from prayer, He went forth to drink to the dregs that chalice of His Father's Will, which was our own redemption in the shedding of His Blood.

The prayer of Jesus Christ in the Garden was a passing act: the *Prayer of His life* was that unchanging submission to the will of God, of which the prayer in the Garden is the poignant expression. "My meat is to do the will of Him that sent Me."[1] At the beginning, His attitude is declared in the words: "Behold I come to do Thy will, O God."[2] At the end of life, He could assert: "I have finished the work which Thou hast given me to do."[3] Even now after He has ascended into Heaven, Jesus Christ has found a means of renewing throughout time, the perfect offering of Himself to God the Father, by the Sacrifice of the Mass. In each Mass is shown forth His death[4] which was a sacrifice in blood upon the Cross. In each Mass, the same High Priest offers Himself, by the hands of His priests, in an unbloody manner, perpetuates the Sacrifice of the Cross and applies to us the fruits of His Redemption. The soul of that Sacrifice, so to speak, is the interior offering of Christ which was once made manifest by the shedding of His Blood, and by His words upon the Cross: "It is consummated. Father into Thy hands I commend my spirit."[5] That offering of infinite value continues to exist in the heart of Jesus Christ, and, as adoration and thanksgiving, will continue for ever. "For that He continueth for ever, He hath an everlasting priesthood, whereby He is able to save for ever them that come to God by Him, always living to make intercession for us."[6]

The Prayer of the life of Jesus Christ.

The total submission of the human soul of Jesus Christ to the will of God the Father had its most perfect imitation in the *prayer and life of Mary*, His Mother. From the moment that she gave her consent to the Incarnation, her words, "Behold the handmaid of the Lord. Be it

The Prayer of the life of Our Lady.

[1]John iv, 34. [2]Hebr. x, 9. [3]John xvii, 4. [4]Luke xxii, 19; 1 Cor. xi, 24 –26. [5]John xix, 30; Luke xxiii, 46. [6]Hebr. vii, 24–25.

done unto me according to Thy word,"[1] are almost all that God allows us to know of the attitude of her life. It is, indeed, enough, for it tells of the most perfect union between God and Mary, between the Mother and the Son.

The Prayer of our life. Our attitude is meant by God to be the same.[2] He it is Who has taught us to pray : " Thy will be done on earth, that is, by us, as it is done in Heaven." By grace it is possible for us, in imitation of Jesus Christ and His Virgin Mother, " always to pray,"[3] according to His command. It is open to us, at all times and in all things, by a will that never withdraws its devotedness from God, to choose only what is the blessed will of God. It is possible, with the aid of grace, to live in a state of loving dependence upon God in which our very needs become, without words, our silent prayer.

No doubt we have sinned and we know our capability of further sin. Therefore is *penance*, in the Christian life, the necessary foundation of true prayer. Our life is now and, will continue to the end, to be the daily penance of taking up the Cross of Jesus Christ.[4] And by that Cross is meant the denial to ourselves of everything that runs counter to the will of God. The sadness of our daily self-denial is effaced by the joy of the grace of our redemption. We have been redeemed by the Blood we now rejoice to call " Most Precious,"[5] though, by our sins, we rated it very mean indeed, when we treated Him so disdainfully in the Passion.

The prayer of those who have been redeemed to grace by Jesus Christ, the constant attitude of our soul, must then be contrite and very humble. The spirit indeed, He Himself has warned us, may be willing, but human nature or the flesh is weak.[6] This knowledge of our human wretchedness can, by the virtue of our humble prayer, become our strength ;[7] we no longer depend on our own poor sufficiency. We cast all our care on God.[8] And God, we have seen by Faith, is Supreme, is sole Creator, is

[1]Luke i, 38. [2]John xvii, 20–21 ; 1 Thess. v, 10 ; Rom. xii, 12. [3]Luke xviii, 1. [4]Matt. x, 38–39 ; xvi, 24 ; Mark viii, 34–35 ; Luke ix, 23. [5]1 Petr. i, 18–19. [6]Matt. xxvi, 41 ; cf. John iii, 6 ; vi, 64. [7]Philipp. iv, 13 ; 2 Tim. ii, 1. [8]Ps. liv, 23 ; Matt. vi, 25–34 ; 1 Pet. v, 7.

Author of all our good, but most of all is God our Father. "With Him all things are possible." In the confidence and wisdom of the humble prayer of Jesus Christ we can have strength to say, in every circumstance of human life : "Not what I will, but what Thou wilt. Thy will be done."

Chapter III

THE HOLY SACRIFICE OF THE MASS

The Mass :
Central
Act of the
True
Religion.

OUR faith teaches us that the central act of the true religion of Jesus Christ is the Holy Sacrifice of the Mass. For that reason we are obliged by the Church to assist at Holy Mass on Sundays and the greater Feast Days. From our childhood, we have accepted as our bounden duty this serious obligation and by the time that each of us has reached ripeness of age, the number of occasions on which we have been present at the Holy Sacrifice is a surprising total. It is, then, well for each Catholic to ask himself the question that later will be put to him at Judgment : Have I grown, with the passage of the years, in understanding and appreciation of the Mass ? It is happily possible for all persons, even for the young and the unlearned, fruitfully to assist at the Sacrifice of the Mass. We cannot, however, claim that we worthily love Our Divine Redeemer, Who shed for us His precious Blood, if negligently we leave unopened the treasury of the Mass.

When one considers the accurate meaning of Holy Mass, one finds that it is useful or rather, necessary, to have explained the nature of sacrifice in general. The words one uses and the ideas that these words express at first seem difficult. Yet it must be remembered that persons of every age and type have always assisted at the offering of sacrifice. It must then be easy for everyone to grasp that which a sacrifice is meant to signify. In this context, it is not hard to employ figurative language or to describe the Mass, especially in its effects, by the use of highly-coloured phrases. It will, however, be found that the sober accuracy of the language in which the Church sets forth her teaching, if at first it tastes uninteresting, is, in the long run, the only satisfying food, on which genuine devotion can be kept alive and nourished to maturity.

Properly speaking, a sacrifice is an outward and public *The meaning of Sacrifice.* act of religion, which is done in honour of God alone, in order that men may admit and reverence His complete dominion. In a true sacrifice, accordingly, an offering is made to God to show forth man's total dependence on the Creator. That dependence of the creature reaches to man's existence, to his activities and to his final destiny : it covers all his being, either as an individual person or as a member of society. Only by offering himself totally to God, in mind and will and body, can a man properly acknowledge his utter dependence on his Creator. Only by a visible, outward ceremony can a man duly express the hidden dispositions of his soul towards God. Hence the full surrender of his being to God was expressed by the outward external offering of some visible thing, which was set apart for God alone and was taken to represent the being and the life of man. In the history of sacrifice, we find that some destruction of the visible thing thus offered or of the victim, as it was called, has always taken place. Man, then, set apart for God alone and, in some way destroyed, a creature, over which he himself had dominion, as a visible sign and proof that, in lowly subjection, he offered his existence and activity to God, Who is the absolute owner of creation.[1]

It is in the nature of man to offer sacrifice. Even if God had not Himself in person intervened to establish rites of sacrifice, some form of sacrifice would have been necessary to enable men to manifest due reverence to their Creator and to secure from human society a public admission of the supreme majesty of God.

It is not, indeed, the value of the thing itself offered to God that is chiefly to be considered in sacrifice, nor yet the full destruction of the victim, but rather the aptness of the rite or ceremony to express visibly man's inner attitude of adoration.

Moreover, since no created thing is of its nature suited to signify the peculiar honour owed to God, it follows

---

[1] Exod. xxii, 20 ; Hebr. v ; ix, 22 ; Deut. vi, 13 ; cf. Matt. iv, 10. Cf. St. Thomas *Summa. Theol.*, ii, ii, quest. 84, 85.

that the rite of sacrifice must be fixed by God's authority as the sign suitable for expressing man's acknowledgement of the Sovereign Creator. Further, a person must be designated and set aside, who, in the name of human society, will perform the ceremony of sacrifice. Hence, we find in the Old Law that God Himself chose certain rites as suitable for sacrifice, with shedding of blood or some equivalent destruction and named Himself one tribe of Israel as priests to offer Him due sacrifice.[1]

The purpose of Sacrifice.

The first purpose, accordingly, of sacrifice is to admit and reverence the infinite majesty of God. Man, however, is a sinner and for that cause stands in the debt of his Creator. The offering, therefore, and sacrifice to God of a victim take on the additional meaning of repentance for the sins that merit the just punishment of God. Further, it is not possible for man to know and praise the Creator, without also giving thanks to Him that He has created us and kept us in existence, and without at the same time acknowledging that it is to Him we must look for the answer to our prayers. For these reasons, in fine, a sacrifice takes on the character not only of an act and sign of adoration, but also of an act and sign of satisfaction for our sins, of thanksgiving for God's benefits and of petition for our every need.

The Sacrifice of the Mass.

These somewhat difficult ideas become easy to grasp, when one considers the Mass, the Sacrifice of Jesus Christ, for at once we meet the adorable Person of the Divine Redeemer, God made Man. All the sacrifices of the Old Law ordained by God had been the types of Him Whom at last men saw and heard in human form, in the towns and countryside of Palestine : they had been dim figures of the unique Sacrifice of Jesus Christ upon Mount Calvary.[2] Our Divine Lord Jesus Christ, constituted by God High Priest from all eternity,[3] in shedding His Precious Blood on the Altar of the Cross, offered Himself to God, in sacrifice, as a victim for our salvation. By that single sacrifice of the Cross our redemption has been once for all accomplished, satisfaction has been fully made to God for sin,

[1]Levit. i–viii ; Hebr. vii.   [2]Council of Trent, Session 22, chap. 1.
[3]Ps. cix, 4 ; Hebr. x, 5–9.

all merit has been won completely.[1] Christ died for all, that they also who live may not now live to themselves unregenerate in sin, but in holiness with Him Who died for them. We are sanctified by the oblation of the Body of Jesus Christ once. Offering one sacrifice for sins, He for ever sitteth on the right hand of God.[2]

Our Divine Redeemer, in His mercy, found a means of establishing a Sacrifice which would not only recall and represent His death but also apply to each and every man the Saviour's merits and satisfaction. And by the same Sacrifice so instituted mankind would be enabled to offer to God unceasingly a perfect tribute of public adoration. This is the unique and holy Sacrifice of the Mass. For, on the night before He died, Our Divine Lord instituted the Sacrifice of the Eucharist or Mass, by which in an unbloody manner, His Body and Blood would be offered to God beneath the appearances of bread and wine. " And whilst they were at supper, Jesus took bread and blessed and broke and gave to His disciples and said : Take ye and eat. This is My Body. And taking the chalice, He gave thanks and gave to them, saying : Drink ye all of This. For this is My Blood of the New Testament which shall be shed for many unto remission of sins."[3] At the Last Supper, He Who is a Priest for ever according to the order or manner of Melchisedech[4] ordained His Apostles priests and commanded them and their successors in His priesthood to offer the Sacrifice of His Body and Blood until the end of time. " Do this for a commemoration of Me."[5]

The Mass a perfect tribute of Adoration.

This, then, is the unique excellence of the Mass that, being a true and proper sacrifice, it represents and recalls the Sacrifice of the Cross. In substance the Mass is the same as the Sacrifice of the Cross. The same Priest, Jesus Christ, continues to offer Himself to God the Father by the ministry of His lawful priests. The same Victim, Jesus Christ, is now truly present on our altars under

The Mass the same as the Sacrifice of the Cross.

[1]Eph. v, 2 ; Tit. ii, 13 ; Rom. v, 8–9, 19 ; viii, 32 ; Matt. xx, 28 ; Mc. x, 45 ; and John iii, 14–16. Trent. Sess. 22, chap. 2. [2]2 Cor. v, 15 ; Hebr. x, 10, 12. [3]Matt. xxvi, 26–28. [4]Gen. xiv, 18 ; Hebr. v, vii. [5]Luke xxii, 19 ; 1 Cor. xi, 26.

the appearances of bread and wine. Only the manner of offering differs in the Mass from that in the Sacrifice of the Cross. In death upon the Cross, the Precious Blood was physically shed and separated from the Body. To-day upon our altars, the Precious Blood is shed for us and separated from the Body, not indeed physically, but sacramentally, under a sign or symbol that expresses death : the separate consecration of the substance of the bread which now becomes His Body, apart from and previous to the consecration of the substance of the wine which now becomes His Blood.

The purpose of the Sacrifice of the Mass.

The purpose of the unbloody offering which Jesus Christ makes of Himself and of His Church to God in Holy Mass is not different from that which He made with the shedding of blood upon Mount Calvary. For this the Church teaches is the clean oblation of which the Prophet long ago made mention : " From the rising of the sun even to the going down, my name is great among the Gentiles : and in every place there is offered to my name a clean oblation."[1] Thus the Holy Sacrifice is an unceasing fount of adoration.

The Mass, too, is the endless thanksgiving made by Jesus Christ and His Church for all the benefits of God, our Creator and our Father. " He gave thanks,"[2] says the Sacred Scripture, referring to the institution of the Blessed Eucharist. The very name of Eucharist means thanksgiving. That the Mass is equally a sacrifice of appeasement to God is the constant teaching of the Church. Christ Himself has told us that in the Sacrifice of the Eucharist His Body is given for us, that His Blood is shed for many, unto the remission of sins.[3] And if Holy Mass is instituted for the pardon of sin, it must aim no less at obtaining from the mercy of God the other needs which follow upon our state of fallen creatures. The purposes, therefore, of the Holy Sacrifice are exactly similar to those for which Our Saviour offered Himself on the altar of the Cross.

[1]Malach. i, 11. [2]Matt. xxvi, 27 ; Luke xxii, 17. [3]Luke xxii, 19 ; Matt. xxvi, 28 ; Mark xiv, 24.

The effects of the Holy Sacrifice correspond without change to those of the Sacrifice of the Cross. If we consider those effects in regard to God, we cannot fail to gain fresh knowledge of and esteem for Holy Mass. For the Mass is a never-ending Source of perfect adoration and thanksgiving and reparation and petition. In the Mass it is God made Man Who is Himself the Principal Offerer. In the Mass it is Jesus Christ Himself Who offers Himself to God, under the appearances of bread and wine. By reason of the infinite dignity of Him Who offers, because the Victim offered is of infinite worth, the Mass cannot fail to produce the effects for which it has been instituted. Unfailingly, independently of the holiness of human celebrant or assisting faithful, each Mass will always pay to the Blessed Trinity a limitless tribute of praise and thanks. Each Mass infallibly gives God a greater reparation than all the wrong that sin of men and Angels could inflict upon the Divine Majesty. Each Mass unerringly obtains remission of sins and grace of every kind that makes for man's salvation. Such is the glory and the worth of Jesus Christ, true God, true Man, Divine Redeemer of mankind.

The Effects of Holy Mass in regard to God.

The effects of Holy Mass, in regard to us sinners, are measured by the disposition of our souls. As a sacrifice of reparation, the Mass obtains for those, who are not obstinate in resisting God, the graces by which they are led to genuine repentance and to the fruitful reception of the Sacraments. In like manner, the Holy Sacrifice remits, immediately and unfailingly, for the living and the dead, the temporal punishment due to sin, in the measure of the charity of those who assist at Mass or for whom the Mass is offered. As a sacrifice of supplication, the offering of Jesus Christ in Mass cannot fail, of itself, to obtain the graces and the temporal benefits we need for our salvation. But it must be remembered that Holy Mass avails to win for us that only which the Providence of God sees fit to give, in proportion to the fervour and the perseverance of our prayers.

The Effects of Holy Mass in regard to us.

It follows that they benefit most fully by the Holy Sacrifice who properly unite with Jesus Christ in the offering of Himself in Mass. The efficacy of the Mass is infinite in that the dignity of Jesus Christ, Principal Offerer and Victim, is infinite. The efficacy of the Mass is infinite in that it applies the boundless merits of the Cross, without being limited by the number of the souls who draw the grace of Christ from out this treasury. But they draw greatest grace who assist at Mass with deepest faith and firmest adherence to the loving Will of God.

Union with our Divine Redeemer in the Offering of Himself.

There are many methods of assisting fruitfully at the Holy Sacrifice ; and all are good. One attitude of soul, however, we would emphasise beyond all others : the effort to unite ourselves more closely with the offering of Himself which Our Divine Redeemer makes to God in the Sacrifice of the Mass. This attitude is a conscious understanding of the truth that by the character of Baptism, by the grace of Christ, we are members of that Body of which Jesus Christ is Head.[1] It is then a disposition of complete surrender to the claims of God. It is a readiness to carry the Cross of His Will in all the aspects of our life. It is a permanent inclination to do always that which is pleasing to God the Father after the model of Our Saviour, Jesus Christ.[2] In the first instant of His existence as man, He declared His oblation of Himself to God : " Holocaust for sin did not please Thee. Then said I : Behold I come to do Thy Will, O God."[3] In the moment of His death, He declared that He had finally accomplished all that Will : " It is consummated."[4]

Our Blessed Lady as our Model at Holy Mass.

This union with the offering of Jesus Christ in Holy Mass is by the grace of God easy to all. Even a child can understand it, while the unlettered, and especially those who suffer, can here outstrip the learned in their contrition and their fervour. This is that disposition of soul which was most perfectly possessed by Our Blessed Lady. At the Annunciation, Mary, in accepting to become the Mother of the Saviour, offered herself to God, in fullest union with Her Divine Son, to do the will of God as His lowly handmaid.[5] From that moment, each successive trial of her life only served to increase the depth and merit of her sacrifice. At the Presentation, she heard the words

[1] I Cor. xii, 12–13 ; vi, 15 ; Eph. i, 22–23 ; v, 23 ; Coloss. i, 18.
[2] John viii, 29 ; v, 30. [3] Hebr. x, 6, 9. [4] John xix, 30. [5] Luke i, 38.

of Simeon, which, foreshadowing the Cross, transfixed her soul.[1] In the Three Days' Loss, in the Home of Nazareth, in the Public Mission, she was being made ready for the final agony of the Passion and the Cross. Standing beneath the Cross, she offered herself in union with her Son, Whom she fully knew to be the Saviour, in the unique Sacrifice which was the redemption of mankind.[2] It is because she was so closely linked with Jesus Christ in the offering of Himself on Calvary, that the Mother of the Divine Redeemer is now the universal Mediatrix who intercedes for human kind and distributes all the graces of Christ.

No grace more precious—unless it be the grace of final perseverance—can be won for us by Mary's intercession than the enduring union of our mind and heart and soul with Jesus Christ, in the perfect worship of the Holy Mass. *Union with Jesus Christ in Mind and Heart.* This is that "spirit of lowliness and sorrow of heart" of which mention is made at the Offertory, and for which we are prepared by the confession of sin at the beginning of Mass, by the petition of all the Collects and by the instruction of the Epistle and Gospel. In such an attitude of humble adoration, we acknowledge in the Preface that through Jesus Christ all benefits come to us from God. Before the Consecration as suppliants, in union with the glorious ever Virgin Mary, Mother of Jesus Christ, our God and Lord, together with all the Saints, the Pope, our Bishop and all who make profession of the one true Faith, we beg to present to God the Father the Host and Chalice about to be consecrated as the sign or offering of submissive adoration made by us His servants and by all the family of His Church. After the separate Consecration, symbol of death, by which the Body and Blood of Jesus Christ become truly present on the altar, "as servants of God, His holy people, we offer by the hands of the priest to the most excellent majesty of God the pure and holy and spotless Victim, the holy Bread of eternal life, the Chalice of eternal salvation." We most humbly beg "to be filled with all heavenly graces and blessings through Christ

[1] Luke ii, 34–35. [2] John xix, 25–27.

Our Lord." As sinners we entreat Him to grant us " some part in the fellowship of His elect, not, indeed, in consideration of our merits, but according to the kindness of His pardon through Christ Our Lord." For, we confess, through Jesus Christ all honour is paid to the Most Holy Trinity and good things of salvation secured to men. Continuing in the prayer of Christ Himself, we petition God that He may be known on earth, that we may do His Will, and obtain the graces necessary to be free from sin and peaceful through Jesus Christ. Then addressing ourselves directly to the Divine Redeemer, Who taketh away the sins of the world, in the prayers before Communion, we beg that Jesus Christ may not regard our sins, but may look upon the faith of His Church and make us to cleave at all times to His commandments.

To assist at Holy Mass in the disposition that these prayers evoke is to unite ourselves completely with the offering made by Jesus Christ upon the Cross and renewed perpetually in the Holy Sacrifice. We should, then, seriously endeavour to understand more clearly the meaning of the Mass, so that, being united with Jesus Christ, our God and Saviour, our lives may be made entirely subject to the Will of God and the teaching of His Church.[1] It is our very earnest desire that we who are privileged to assist at Mass so often may, by the intercession of Our Blessed Lady, more fully submit to God in contrite adoration, more humbly thank Him for His benefits and more completely satisfy for our sins, so that, in each and every aspect of our daily lives, we may " more lovingly adhere to His commandments nor ever be separated from Him," by the merits of the Sacrifice of " the one Lord Jesus Christ, only begotten Son of God, Who for us men and our salvation came down from Heaven and became incarnate by the Holy Ghost of the Virgin Mary, and was made man and was crucified for us."[2]

[1] Cf. John xiv, 23. [2] *Credo* of the Mass.

Chapter IV

THE BLESSED SACRAMENT

WHEN we think of Our Divine Redeemer, Jesus Christ, we are apt to picture Him as living at a given moment of time, in a little country, among a privileged, few persons. Yet, He came on earth for the salvation of each man, who should be born throughout succeeding ages of time. He ought to be at hand, we feel, for each of us. We have need of certainty. We have urgent need of courage and of present help. It were little use to us that some men and women in Palestine heard His voice and saw His miracles and believed in Him. It is our own necessity that presses on us and drives us outwards, to look for the aid that we know by experience we cannot find within ourselves. Such an aid we have at hand in the Sacraments of Jesus Christ.

We have no reason, then, to envy the men and women of Palestine. They saw, no doubt, what we shall see, one day in Heaven. But, we possess the power and presence of Jesus Christ in all His Sacraments. We have Him closer to us than we can appreciate. The woman who touched the hem of the garments that He wore, experienced His power. We, in the touch of the ordinary things that He Himself has chosen, are made holy by His grace. God chose a human body in which to redeem us. Before He left the earth, He chose the simple things of water and oil and bread and wine, to be the means of holiness. By His death on the Cross He has redeemed us ; by the Sacraments of His Church, in the touch of common things made holy by His choice and power, He gives to each soul the fruits of that redemption. No stage of human life has been omitted by our most kind Redeemer.[1] At birth, there is Baptism giving new life of sanctifying grace. In youth, there is Confirmation, lending vigour for the combat against rising passion. From the

The Grace of the Sacraments.

[1]Cf. St. Thomas, *Summa. Theologia*, pars. III, quaest. 61, art. 1, art. 5.

97

dawn of reason, there is the sweet healing of the Sacrament of Penance, in which every sin can have His pardon. To found the Christian home, there is the blessing and the strength of Marriage. To govern His Church and sanctify the faithful, He has provided the Sacrament of Order. To remove the vestiges of sin, He has given us the last Anointing. To be the food of our soul, in daily life and in the hour of death, He has given us the Sacrament of Sacraments, Himself. beneath the ordinary appearances of bread.

The Blessed Sacrament in our times.

We have, indeed, no reason to envy those who lived on earth, in the time of Jesus Christ. We have less reason to bewail our lot, because, by His Will, we are asked to spend this life's brief day, in an age of unexampled evil. The Most Holy Sacrament of the Body and Blood of Jesus Christ was the staff of life, in the earliest persecutions of the infant Church. To-day, by the direction of successive Popes, the use of the Blessed Sacrament has been made available to an extent unknown for centuries. In his Encyclical, *Mirae Caritatis*[1] on the frequent reception of the Blessed Eucharist, Pope Leo XIII explained to all the Faithful the charity of Christ which had given us the Blessed Sacrament : " that charity which Christ had brought into the world and with which He would have all hearts on fire." It was reserved to the fiery zeal of Pius X,[2] a few years later, to allow the Faithful and, especially the children, to receive Our Divine Lord in Holy Communion, frequently or even every day. Who can measure the effect upon the world of that prophetic action ? To meet the unseen approach of enormous evils, mankind has again been given the strength of Jesus Christ Himself in the Sacrament of His love. Thus, has the " mystery of Faith "[3] again become for unnumbered Catholics the hearth at which, each morning, they can rekindle their Faith and increase their charity.

The Fore-shadowings of the Blessed Sacrament in the Old Testament.

This mystery of Faith is so hidden from human minds[4] that there is no possible method of discovering it apart from

[1]May 28, 1902. [2]Decrees, *Sacra Tridentina Synodus*, December 20, 1905, and *Quam Singulari*, August 8, 1910. [3]The exclamation of the Church at the Consecration of the Mass. Cf. 1 Tim. iii, 9. [4]Cf. Eph. iii, 8—9.

God's own declaration. Looking back, under the guidance of the Church, we can see Foreshadowings of the Blessed Eucharist in the Old Testament. But we understand them to be hints only, now that God has spoken. There was the sacrifice of Melchisedech in bread and wine.[1] There was later the strange prophecy of the Psalmist that the Messiah would be a priest after the manner of Melchisedech.[2] There had been the Manna, a miraculous bread provided for the chosen people in the desert.[3] There was the Paschal Lamb, in particular, which was eaten by all the people and which, by its blood, protected Israel from the Angel of destruction.[4] The priest had given David " no common bread, but holy bread," which could be given only to the clean.[5] A clean oblation had been mentioned, which would be offered to God from the rising of the sun to the going down thereof.[6] An Angel had given Elias mysterious bread because " he had yet a long way to go," and in the strength of that bread, the despair of the Prophet had given place to courage.[7] In none of these images could the ingenuity of man discover the type of that which Jesus Christ would give out of the inscrutable " riches of the wisdom and the knowledge of God."[8]

In fact, we may reverently trace in the words of Our Divine Master to His disciples His expectation of their failure to understand the Blessed Sacrament, even after He had most plainly spoken : " I have spoken to you earthly things and you believe not : how will you believe if I shall speak to you heavenly things ? "[9] There was a certain preparation of the disciples through the miracles of healing : He was seen to possess almighty power.[10] His teaching was singular, as of one having authority.[11] His goodness was such that multitudes flocked after Him, to hear or only to see Him.[12] It was such a very great multitude that inspired the immediate introduction of His promise to give the Blessed Sacrament. With five

---

[1]Gen. xiv, 18. [2]Ps. cix, 4. [3]Exod. xvi, 4, 15 ; Wisd. xvi, 20–21. [4]Exod. xii ; cf. *Summ. Theol.*, iii, q. 73, a. 6. [5]1 Kings xxiv, 4–6. [6]Mal. i, 11. [7]3 Kings xix, 7–8. [8]Rom. xi, 33. [9]John iii, 12. [10]Matt. iv, 23–24; ix, 6. [11]Matt. viii, 29. [12]Matt. xiv, 13–14 ; Mark iii, 10 ; Luke v, 1.

loaves and two fishes he had fed five thousand, but as yet no man could guess His meaning.[1]

The Promise of the Blessed Sacrament. Then suddenly, after this miracle, He rebuked the disciples for having followed Him only because He had fed them : " Labour not for the meat that perisheth, but for that which endureth, unto life everlasting, which the Son of Man will give you." The disciples were roused to ask for a sign that they should see and believe. And Jesus promised them the Blessed Eucharist : " the bread of God that cometh down from Heaven, and giveth life to the world." " Give us always this bread," they asked, but they did not understand the vastness of their request that they who had the Faith would repeat, until the end of time. And Jesus said to them, " I am the bread of life. He that cometh to Me shall not hunger and he that believeth in Me shall never thirst." Our Divine Master had read the hearts of His disciples, for at once He rebuked them again: "But I said unto you that you also have seen Me and you believe not." If they did not believe in the Redeemer, Whom they saw with their eyes of flesh, they would not believe that the same Redeemer could be the bread of life. " The Jews therefore murmured at Him because He had said : I am the living bread which came down from Heaven."[2]

It is for the healing of our unbelief that God permitted such a scene. The mystery of Faith is in the power of God alone to reveal. " Murmur not," said Jesus, " no man can come to Me except the Father Who hath sent Me, draw him. Amen, amen I say unto you ; he that believeth in Me hath everlasting life." Then follows in sentence after sentence the declaration, from which the Church has drawn the faith and hope and love of all its life[3] : " I am the bread of life. Your Fathers did eat manna in the desert : and are dead. This is the bread which cometh down from Heaven : that if any man eat of it, he may not die. I am," He repeats with emphasis, " the living bread, which came down from Heaven. If any man eat

---

[1]John vi, 9 ; Mark vi, 52. [2]John vi, 26–41. [3]Cf. Pius XII, Broadcast to Euch. Congress, El Salvador, November 26, 1942. Cf. *Summ. Theol.*, III, q. 83, a. 4.

of this bread, he shall live for ever : and the bread that I
will give is my flesh, for the life of the world."[1]

The human understanding of the Jews could not grasp
His meaning ; none the less, more solemnly still did He
assert the reality of this Bread from Heaven ; " Amen,
amen, I say unto you : except you eat the flesh of the Son
of Man and drink His blood, you shall not have life in
you. He that eateth My flesh and drinketh My blood hath
everlasting life, and I will raise him up in the last day."
And the reality of that food and drink is such that its effect
is not reserved until the final day of judgment : " He that
eateth My flesh and drinketh My blood abideth in Me
and I in him." It is a food and drink that incorporates
us with Christ. It is more : it is a life, by which in some
strange way we live by Christ, as Christ Himself lives
by the Father : " As the living Father hath sent Me and
I live by the Father : so, he that eateth Me, the same also
shall live by Me."[2]

In face of such a mystery, the flesh, or merely human
intellect, profiteth nothing.[3] And after these words,
" many of His disciples went back and walked no more
with Him."[4] Should we have been among that number,
had we assisted at that scene ? Perhaps the weakness of
our present faith in the Most Holy Sacrament of the Altar
could supply an answer. Yet, by God's mercy, we are
found among those who have come to Christ, because
it has been given to us by His Father. It is the gift for
which eternity will not be long enough to give our little
thanks. " Lord," we can say, in the light of Faith, with
St. Peter, " to whom shall we go, except to Thee ? Thou
hast the words of eternal life."[5]

Having promised the Blessed Eucharist, Our Divine *The*
Lord kept silent for about a year. When next He spoke, *Institution*
it was on the night before He died. The disciples could *of the*
not have linked the Bread of Life with His death upon *Blessed*
the Cross. In fact, though He had most clearly stated *Sacrament.*
that He was going up to Jerusalem to suffer and to die,
they could not accept the mention of His death.[6] But,

[1]John vi, 43–52. [2]John vi, 54–58. [3]John vi, 64. [4]John vi, 67. [5]John vi,
67–69. [6]Matt. xvi, 21–22 ; Mark viii, 31–33.

"knowing that His hour was come, that He should pass out of the world to the Father, having loved His own who were in the world, He loved them unto the end."[1] This is the hour at which He chose to institute the Blessed Eucharist. "And whilst they were at supper, Jesus took bread and blessed and broke and gave to His disciples and said : Take ye and eat. This is My body, which is given for you. Do this for a commemoration of Me. And taking the chalice, He gave thanks and gave to them saying : Drink ye all of this. For this is My blood of the New Testament, which shall be shed for many, unto the remission of sins."[2]

It is Our Divine Lord Himself Who has described the greatest proof of love : "greater love than this no man hath that a man lay down his life for his friends."[3] That proof of love He gave by dying on the Cross : it was first of all to redeem us, that He gave His life on Calvary.[4] This infinite love of God found a means for giving us a gift greater than even His human life : The Body that was given for us, in the Sacrifice of the Cross, the Blood that was shed for us, in remission of our sins.

We shall never understand the love that gave the Blessed Sacrament. When we think of love in God, we speak of a limitless desire and almighty power to benefit ; we refer to the unfathomable wisdom of His providence. But, we are set at such a distance from Him that our faltering thoughts are only the effort of a child to spell His goodness. Even the Apostle of love, St. John, who rested his head on the Sacred Heart of God made Man, looks for no words to describe the love of Jesus Christ ; he is content to state the fact : "God so loved the world as to give His only-begotten Son.[5] God is love.[6] He loved unto the end."[7] And when God made Man described the Blessed Sacrament, He too, we may reverently say, was pleased in the simplest words to name His gift : "This is My Body, Take ye and eat. This is My Blood. Drink ye all of this.

---

[1]John xiii, 1. [2]Matt. xxvi, 26–28 ; Luke xxii, 19 ; cf. Mark xiv, 22–24; 1 Cor. xi, 23–26. [3]John xv, 13. [4]1 John ii, 2 ; Matt. xx, 28 ; Tit. iii, 14 ; Eph. v, 2 ; Apoc. i, 5. [5]John iii, 16. [6]1 John iv, 16. [7]John xiii, 1.

I am the Bread of Life. He that eateth My flesh and drinketh
My Blood abideth in Me and I in him. He that eateth
Me, the same shall live by Me. And I will raise him up
on the last day."

In dealing with what the Church herself has solemnly *The Reality*
called the Mystery of Faith, we are, in God's mercy, guided *of the*
Blessed
by the infallible teaching of His Church. From the beginning, *Sacrament.*
our Holy Faith has taught that in the Blessed Sacrament,
under the lowly appearance of bread, we receive the substance of the Body and the substance of the Blood of Jesus
Christ, True Man, True God, with his Soul and His
Divinity.[1] Nor have we any doubt about the purpose of the
Gift that we receive : this Bread gives life, of such a kind
that we abide in Christ, by union of our soul, and live by
Christ, in the virtue of His love.

" He that eateth My flesh and drinketh My blood *abideth* *The Effects*
in Me and I in him " : in these words, the Church teaches us, *of the*
Blessed
Jesus Christ refers to the primary effect of worthily receiving *Sacrament.*
the Blessed Sacrament : we are united with God made Man
in such a closeness of sanctifying grace and charity that we
are, so to speak, spiritually transformed into Christ, as our
food is changed into ourselves.[2] Grace and truth came on
earth through Jesus Christ.[3] When Jesus Christ Himself
comes by the Eucharist into our souls, He floods our being
with the grace by which we share more deeply still in the
very nature of God Himself.[4] Nor can sanctifying grace
and charity be given us in single measure ; the virtues and
the gifts of God the Holy Ghost flow into us to be the power
of energy in our attempt to live by Christ.[5]

And since the Blessed Eucharist is a Sacrament of union,
we cannot receive the true Body and Blood of Jesus Christ
without at once being intimately united to all the members
of the Church, who share with us this Banquet and are joined
with us in the love of God made Man.[6] Therefore, Our
Divine Master, as soon as He had instituted the Blessed

[1]Council of Trent, Sess. 13, Can. 1, 2, 3. [2]Council of Florence, *Decr.*
pro Armenis ; Trent. Sess. 13, ch. 2 ; Cat. Council of Trent, quest.
45–52. [3]John i, 14, 17. [4]1 Pet. i, 14 ; Rom. viii, 17. [5]1 Cor. xiii, 13 ;
Rom. v, 5 ; 2 Pet. i, 4–8 ; Rom. viii, 14. Cf. *Summ. Theol.*, Ia. IIae. q.
65, a. 3 ; q. 66, a. 2 ; q. 68, a. 5. [6]1 Cor. x, 16–21 ; Trent. Sess. 13,
ch. 8.

Eucharist, gave the disciples a new commandment, His precept, that they should love each other, as He had loved them. The prayer He uttered speaks of a union which imitates the oneness of the Father and the Son : " that all may be one in charity as Thou Father in Me and I in Thee : that they too may be one in Us." [1]

" He that eateth me, *the same shall live by Me.*" Our Divine Lord comes to us in this Sacrament under the form of food. What food can do to the body, all that and more this Bread of Life is capable of effecting in our soul.[2] The Blessed Sacrament sustains our life of grace in that it communicates the enduring power of charity. Thus it rouses the soul not only to avoid the death of sin, but to seek in sentiment and act, a closer likeness to the life of Jesus Christ. This Sacrament increases our spiritual life, because it strengthens and perfects the intimacy of our converse with God Himself.[3] And stirring the will to acts of fervent love, the Eucharist repairs the damage done by venial daily faults.[4] It would be strange if the privilege of our union with God made Man should fail to delight the heart ; the Blessed Sacrament, because it is a Bread containing in itself all sweetness,[5] is apt, of its power, to produce at times a spiritual gladness in the will of the well-disposed communicant.

" He that eateth My flesh and drinketh My blood, *hoth eternal life and I shall raise him up on the last day.*" In receiving the Blessed Sacrament, we share in a union with Jesus Christ which, because of the sanctifying grace and charity He communicates, is already on earth the beginning of eternal life. This Food is given us precisely that we may not fall from grace on earth, but that, in its strength " we may walk for the forty days and the forty nights " of mortal life, " unto the mount of God." [6]

Preparation for Holy Communion.   One might think that it would be natural to approach the Blessed Sacrament with great fear. Our Divine Lord

[1]John xiii, 34, 35 ; xiv, 20 ; xvi, 15 ; xvii, 21–22. [2]Council of Florence, loc. cit. [3]I John iv, 16 ; cf. *Summ. Theol.*, IIa, IIae. q. 17, a. 6, ad 3 ; and q. 24, a. 8 and a. 9. [4]*Summ. Theol.*, III, q. 79, a. 1 ad 2 ; q. 87, a. 1. [5]Wisd. xvi, 20 ; *Summ. Theol.*, III, q. 81, a. 1, ad 3. [6]3 Kings xix, 8 ; John vi, 55 ; St. Ignatius, *Ad. Eph.*, 20, 2 ; *Summ. Theol.*, III, q. 79, a. 2, ad 3.

would seem to have forestalled our weakness, for in all that touches the Most Holy Sacrament, the Church maintains a very great simplicity of rite. Reverence there must be of adoration and love ; but the ceremony is unobtrusive and very silent. His coming is as quiet as on the night when He was born, in the hiddenness of a stable in Bethlehem.[1] We are thus instructed by the infallible Church to worship and receive Him, not with emotion but by Faith. The words which she uses in distributing Holy Communion admirably prepare us to give Our Divine Lord a more proper welcome.

"Behold the Lamb of God. Behold Him Who taketh away the sins of the world." [2]

These are the words of St. John the Baptist as he gave witness to the Saviour of the world. They are a most loving act of humble faith. It is easy to forget that we were given the Blessed Eucharist on the night before He died to redeem us from our sins. We look on Him Who has been slain to give us life. The Bread that is broken to us is the Body that hung in death upon the Cross, but now has risen and sitteth at the right hand of God.[3] Nor could we receive that Sacred Body to-day in Holy Communion, unless the Sacrifice of Calvary were renewed each day in Mass.

"Lord, I am not worthy that Thou shouldst enter beneath my roof." [4]

This is the cry of the Centurion in the Gospel-story, who sought from Christ the cure of the boy he loved. How strange that the infallible Church should choose this prayer ! She has not placed upon our lips the burning confession of St. Peter [5] ; nor the ardent words of the Beloved Disciple,[6] nor yet the utterance of St. Mary Magdalene, who loved Him much.[7] She has given us the lowly confession of a pagan whom grace had truly taught. We can repeat the words of the Centurion with vivid faith in the Divinity of Jesus Christ, Who would enter under our roof, and in particular, with sorrow for the sins which make our home unworthy to receive Him.

---

[1]Luke ii, 6–7. [2]John i, 29. [3]Mark xvi, 19 ; Matt. xxvi, 64. [4]Matt. viii, 8. [5]Matt. xvii, 4 ; xvi, 6. [6]John xxi, 7 ; Apoc. xxii, 20. [7]John xx, 16 ; Luke vii, 47.

" Yet, say only a word and my soul shall be healed."
Only the confidence that knows the loving heart of Jesus
Christ could speak these words. In the memory of all we
ever learned of the goodness and kindliness of God made
Man, we dare to hope. Despite our sins, despite the power
of sinning that will remain in us, we look for healing from
the Saviour of mankind. And because He calls us, we
approach.

" May the Body of Our Lord Jesus Christ guard
thy soul unto everlasting life."

It is His presence in us to which the Church refers at the
moment of receiving Him, His power to guard our soul, His
gift to keep us unto everlasting life ; for it is He Who comes
to us rather than we to Him ; He will transform us into
Himself.

Thanksgiving after Holy Communion. What each soul shall say to Our Divine Lord after Holy
Communion must depend on age and experience and grace.
No set form of words, especially another's words, is required
to express our welcome. The state of soul and the particular
need will suggest the words of gratitude and petition. But,
as in our preparation, we are helped by the attitude of the
Church, so, in our thanksgiving, we can humbly watch the
salutation of the Church, when the Blessed Sacrament has
been distributed.

" O Sacred Banquet," she exclaims, " in which Christ as
Food is taken, and the memory of His Passion is recalled,
the soul is filled with grace and a pledge of future glory is
bestowed on us." [1]

" O SACRED BANQUET IN WHICH CHRIST AS FOOD IS TAKEN "

The Church's exclamation is an act of Faith. On receiving
Jesus Christ, we, too, should bend ourselves, in all the powers
of our being, before the Everlasting God Who has visited
us, in the reality of His Flesh and Blood, His Soul and His
Divinity. " I do believe, Lord. Help my unbelief," [2] is
the prayer that our daily heedlessness and coldness demand,

---

[1] *Rituale Romanum,* Tit. IV, cap. ii ; cf. *Summ. Theol.,* III, q. 79, a.
7. [2] Mark ix, 23.

for here we have Jesus Christ, yesterday, and to-day and the
same for ever,[1] unchanged since the days of His mortal
life on earth. In our hearts we possess the Food " in which
dwells all the fulness of the Godhead corporeally." [2]

" AND THE MEMORY OF HIS PASSION IS RECALLED "

Our Holy Communion is no mere memory however vivid
or however tender of the Sacred Passion. By His command
we have received the Eucharist, in which most really is
renewed the Sacrifice of the Cross. There is no Blessed
Sacrament without the Holy Sacrifice of the Mass. The
consecrated Host that we receive, in showing forth His death
until He come,[3] is none other than the Lamb that was slain
on Calvary. Now, in the moment of our partaking of Himself the Victim, He applies to us the fruits of His redemption ; and chiefly the fruits of perpetual immolation.[4] From
the first moment of the Incarnation Jesus Christ offered
Himself to do the will of God, which meant His death for
our salvation.[5] To-day, in the Heart of Jesus Christ that
disposition of utter submission to the will of His Heavenly
Father persists unchanged. For the Lamb of God, the Victim
for our sins, is seen by St. John in the Apocalypse, " standing
and as it were slain " [6] : standing because He dieth now no
more,[7] but is eternal ; and slain, because His immolation
is till the end of time mystically renewed in the Eucharistic
Sacrifice. We cannot meditate sufficiently the import of
these thoughts suggested by the Blessed Sacrament. Our
first desire must be to imitate the offering of the Lamb, in
our total submission to the will of God,[8] and in the crucifixion of our sinful desires by daily self-denial.[9] Only at
such a price can we follow Jesus Christ. Only by suffering
with Him, in His life as Victim for our sins, can we rise with
Him and be glorified with Him.[10] " He that eateth Me, the
same shall live by Me."

[1]Hebr. xiii, 8. [2]Col. ii, 9. [3]1 Cor. xi, 25. [4]Heb. x, 10. [5]Heb. x, 5–10.
[6]Apoc. v, 6. [7]Rom. vi, 9. [8]John xiv, 21. Cf. *Summ. Theol.*, IIa, IIae,
q. 186, a. 6, ad 2. [9]Matt. xvi, 24 ; Mark viii, 34 ; Luke ix, 23. [10]Rom.
viii, 17 ; 2 Tim. ii, 11–12 ; cf. *Summ. Theol.*, III, q. 79, a. 2,
ad 1.

"THE SOUL IS FILLED WITH GRACE"

Grace and the effects of grace within the soul must be
unseen. But we know on His word, that He has given us
His Flesh to be the Bread of Life. We know by Faith that,
in receiving Him, our souls can be flooded with His grace ;
we believe that in each Holy Communion He penetrates our
being and transforms us into Himself. Each person comes
to Holy Communion with very different needs and each
is answered in a different manner. At times we may feel
the solace of His presence. Sometimes, to win us from
undue attachments to things created, He will give us the
sense of the sweetness of His presence.[1] Or, after the storm
of passion and sadness, He may produce in our hearts a very
great tranquillity.[2] More often, as we grow in genuine
charity, the influence of the Blessed Eucharist will be per-
ceived in a certain vigour making more easy the effort to
be virtuous. And, as we advance in union of Faith, His
presence will be more unfelt, but in the depths of our being,
He will teach us to make our choice by light of Faith : He
will produce in our will a habit of sacrifice in union with
Himself, the Lamb of God and Victim. In particular, He
will deepen in us the habit of divine charity, and with it the
gift of wisdom, until gradually, by instinct, as it were, we
choose whatever is His will.[3] To reach the state in which
the virtues of the life of Our Divine Redeemer can become
our own, we need great courage.[4] We need the courage of
patience through the daily trials that we cannot turn aside ;
courage of frankness when we ought to speak or act for God ;
courage of silence in the face of calumny and treachery.
So many are afraid ! So many are cast down by failure !
But our fear and our dejection are the reason for this Bread
of Life. " The Bread that I will give is My flesh for the life
of the world." Our confidence in that strong word of God
is the beginning of our courage.[5] At the moment of our
receiving Jesus Christ, we have within our heart the living

---

[1]Ps. xxxiii, 9. [2]Job iii, 22 ; Matt. viii, 26. [3]John xv, 1–11 ; cf. *Summ.
Theol.*, IIa, IIae, q. 45, a. 5 ; St. Francis de Sales, *Love of God*, Bk.
II, ch. 22. [4]Cf. *Summ. Theol.*, IIa, IIae, q. 123, a. 3, ad 6. [5]Cf. Acts
xciii, 10 ; Rom. viii, 31 ; Esther xiv, 19.

Saviour, Who reassured us : " Have confidence, I have overcome the world. Fear not, It is I. I will refresh you." [1]

" A PLEDGE OF FUTURE GLORY IS BESTOWED ON US "

Even the dust of a Christian who has been nourished by
the Blessed Sacrament is quite different from that of any
other person : it is holy before God because it has received
the glorious Body of the risen Christ. How much more holy
is the soul that on earth has been so intimately united with
Christ " the Resurrection and the Life." [2]   It is God Himself Who has said to us : "He that eateth My flesh and drinketh
My blood, hath everlasting life." The Blessed Sacrament
worthily received begets in the soul a great increase of
sanctifying grace. But, grace is a share in the nature of
God Himself, and as such, is the germ of everlasting life. He
that eateth this flesh, abideth in Christ, by the virtue of
divine charity. To be endowed, by reason of the Blessed
Sacrament, with sanctifying grace and charity, is thus to
possess the pledge of future glory, which Jesus Christ
Himself bestowed.

Whatever care we give to our preparation and thanksgiving, we shall always feel that our little effort is unworthy
of the dignity of the Sacrament. And, as life advances, we
shall appreciate more keenly the truth of the Centurion's
plea that he was not worthy to receive His Lord beneath
his roof. [3] It is then natural that we should seek the aid of
one who knew Him best and loved Him most intensely. No
one can help us more efficaciously than the Mother of the
Son of God Who comes to us. Her purity from the first
instant of her life was stainless. Her faith, at the moment
of the Incarnation gave Him to us to be our Saviour. [4] Her
humility in the utterance of her canticle, was the deepest
tribute to the infinity of God. [5] Her charity increased at
every moment of her life with Him, until she could, without
dying, stand beneath the Cross and lay her Saviour in the
tomb. [6] And now, in Heaven her glorious power of intercession has limitless sovereignty over the Heart of Jesus

*Our Lady
and the
Blessed
Sacrament.*

[1]John xvi, 33 ; Matt. xiv, 27 ; Luke xxiv, 36 ; Matt. xi, 28. [2]John
xi, 75.   [3]Cf. Luke xviii, 13 ; *Summ. Theol.*, IIa, IIae, q. 24, a. 8 ;
q. 184, a. 3 ; St. Francis de Sales, *Love of God*, Bk. III, ch. 6. [4]Luke
i, 38. [5]Luke i, 46–55. [6]John xix, 25 ; 40–42.

Christ. " In her is the spirit of understanding, holy, active and sweet." [1] With whom, more dear to God, could we approach the Blessed Sacrament ? With whom more fittingly could we make our plea for grace in urgent need ? To His Mother the Son can truly say : " All that I have is thine." [2]

The Blessed Sacrament and Death.

" This is the bread which cometh down from Heaven ; that if any man eat of It he may not die." The Blessed Sacrament is the food which strengthens us through life, lest our soul may lose the life of grace. There is for each of us a final hour, in which we must not faint on the way, on which eternity depends ; and it cannot be that the mercy of Our Saviour would forsake us in the final urgency of our weakness. Death may be very swift in its approach. More often, the closing day of life has a long twilight and a darkened evening. In such a space, God gently looses all our moorings. Already, in the irksomeness of pain, He is, to use St. Gregory's phrase, found knocking at our gate. As He withdraws our heart from things created, He knows how to fix our love upon the world to come. In a secret way, He draws us to seek in Him our rest and proper home. Throughout these days the Blessed Sacrament becomes, if not to our emotions, at least to our deeper life of faith and love, the strength and solace of the Sacred Heart.[3]   And at the end, before He comes to judge us, as we wait for Him pardoned and cleansed of sins' last vestiges, none other than Himself is the strength and courage of our final journey.

The Blessed Sacrament and Heaven.

In Heaven we shall need no more the Blessed Sacrament, for the former things are passed away.[4] When that which is perfect is come, that which is in part shall be done away.[5] He Who on earth had made Himself to be our Bread of Life, and had promised to raise up us, is Himself the everlasting life.[6] The Lamb that was slain shall rule us : and shall lead us to the fountains of the waters of life, and God shall wipe away all tears from our eyes.[7]   And we shall see His face.[8] Beholding the glory of the Lord with open face, we shall be transformed into the same image,[9] because we shall see Him as He is, face to face.[10]

[1]Wisd. vii, 22. [2]Luke xv, 31. [3]Gal. ii, 30 ; cf. *Summ. Theol.*, IIa, IIae, q. 184, a. 2. [4]Apoc. xxi, 4. [5]1 Cor. xiii, 10. [6]John vi, 40 ; xi, 25. [7]Apoc. vii, 17. [8]Apoc, xxii, 4. [9]2 Cor. iii, 18. [10]1 John iii, 2.

Chapter V

SORROW FOR SIN

AT the approach of Lent, the Church vividly reminds us of our mortal condition. On Ash Wednesday she marks our brows in the sign of the Cross with ashes : " Dust thou art, and unto dust thou shalt return." The words she borrows are those of God Himself in the Garden of Eden, when, in punishment of sin, He condemned our first parents to a life of toil and sorrow, until by death they " should return to the earth out of which they had been taken."[1] It might seem a needless thing to remind us that we shall die. With a wisdom given by God the Holy Ghost, the Church unfailingly brings to mind the sentence of death, under which every man lives. At the same time, since by " sin death entered into the world," [2] the Church summons us to repent of all our sins, while yet the mercy of God is disposed to grant us the grace of sorrow and amendment. " Let us amend for the better in the things in which through ignorance we have sinned, lest being suddenly overtaken by the day of death, we seek a space for repentance and find it not. Hearken, O Lord, and have mercy, for we have sinned against Thee." In this prayer of Ash Wednesday is found the story of mankind and the unending call of God to return to Him in penance. " Be converted to Me with all your heart. Turn to the Lord, your God, for He is gracious and merciful." [3]

The Old Testament, which the Church uses so frequently *In the Old* in the Mass during Lent, might seem to be but the recital *Testament.* of the unfaithfulness of God's chosen people. It is much more the touching narrative of the patience wherewith God chastised His people unto sorrow, in a long preparation for the Divine Redeemer Who should save them from their sins. Thus Abraham is seen to intercede with God for the guilty cities,[4] and Moses, by his penance, succeeds in saving

[1]Gen. iii, 19. [2]Rom. v, 12. [3]Joel, ii, 13. [4]Gen. xviii, 22–33.

all his people[1]. The Prophets in succession urge repentance in order to avert God's anger. By the sufferings which are a penalty for sin, God breaks the pride of sinners. " I have broken their heart that was faithless and revolted from Me. They shall know that I am the Lord." [2] Solomon, at the dedication of the Temple, prays that " if the people have sinned and been afflicted and, by reason of their afflictions, do penance in their hearts and be converted from their sins, then may God hear them and, as He shall see their hearts, forgive them their sins." [3] Time after time in the Sacred Writings the readiness of God to pardon the truly penitent is emphasised. " I will forgive their iniquities and I will remember their sin no more. Pitying, I will pity," saith the Lord.[4] "If the wicked do penance for all his sins which he hath committed, and keep all my commandments, I will not remember all his iniquities that he hath done. Is it my will (asks the Creator) that a sinner should die and not that he should be converted from his ways and live ? " [5] The Book of Psalms is a sinner's admission of his manifold guilt, the sorrow of a contrite and humiliated heart, a cry for mercy to the heart of God, in whom alone is the hope of peace. The Old Testament indeed speaks much of the heavy chastisement of sin, but it is in the Old Testament that we read a prayer such as that of Esther[6] or Daniel[7] or Tobias,[8] filled with the grief of genuine penance, and confident in the tenderness of a forgiving Father. " O how good and sweet is Thy spirit, O Lord, in all things, for by little and little, Thou chastiseth them that err : and admonisheth them, and speaketh to them concerning the things wherein they offend : that, leaving their wickedness they may believe in Thee." [9]

In the Gospels.

When, in the course of time, God sent His last messenger to prepare men for the coming of the Divine Redeemer St. John the Baptist had no other message than that of all the Prophets. " Do penance," said John, " for the Kingdom of Heaven is at hand." [10] Nor was his language less vivid

---

[1]Num. xiv, 20–13. [2]Ezech. vi, 9. [3]3 Kings viii, 35, 39. [4]Jer. xxxi, 34 ; xxx, 20. [5]Ezech. xviii, 21–23. [6]Esth. xiv, 6, 18. [7]Dan. iii, 26–45. [8]Job. iii, 21–23 ; xiii, 1–8. [9]Wisd. xii, 1–2. [10]Matt. iii, 2.

than that of Jeremias or Isaias. " Ye brood of vipers, bring forth fruit worthy of penance." [1] It was the change of heart that was sought, not the appearance of goodness. " And the people," we read, " confessing their sins, were baptised unto penance." [2] This cleansing of the heart made men ready for the preaching of Him Who was to come, Whose shoes, said John, he was not worthy to loose. Jesus Christ would thoroughly cleanse the threshing-floor. His wheat He would gather into the barn ; the chaff He would burn with unquenchable fire.[3] For, St. John confessed : " This is the Son of God, the Lamb of God Who taketh away the sin of the world." [4]

It is indeed strange that the Son of God, at the opening of His public life, should have used the very words of St. John the Baptist concerning repentance :   " He began to preach and to say : Do penance, for the Kingdom of Heaven is at hand." [5] Explaining His mission in the synagogue at Nazareth, He applied to Himself the striking text of Isaias : " This day," He said, " is fulfilled this scripture in your ears : the spirit of the Lord is upon Me. Wherefore He hath anointed Me to preach the Gospel to the poor. He hath sent Me to heal the contrite of heart, to set at liberty them that are bruised." [6]   When first Our Divine Lord sent out the Twelve, the mission He gave them was no different from His own: "Going forth they preached that men should do penance." [7]   On one occasion, solemnly He uttered the dread warning to His disciples : " I say to you : except you do penance you shall all likewise perish." And lest the words might not be correctly grasped, at once, in the same solemn form, He repeated the judgment.[8] At the very end of His life, when speaking to His Apostles, a few moments before ascending into Heaven, " He opened their understanding that they might understand the Scriptures." At this final farewell Our Divine Lord recalled the message of repentance that explained His life and death : " And He said to them : Thus is it written and thus it behoved Christ to suffer and to rise again from the dead, the third day ; and

[1]Ib. iii, 7–8 ; Luke iii, 7–8. [2]Matt. iii, 6 ; Mark i, 5. [3]Matt. iii, 11–12 ; Luke iii, 16–17. [4]John i, 34, 29. [5]Matt. iv, 17 ; Mark i, 15. [6]Luke iv, 16–21. [7]Mark vi, 12. [8]Luke xiii, 3, 5.

that penance and remission of sins should be preached in His name, unto all nations." [1]

After the Ascension. How faithfully the Apostles fulfilled the mandate to preach repentance for sin, we can see throughout the Acts of the Apostles. Immediately after the descent of the Holy Ghost, St. Peter in his first sermon rebuked his hearers for their share in the crucifixion of the Son of God. Struck with sorrow, they asked : " What shall we do ? " " Do penance ": answered the Apostle : "be baptised every one of you in the name of Jesus Christ, for the remission of your sins." [2] In his second sermon St. Peter cried out to the people, who had witnessed the cure of the man born lame : " Be penitent and be converted, that your sins may be blotted out." [3] In the presence of the High Priest, the Chief of the Apostles bore this witness to His Divine Master : " Him hath God exalted to be Prince and Saviour, to give repentance and remission of sins." [4] St. Paul teaches that " the benignity of God leadeth us to penance." [5] Baptism for the Apostle is a death to sin, a resurrection to newness of spirit and holiness of life. [6] " A faithful saying," he writes, " and worthy of all acceptation : that Christ Jesus came into the world to save sinners." [7] With St. John, the Apostle of the love of God, penance is equally a stern demand of God. " They shall be in very great tribulation, except they do penance from their deeds." [8] The wicked are thus described in the Apocalypse : " They blasphemed God because of their pains and wounds : and did not penance for their works." [9] Of the elect it is written : " Such as I love, I rebuke and chastise. Be zealous therefore and do penance." [10] Thus in the early Church to " teach and preach Christ Jesus " [11] is to announce the message of repentance unto the remission of sins.

The Mind of the Church. Nor has the mind of the Church in any sense changed during two thousand years. The priest, in his preparation for Mass, begins : " Remember not, O Lord, our sins nor the sins of our forebears ; neither do Thou take vengeance for our sins." The Mass itself commences with an avowal of

[1]Luke xxiv, 45–47. [2]Acts ii, 38. [3]Acts iii, 19. [4]Acts v, 31. [5]Rom. ii, 4. [6]Rom. vi, 4–14 ; 22–23 ; Col. ii, 1–10. [7]1 Tim. i, 15. [8]Apoc. ii, 22. [9]Ib. xvi, 11. [10]Ib. iii, 19. [11]Acts v, 42.

our guilt as sinners; its prayers are filled with the entreaties
of the Church for purification. "Visit, we beseech Thee,
O God, and purify our consciences, that Jesus Christ, Our
Lord, Thy Son, on coming to us, may find in us a dwelling-
place made ready for Himself." "O God, to Whom all
hearts lie open and every will doth speak and from Whom
no secret is concealed, purify, by the outpouring of the Holy
Ghost, the thoughts of our heart." Immediately before the
Consecration, the Church prays that God in His mercy would
snatch us from eternal damnation. At a moment when it
might be thought that the soul was pure, the Church, at
Holy Communion, makes the priest repeat the humble confession of the Centurion : " Lord, I am not worthy that Thou
shouldst enter under my roof : yet, say only the word,
and my soul shall be healed." [1] Before the Faithful are
communicated, the priest holds up the Sacred Host for
adoration and the prayer he recites is not an act of fervent
charity but the words of St. John the Baptist that remind
us of our sins and our utter dependence on the Redeemer :
" Behold Him, the Lamb of God : behold Him, Who taketh
away the sins of the world."

We are tempted to wonder at this emphasis on our sinful *Our*
condition and on the need for sorrow for our sins. It is that *Sinfulness.*
we do not understand how often and how insistently Our
Divine Master spoke of our sinfulness before God. We are
apt to put aside His words as having been addressed to a
people, distant in time and country and living in a pagan
world. We forget that the teaching of Jesus Christ is meant
for each and every man, at whatsoever time he may be born
on earth. We fail to believe that He Who spoke "knew
all men, and knew what was in man." [2]

Thus, there is not an aspect of our fallen condition that
has escaped the notice of our Divine Saviour. His sermons
and parables and encounters with the people of His time
reveal the full extent of human negligence and malice. God
alone is good,[3] Our Divine Master teaches ; men are wicked
debtors to God, who have not wherewith to pay. [4] The

[1] Matt. viii, 8 ; Luke vii, 6. [2] John ii, 24–25. [3] Matt. xix, 17 ; Mark
x, 18 ; Luke xviii, 19. [4] Matt. vii, 11 ; xii, 34 ; vi, 12 ; xviii, 23–27 ;
Luke vii, 42.

grosser sins of injustice and sensuality are referred to in the Parables of the Unjust Steward and the Unjust Judge and the Prodigal Son. But the condemnation of Our Divine Lord bears for the most part upon the neglect of God in human life. Men have set their hearts on the visible things of the earth. " Where their treasure is, there will be their heart ; " [1] and, in practice, they have forgotten God. Thus are " they choked with the anxieties and riches and pleasures of this life." [2] " The light that is in them becomes darkness." [3] God, Who alone must be adored [4] and served, is despised, for " no man can serve two masters." [5] " God knoweth your hearts, warns Our Divine Master ; that which is high to men is an abomination to God." [6] Our sin, too, He shows in the Parable of the Prodigal Son, takes on the character of a heartless ingratitude. " God came unto His own," we read, " and His own received Him not." [7] But sin becomes in its effects still more terrible, when it generates the wilful blindness that hates the light of Jesus Christ. " And men loved the darkness, for their works were evil." [8] Such a darkness of soul makes of man a bond-slave, controlled and even possessed by Satan[9]. The sinner can reach the wickedness of hating God. When the enemies of Jesus Christ, urged on by Satan, crucified the Son of God, in envy and in hatred,[10] for one moment it might have seemed that the sin of man had triumphed. But in that very moment, God, in His unspeakable love, used the hatred of man to accomplish the work of our redemption. The shedding of the Precious Blood was the price of the remission of all our sins.[11]

The Mercy of Our Divine Redeemer.

The mercy of the Sacred Heart towards sinners was frequently made evident during Our Divine Lord's life. He wept over Jerusalem that had slain the Prophets, who troubled its peace by their call to penance. In the end, the same Jerusalem would crucify Himself : " if thou hadst known, and that in this thy day, the things that are to thy peace :

---

[1]Luke xii, 34 ; Matt. vi, 21. [2]Luke viii, 14 ; Matt. xiii, 22. [3]Matt. vi, 23 ; Luke xi, 15. [4]Matt. iv. 10. [5]Matt. vi, 24 ; Luke xvi, 13. [6]Luke xvi, 15. [7]John i, 10. [8]John iii, 19. [9]John viii, 34 ; xiii, 27 ; 1 John iii, 8 ; Matt. xii, 29 ; Eph. vi, 12. [10]Matt. xxvii, 18 ; Mark xv, 10 ; Acts ii, 23. [11]John i, 7 ; Apoc. i, 5 ; Eph. i, 7 ; Luke xxii, 20.

but now they are hidden from thy eyes." [1] He pardoned the Magdalene.[2] He had pity on the multitude, for that they lay like sheep without a shepherd.[3] He had cried out : " if any man thirst, let him come to Me, the fount of living water, and drink." [4] He had invited the weary souls of sinful men : " Come to Me all you who labour and are burdened, and I will refresh you. My yoke is sweet and my burden light." [5] Looking down from Calvary, He had pleaded for forgiveness even for those whose wilful blindness had nailed Him to the Cross.[6] Yet, in a sense, at no moment did the unrequited mercy of His all-loving Heart pour gentler balm on humankind than when He said to His Apostles, just before He departed from the earth : " Receive ye the Holy Ghost, whose sins ye shall forgive, they are forgiven them : whose sins ye shall retain, they are retained." [7] At that moment we were given His Sacrament of sorrow.

All supernatural sorrow for sin must find its origin in Faith.[8] It is not a mere regret that we have failed, much less a grief that we have lost the chance of sinning again. It is a lowly avowal of sin, made with the help of grace. True sorrow turns from sin ; it detests it as an offence against Almighty God. Thinking on the infinite majesty of God, Whom sin despises, our sorrow rejects the sin as an evil greater than any other evil. And, as in every mortal sin there is the same offence to God, sorrow must reject all mortal sins. Reflecting on the fulness of the evil, as our holy Faith reveals it, our sorrow understands that sin deprives us at once of sanctifying grace, and, excluding us from the company and friendship of God, merits the eternal punishment of Hell.[9] But sorrow can reach an even greater height, with the aid of grace. If we consider that sin revolts against God, our Creator, and our Father, Who is Himself all-good ; if we reflect that sin has caused the death of God made man, and that the proof to us of God's unspeakable, nay infinite, goodness is His death to save us from all sin,

True Sorrow for Sin.

[1]Luke xix, 40. [2]Luke viii, 47. [3]Mark vi, 34. [4]John vii, 37. [5]Matt. xi, 28–30. [6]Luke xxiii, 34. [7]John xx, 22–23. [8]Cf. Council of Trent, Session xiv, ch. 1–9. *Summa Theol.*, 3a, qq. 85–87. [9]Trent. Sess. xiv, ch. 4, cf. *Summ. Theol.*, 2a, 2ae, q. 19, a. 2, and a. 4.

then sorrow is become an act of perfect love which reconciles us to God. Only love returned can compensate for love refused. And thus in perfect contrition there is no longer the mere anxiety of justice to repair a sin against the majesty of God, but rather the charity that clings to God, with all one's heart, as infinitely good, and strives to repair the insult to God Who is our Father, Our Redeemer and our Friend. [1]

The Sorrow Needed for the Sacrament.

Such a sorrow is not based on emotions : it rests on Faith. " They shall know that I am the Lord their God." True sorrow is an understanding of sin as an offence against God. It springs from the will which, assisted by grace, turns away from sin in order to submit to God completely. " I will give you a new heart, and I will cause you to walk in My commandments." How perfect our sorrow is, only the eye of God can fathom. We, who know our own fickle heart and feeble love of God, might well doubt the value of our sorrow to wipe away all sins in perfect charity. But God, in His unending mercy, does not leave us to wonder whether our sins have been forgiven. He has given us the Sacrament of Penance, and in that Sacrament He does not exact the perfect sorrow of contrition. He Who, " knows what is in man," is pleased to accept the sorrow that considers sin chiefly as an offence against God, which deprives us of grace and deserves the eternal loss of God. Without genuine sorrow inspired by Faith, there cannot in fact be any Sacrament of Penance. But we may well ask if God could have made more easy the conditions of sorrow for that Sacrament. Few things can prove to us more cogently the endless love of the Sacred Heart of Jesus than the ease with which we can receive, and know with certainty that we have received, forgiveness of all our sins in the Sacrament of sorrow.

In Preparation for Absolution.

Because the fruit of the Precious Blood is easy to receive in this Sacrament, we should be all the more careful to prepare our hearts for absolution. By our sins, be they grave or venial, we have offended God. Suppose that Jesus Christ were to examine my conscience and recount my sins,

[1]Trent, loc. cit., cf. *Summ. Theol.*, 1a, 2ae, q. 113, a. 2 and a. 5.

as He numbered the insults that He had received in the
house of the Pharisee. One day He will detail all my sins
in the judgment, immediately after death. To-day as we
prepare for absolution, let us each kneel down before Him
and pray that He may look on us as He looked on the
Magdalene, on the woman taken in sin and on St. Peter.
May He never look on us as He looked on Judas, who turned
for ever from His love ! If our sins be those that spring
from discouragement and human respect, let us kneel before
Our Divine Redeemer as He prays in agony in the Garden.
If our faults be those that offend against chastity in ourselves
or in others, let us kneel before His blood-stained Body in
the scourging at the Pillar. If our offences are sins of pride
or faults against charity, let us kneel before Our Saviour,
mocked and spat upon and crowned with thorns. If we
must bewail the relapse into sin, let us kneel before the
dying Saviour, as He struggles to Calvary and falls beneath
the burden of our wickedness. And at Calvary, one and all
can kneel before the Crucified ; there is not one of us who
has not helped to crucify Him, because there is no sin of
man that has not had its share in His Passion and redeeming
death.[1]

Thus to examine our consciences before Our loving *Absolution*
Saviour, in the stages of His Passion, is already to prepare
our hearts for the act of genuine sorrow, which turns from
sin as evil and clings to God, resolved with His grace never
to sin again. When we kneel,[2] as befits a sinner, before the
priest who receives our confession and adjudges our guilt,
we kneel before Jesus Christ Himself. As in the Consecration
at Mass the priest, who takes Christ's place, says : " This is
My body," so in the Sacrament of Penance, the priest
declares : " *I* absolve thee from thy sins." It is Jesus Christ
Himself Who absolves us in this Sacrament as truly as when
He stretched forth His hand and raised from death the
widow's son of Naim.[3] While we make our humble admission of sin, while we reject with detestation all sin which
helped to crucify Him, while we determine with His grace

[1]Cf. *Summ. Theol.*, 3a, q. 46, a. 5 ; q. 49, a. 1–5. [2]Cf. In 4 dist. 17, a.
3, q. 4. [3]Luke vii, 14–15.

never to sin again, it is Our Divine Lord Himself Who declares as long ago in the days of His life in Palestine : "Thy sins are forgiven thee. Go in peace and sin no more." [1]

To Sin no more.

To sin no more is the privilege of the Blessed, who are with God. We do not doubt God's mercy, nor the full forgiveness of the Sacrament of Penance, but we know that we have sinned and we greatly fear that we shall sin again. Yet, here and now, in the act of sorrow that we make, we recognise the evil of our sin : we wish that we had never offended God : we long never to sin again ; we bring our will to bear on the flight from such occasions as we know could induce us to repeat our sin. We know that it is precisely on the sins that we have confessed with sorrow that the special grace of the Sacrament directs its light and strength. We set our trust no longer in the feeble barrier of our own poor resolutions, but in the Precious Blood of Jesus Christ. To Him in loving humility, we entrust our unstable wills. With child-like love, we confide in the protecting intercession of Our Lady, because He gave her to us on Calvary to be our Mother and our Refuge. [2] To remedy the weakness of our will we accept, together with the penance imposed by the priest, all the suffering of our life, in particular, the pain we shall undergo in avoiding further sin. [3] Our temptations do not soil us, but they harass and discourage us. They can be made a reparation for the past and a confiding act of love, if, in union with Our Divine Lord in the Agony at Gethsemane, we turn at once to God and protest that by His grace we choose His Will, whatever suffering it may cost us in body or in soul : "Not my will, Lord Jesus, but Thine alone, now and at every moment and for always."

Abiding Sorrow.

True sorrow restrains from further sin. " Wash me yet more from my iniquity," [4] prayed the Psalmist, and the Church continues to repeat his prayer. When we have knelt before our loving Lord in all the scenes of His bitter Passion, we must share His horror of sin as an offence against the all-holy God. When we have knelt beside Our Lady of Sorrows at the foot of the Crucifix, something of her grief

[1] Matt. ix, 2 ; Mark ii, 5 ; Luke v, 20 ; vii, 48. [2] John xix, 26. [3] Cf. *Summ. Theol.*, 3a, q. 90, a. 2. [4] Ps. L. 4.

at sin passes into our heart and soul. By a refinement of
grace, our conscience gradually becomes more delicately
sensitive. The knowledge of our failures purifies our pride
and urges us to the reparation of a greater love. " All the
day, in a sense, sorrow is in our heart," [1] but the grief
is become a sweetness, for it rests upon the confidence of
sin forgiven in His sacrament of sorrow.

It is a sad, strange fact that, when we shall have come into
the vision of God in Heaven, and can no longer sin, we shall
see at once the Five most Precious Wounds of Jesus Christ.
In eternity and for eternity, we shall remember that we
have sinned. He has kept in His hands and feet the trace
of the nails, and in His side the wound of the lance,[2] that we
may for ever praise the mercy of the Sacred Heart, Which
shed its blood to be the remission of our sins.

[1]Ps. xii, 2. [2]John xx, 27 ; Hebr. x, 14, 15, 24.

Chapter VI

EPISCOPAL CONSECRATION*

" Thou shalt make them princes over all the earth."—Ps. 44, 17.

IT is a singular grace to assist at this ceremony of Episcopal consecration. The Church is lavish of her many-sided symbolism, when she crowns her princes ; but throughout this function her insistence upon *Faith* is perhaps the most striking feature of her liturgy. We have heard the Bishop-Elect being questioned upon his faith in the Holy Trinity, in Our Divine Lord and in the Church. We have listened to the consecrating prelate answer in turn : " May this thy Faith be increased by the Lord unto true and everlasting blessedness." In the splendour of the Pontifical vestments we are bidden by the Preface to see the inner glory of the grace of fullest Priesthood. The Episcopal ring is called "the sign of Faith," inasmuch as the Bishop has for task to keep his spouse, the Church, inviolate, by the stainless orthodoxy of his teaching. When the hands that give the Holy Ghost have been imposed, and when the help of God the Holy Ghost has been again invoked, the consecrating prelate anoints the head of the new Bishop in the name of the Most Holy Trinity unto the fulness of " constancy in *Faith*, singleness of charity, sincerity of peace," that he may love the Faith nor ever abandon it, being overcome by flattery or fear. May he not, continues the prayer, set light for darkness nor darkness for light before the people God will give him. Nay, God Himself will be his authority, God his power, God his steadfastness. May this anointing, asks the Consecrator, so penetrate his soul that the power of God the Holy Ghost may fill his being ; it is the fulness of the sovereign Priesthood of our anointed Saviour.

*Sermon on the occasion of the Episcopal Consecration of Most Reverend Joseph Byrne, D.D., C.S.Sp., at Rockwell College, March 19th, 1933.

To-day, as we view this ceremony, our thoughts of Faith go back at once to that primary anointing which is the source of all our grace. The Fathers speak of Christ as *the* anointed, because the union of the Divinity with the Humanity is the anointing, so to speak, of His Humanity. By reason of this union of the Person of God the Son with human nature, Jesus Christ is sanctified with an uncreated and substantial holiness. This unique union, greatest of graces, is the fount of every blessing, because it gives us Jesus Christ, true God and true Man. " How hath not God given us all things with Him?" In virtue of this personal union of the Divinity and Humanity, Jesus Christ is constituted Priest, sole mediator between heaven and earth. Called by God a High Priest, He reunites once more the broken bonds of friendship between God and man. " Christ is yours," says St. Paul, " and in Him you have the hope of glory." Jesus Christ is ours because He is our Saviour. God, from eternity, has chosen Him to raise up sinful man to the life of grace, and in His person to give back to God the homage of praise which sin had taken from the earth. High Priest of the New Covenant, in His Priesthood He has offered the Sacrifice of Himself on Calvary, by which God now is perfectly adored and adequately satisfied. Only Christ, the High Priest, can institute the perfect worship, by which the homage of our adoration shall rise up to God, in confident assurance of His mercy. Only Christ is Head of all the Church, which is His Body. He only is the vine which to the branches gives the sap of God's own life. Only Christ, in Whom dwells all the fulness of God's grace, can institute the means of grace which shall for ever operate the salvation of the world. Jesus Christ is henceforth sole High Priest. Those men to whom, by the Sacrament of Order, He gives a share in His Priesthood, have power, only because they act in the Person of Christ, and because Christ acts most truly in them and through them. Now the fulness of this Priesthood is the exclusive property of a Bishop.

It might well appear that there is nothing greater than the power conferred on a simple priest. Is it not the most sacred dignity that man can have, that of consecrating the

Eucharist ? To take the place of Jesus Christ, on Calvary as He offers Himself in sacrifice, is to stand where Christ, raised above all, draws all things to Himself ? True, *this* power is equal in Priest and Bishop and Pope. But it is of Faith defined that the Bishop is superior to the Priest in power of sacred ministration. The priestly character, once indelibly received at Ordination, is, in Episcopal Consecration further determined, made more perfect in view of the sacred ministrations, which the Bishop alone is competent to perform. Only the Bishop can confer the Sacrament of Order : the Priests whom he ordains are truly his sons in the Priesthood. He is the fount of spiritual power in his diocese, from which flows all the power of the Priesthood and all the grace of Sacraments which Priests administer in the name of Christ. The Bishop is thus the father of the children of the Church, who are born to God in Baptism. By the Sacrament of Confirmation he elevates these Christians to the rank of champions of the Faith. By him alone the temples of God and vessels of the Sanctuary are set aside by distinctive consecration. He is the symbol of the unity and fecundity of Catholic worship. A Priest already, he is now become, by fulness of the Priesthood of His Master, a High-Priest.

But further, the eyes of Faith see in Jesus Christ a Ruler and a King. By His Priesthood He justifies and sanctifies : by His Kingship He governs the Church, which is His Body in the spiritual order and, where the interests of grace require it, in the temporal sphere. To Jesus Christ as King it belongs to set before the faithful both the goal to which they shall ever tend and the means by which they shall attain their supernatural end. To Jesus Christ as King it appertains to determine sanctions, to assign reward and punishment. To Jesus Christ as King it finally belongs to conquer souls by active war against evil and by untiring defence of His faithful subjects. Thus Jesus Christ is King in view of the salvation of mankind. His domination covers every creature, whether in the visible Church or outside the Church. Therefore the Kingship by which He rules is ever allied most closely with the Priesthood by which He sanctifies.

To the apostles Jesus Christ gave His power of Kingship:
" As the Father hath sent Me, so I send you." They are
the princes who will assure to the Church its living unity
and its common good. Since, however, in the course of
years, the apostles would die, Jesus Christ designed that
they should for ever have successors, and these successors,
in whom the twelve apostles truly live, are our Catholic
Bishops.

Thus, by Divine Right, the Bishops are superior to the
Priest in power as Rulers. They only are established by
Jesus Christ for the ordinary government of the faithful.
It is of the very constitution of the Church of Jesus Christ
that the Church shall ever have for ordinary Rulers, Bishops.
This is their principal prerogative :—" The Holy Ghost
hath set you Bishops to rule the Church of God."

" Set in the tower of the Church," as Origen puts it,
the Bishop is teacher of the Faith. By his commission,
priests are permitted to instruct the faithful ; they teach
that of which the Bishop is divinely constituted guardian.
In subjection to the Bishop, sins are validly forgiven or
retained. Lieutenant of Christ, the Sovereign Ruler, the
Bishop, in Christ's Name, exercises over his subjects an
external, visible government. He gives precepts and makes
laws, he judges the guilty and imposes sanctions. In the
Ruler, who is the Bishop, Jesus Christ is truly King. As
by his plenary priesthood, the Bishop initiates the life of
grace within his diocese, so, by his authority to rule, he
directs the supernatural activity of his subjects.

It is not that the episcopal character received in Consecration, of itself, formally includes this authority to rule
the Church of God. Rather it is that the Episcopal character is, by Divine Institution, capable of receiving this
authority or jurisdiction. Now in the design of Jesus Christ,
one only is Ruler on earth, possessed of Supreme and
Universal jurisdiction : Peter, Chief of the Apostles. To
Peter alone Christ gave personally and immediately,
absolute Primacy : on Peter, as upon the foundation of
the Church, the College of Apostles rests. Peter alone is
Pastor of all the flock : of shepherds and of sheep. This
Primacy, willed and forever instituted by Jesus Christ,

Peter transmits to his successors. It is thus from the successor of St. Peter, not immediately from God, that every Bishop, successor of the Apostles, receives his jurisdiction or authority to rule.

That each Bishop should thus derive his jurisdiction from the fulness of power that exists in the Supreme Apostolic Ruler is to the eyes of Faith a beautiful necessity of Divine Wisdom : it is also a law of the Constitution of the Church of Christ. The lawfulness of authority must ever be visible and plain : for it depends upon the mission received from Christ by the apostles. Now the apostolic character of all authority in the Church appears in this, precisely, that all power of government descends from that single See of Rome, in which through an unbroken chain of Rulers, the self-same mission, given it immediately by Christ Himself, now exists and is forever perpetuated.

We of the Faith have no need painfully to search out texts of Sacred Scripture or documents of history. By the favour of God we recognise the living fact of the Church which is One and Apostolic, by very reason of the supreme authority of the living successor of St. Peter, Pius XI. To-day the very name of Pius XI awakens all the consciousness of our grateful love and dutiful subjection, brings to our mind the full meaning of the Apostolic See of Peter. To-day by the authority of Pius XI, the living successor of St. Peter, a new successor to the apostles has been consecrated, at the hands of one who is himself a legitimate member of the Hierarchy, long since established through St. Patrick by immediate mandate of the Vicar of Jesus Christ. To-day we celebrate " our peace and communion " with the Holy See.

It is a touching feature of this morning's ceremony that the Vicar of Jesus Christ, successor of St. Peter, who, of his plenary Apostolic power, has given to the newly consecrated Bishop, rightful authority to rule the Church in distant Africa, should be himself peculiarly Pope of Catholic Missions. Among the many titles of our Pope to greatness, this especially I may say, endears him not only to this Missionary Congregation of the Holy Ghost, but also to the apostolic Irish Nation.

It is not merely that Pius XI has been incredibly active in the organisation and expansion of the mission-field; nor that he has so frequently urged us to love the Missions. Rather, I submit, Pius is Pope of the Missions precisely because first of all he is Pope of the Mystical Body of Christ. To Pius it has been reserved to trace out for mankind that vast synthesis of Catholic teaching, in which we reverently trace the abiding presence and assistance of God the Holy Ghost. To Pius has been granted the glorious task of setting forth with dauntless courage, the true relations of the Church of Christ to every form of human society and every form of human activity. It is of this mighty programme that Pius is the Pope and it is because he untiringly commissions his envoys to bear *this* his teaching to the uttermost ends of the earth that Pius XI is the Pope of Catholic Missions.

Through the newly-consecrated Bishop, the voice of Pius and of Peter, nay of Jesus Christ Himself, will now be heard by the pagan tribes of Kilima that are grouped around the wondrous, snow-clad mountain, lovely image of the tranquil grandeur of the eternal God, and of the steadfast permanence of the One, True Church. For the furtherance of the Bishop's glorious task, we join our prayers, in mingled joy and sorrow, with the throbbing accents of the Church, as here this morning she entreats for the newly-consecrated:—"May his footsteps, O God, be beautiful by reason of the Office Thou hast entrusted to him: the announcing of Thy peace, the announcing of Thy glad tidings. Grant him, O Lord, the ministry of reconciliation in word and deed. Let his word and his preaching be in the showing forth of spirit and of power, not in the persuasive words of human wisdom. Grant him, O Lord, the keys of the Kingdom of Heaven, that he may use, not glory in, the power which Thou dost give unto building up, not unto our destroying. Whatsoever he shall have bound on earth, may the same be bound in heaven, and whatsoever he shall have loosed on earth may that in turn be loosed in heaven. May he be thy servant, faithful and prudent, whom Thou shalt establish over Thy household that he may give them food in opportune time. Eager in zeal, fervent in spirit, may he detest all pride, may he love humility. May he cherish truth nor ever cast it from him. Give to him his bishop's See, to rule Thy Church and the people Thou hast given him. Grant him in abundance the constancy of Faith, the singleness of Charity, the sincerity of peace. Do Thou be to him authority, Thou his power, Thou his firmness. Blessing and grace be multiplied upon him, that he may ever merit to obtain Thy gracious mercy for his people. Through Jesus Christ, Thy Son, Our Lord, Who with Thee lives and with Thee reigns in the unity of the Holy Spirit, God, for ever and for ever. Amen."

III—The Last Things

Chapter I

DEATH

DURING the season of Lent we have many occasions of remembering Death. It might be thought that we never escape from the sight and memory of death. None the less, the Church makes a special ceremony of this remembrance. " Thou art dust," she declares as the dust of ashes is placed on our brow, " and unto dust thou shalt return." Throughout the weeks that follow Ash-Wednesday, the readings from Sacred Scripture and the prayers of the Mass emphasise the shortness and the sinfulness of human life. It is as if the Church, once each year, urged us with particular insistence to fix our eyes on what we wish that we did not see : death, our own death, certain, final and irrevocable.

It is rather easy to think of death in general, as it affects all other people. There is even a pleasant melancholy in the thought. Nor may it be denied that some of the loveliest images of human literature are concerned with death. There are in nature so many symbols of our transient life : dark night, " with its great gift of sleep," sleep that is " the counterfeit of death " ; the flowers of the field that to-day delight us with their fragrant beauty and to-morrow are withered in decay ; the seasons that gradually rise from the promise of spring to the glory of high summer and sink through autumn into winter's grave. None of these comparisons have escaped the notice of the ancient poets. The flicker of these tender images lights for a moment the cruel sorrow of their pagan life. And then the sadness at the heart of human things masters their souls in the poignant certainty of death.

Images of Death in Nature.

The Church would not turn us from the savour of this poetry of death. Is it not the Old Testament that warns

us that we are walking in a path by which we shall not return?[1]
Job speaks of life as rolled away from us as a shepherd's
tent, cut off as by a weaver.[2] To the Psalmist, man's days
are as grass, as the flower of the field.[3] To the Wise Man our
time is as the passing of a shadow.[4] And it is Our Divine
Lord Himself Who uses the poetry of the homely things
of daily life to make clear the wisdom of His message.[5]
The Church would have us face the reality behind these
images. Death is the penalty of sin : to convince us she
prescribes the penance of Lent for the body in which
we sin. Death is vanquished by the Crucifixion of the
Divine Redeemer : through the season of Lent, then, she
reminds us incessantly of the Passion and Death of Jesus
Christ.

*The Human
Aspect
of Death.*

We must humbly admit that these are not the aspects
of death on which we usually dwell. Rather do we fix on
the merely human side of death, when we allow ourselves
to think at all. We recall the deathbed of relatives and
friends. We feel again the sense of emptiness in the room
of death. We mourn the absence of the presence that filled
our life with its gentleness or strength, its graciousness
or its inspiration. As a result of our experience, we forecast
for ourselves a time of pain, long or short. We shrink from
the parting with all that we knew and loved. We suffer
for the void that we shall make in at least a few hearts.
We fear the loneliness of the journey that we must make
alone. Occasionally, we imagine that the end may be swift.
More often we hope that we shall be given what we call a
reasonable time to prepare. In a vague way, we all trust that
God will be merciful at the end. But, in our heart of hearts,
we all dread death, for it is a separation, absolute and
irremediable, from everything of sight and sound, odour
and touch : it is an end of human life.

*Death in
Divine
Revelation*

What is the light that the Word of God has shed on
death ? " By one man, Adam, sin entered into this world,
and by sin, death "[6]; and so, concludes the Apostle,

[1]Job xvi, 23 ; cf. Wisd. ii, 5. [2]Is. xxxviii, 12 ; cf. Job vii, 6. [3]Ps. lxxxix,
6 ; cii, 15 ; Ecclus. xiv, 18 ; Is. xl, 6–8 ; James i, 11. [4]Wisd. v, 9 and
10–15 ; cf. 1 Paralip. xxix. 15 ; Job viii, 9 ; Ps. ci, 12 ; cviii, 23. [5]Cf.
Matt. vi, 28 ; Luke xii, 27 ; Luke xi, 33 ; xv, 8 ; Matt. xxiii, 37 ; John xv, 5.
[6]Rom. v, 12 ; cf. Ecclus. xli, 5.

death passed upon all men, in that all have sinned. By reason of his human nature, the union of a body and soul, Adam should have naturally died. The seeds of decay are in the nature of material things. But God, in His limitless mercy, had wished to preserve mankind from death. With the gift of sanctifying grace He gave the further gift, unowed in any sense to man, of freedom from death and physical pain. But that gift and the habitual grace from which it flowed were held by Adam for himself and all mankind on the one condition of obedience. " Of the tree of the knowledge of good and evil thou shalt not eat." And God stated most clearly the penalty of disobedience : " For, in what day soever thou shalt eat of it, thou shalt die the death." [1] Despite the fulness of his knowledge and the magnificence of his gifts, Adam chose to disobey. Then God passed judgment : " In the sweat of thy face shalt thou eat bread, till thou return to the earth, out of which thou wast taken : for, dust thou art, and unto dust thou shalt return." [2] Later the Sacred Scripture deliberately adds, as if to confirm the sentence of the Creator : " And Adam died." [3]

Death in the Old Testament.

From that moment there runs like a dark thread throughout the Old Testament the constant reminder of universal death. " For we are sojourners before Thee and strangers, as were all our fathers. Our days upon earth are as a shadow and there is no stay. [4] All things that are of the earth shall return to the earth again. [5] The short years pass by and we are walking in a path by which we shall not return. [6] Nor shall man return any more into his house neither shall his place know him any more. [7] There is no man that liveth always, nor that hopeth for this, for his life that was lent him shall be called for again. [8] And he hath not power in the day of his death." [9]

The small and the great are at one in death. [10] " One man dieth strong and hale, rich and happy. But another dieth in bitterness of soul without any riches. And yet they shall sleep together in the dust. [11] The wicked shall

[1]Gen. ii, 17. [2]Gen. iii, 19. [3]Gen. v, 5. [4]1 Paral. xxix, 15 ; cf. Gen. xlvii, 8–9 ; Ps. xxxviii, 13 ; cxix, 5 ; Heb. xiii, 4 ; xi, 13 ; 1 Pet. ii, 11. [5]Ecclus. xl, 11 ; cf. xii, 5–7 ; xvi, 31. [6]Job xvi, 23. [7]Job vii, 10. [8]Eccles. ix, 4 ; Wisd. xv, 8. [9]Eccles. viii, 8. [10]Job iii, 19. [11]Job xxi, 23, 25–26.

perish without honour, for dreadful are the ends of a wicked race.[1] They shall come to their death with fear at the thought of their sins, and their iniquities shall stand against them to convict them.[2] If their pride should have mounted up even to Heaven, in the end they shall be destroyed like a dunghill and they that had seen them shall say: where are they?[3] The death of the wicked is very evil."[4]

On the contrary, "The just hath hope in death, for the souls of the just are in the hand of God and the torment of bitter death shall not touch them.[5] With them that fear the Lord it shall go well in the latter end, and in the day of their death they shall be blessed.[6] In the sight of men they suffered torments, but their hope is full of immortality. And they shall say in that day of death: "Lo ! this is our God, we have waited for Him ; and they shall be in peace." [7]

The teaching of the Old Testament is summed up in the exhortation of the Wise Man. Saddened at the emptiness of human striving, he warns us : "It is better to go to the house of mourning than to the house of feasting, for in that we are put in mind of the end of all, and the living thinketh of what is to come." [8] For, if a man live many years and have rejoiced in them all, he must remember the darksome time and the many days of final suffering which when they shall come he will say : "they please me not."[9] Therefore the Wise Man urges : "Remember that death is not slow, remember thy last things, forget it not ; for there is no returning. In all thy works, remember thy last end and thou shalt never sin." [10]

Fittingly has the Psalmist resumed the attitude of those who lived under the ancient Law : "Hear my prayer, O Lord, and my supplication : give ear to my tears. Be not silent, for I am a stranger with Thee and a sojourner, as were all my fathers." [11] And he adds the lovely cry of trust which God made Man deigned to repeat upon the Cross : "Into Thy hands, O Lord, I commend my spirit, for Thou shalt save me, O Lord, my faithful God." [12]

[1]Wisd. iv, 19; iii, 19. [2]Wisd. iv, 20. [3]Job xx, 6–7. [4]Ps. xxxiii, 22 ; cf. Heb. x, 31. [5]Prov. xiv, 32 ; Wisd. iii, 1. [6]Ecclus. i, 13 ; cf. Osee xiii, 14. [7]Wisd. iii, 4 ; Is. xxv, 9 ; Wisd. iii, 3. [8]Eccles. vii, 3. [9]Eccles. xi, 8. [10]Ecclus. xiv, 12 ; xxviii, 6 ; xxxviii, 21; vii, 40. [11]Ps. xxxviii, 13. [12]Ps. xxx, 6 ; Luke xxiii, 46.

" God so loved the world," says St. John, " as to give His only-begotten Son, that whosoever believeth in Him may not perish, but may have life everlasting."[1] This is the light that is come into the world of our darkness.[2] He will enlighten us and teach us how to die.

On a very few occasions, the Divine Redeemer inter- *Our Divine Redeemer in* vened to bring back the dead to life. He wished to give a *Face of Death.* most striking proof that He was God, Master of life and death. Thus, too, He forecast His own triumph over death and offered us, who are so saddened by our mortal fate, a pledge of the final resurrection. His Sacred Heart was pierced with sorrow for the penalty of sin. There is a gentleness and compassion shown in the choice of those whom He raised from the dead that is one of the most touching mercies of His Heart. The daughter of Jairus was " an only child, almost twelve years old." [3] The young man of Naim was "the only son of his mother and she was a widow." [4] Lazarus was worthy to be called by Jesus Christ " our friend." [5] We read that the Divine Redeemer, seeing the widowed mother, was moved with mercy towards her and said to her : " Weep not." But for Lazarus, His friend, whom death had claimed, He wept Himself. " And the Jews therefore said : Behold how He loved him." Twice Jesus Christ is shown as weeping : once over the fate of His chosen but faithless city, Jerusalem, and again on the death of His friend.[6]

The Saviour, who had tasted the sorrow of death, instructs *The Teaching of Our* us, many times during His public life, how to die. We shall *Divine Lord* all be harvested, good and evil, in the field of this world.[7] *a) Death is* The net of God let down into the sea of life will gather in all *unexpected.* mankind for judgment after death.[8] If there be one aspect of Our Divine Lord's teaching upon death it is the emphasis upon the suddenness, the unexpectedness of our final hour. At midnight there was a cry made : Behold the bridegroom cometh, go ye forth to meet him. All the virgins had slumbered and slept as the bridegroom delayed, but only the wise were ready, at a moment's notice, with

[1]John iii, 16. [2]John iii, 19. [3]Luke viii, 42 ; cf. Matt. ix, 23–26 ; Mark v, 35–42. [4]Luke vii, 12. [5]John xi, 11. [6]John xi, 35–36 ; Luke xix, 41. [7]Matt. xiii, 30, 39–40. [8]Matt. xiii, 47–49.

trimmed lamps to meet their Lord. " Watch ye, therefore," adds Our Divine Master, " because you know not the day nor the hour." [1]

We are told that we are like to men who wait for their lord when he shall return, that when he cometh and knocketh, they may open to him immediately, their loins girt and lamps burning in their hands. Blessed, He declares, are those whom the Lord when He cometh shall find watching. They are the faithful, the wise and the blessed. [2]   But none can give himself security against that hour, for Our Divine Lord firmly warns : " Take ye heed, watch and pray. For ye know not when the time is. Lest, coming on a sudden, He find you sleeping. And what I say to you I say to all : watch." [3]

That some neglect the command of God to be prepared for death is shown in the parable of the evil servant who said in his heart : "My lord is long in coming." His faith and his hope grew dim. He began to strike his fellow-servants, to be unjust and haughty, to eat and drink with drunkards. " The Lord of that neglectful servant shall come in a day that he hopeth not and at an hour he knoweth not. He shall separate him in death and appoint his portion with the hypocrites." [4]

Again, the rich man, who looked only on the value of his swollen harvests, built greater barns and gathered around him all his goods. To his soul he promised length of days and comforth in wealth : " Take thy rest, eat, drink, and make good cheer." That very night God said to him : " Thou fool, this night do they require thy soul of thee." [5]

b) Death is the end of Merit

Night is an image that Our Divine Lord has used to portray death. It is not the suddenness of that unexpected night that is so frightening, it is its character of darkness that allows no further work of man. " The night cometh when no man can work." [6]   With the separation of the soul and body, there is an end of merit. The state of soul cannot now be changed. The soul must cleave to that which it has chosen as its final lot ; God or the rejection of God. The

[1]Matt. xxv, 1–13. [2]Luke xii, 35–41. [3]Mark xiii, 33–37. [4]Luke xii, 41–46 ; cf. Matt. xiii, 37. [5]Luke xii, 16–21. [6]John ix, 4 ; cf. Gal. vi, 7–10 ; 2 Cor. v, 10 ; Eccles. xi, 3 ; Heb. iii, 13.

wise virgins that were ready go in at once with the bridegroom to the marriage. The door is shut against the foolish virgins once the bridegroom has arrived.[1] When after a long time the lord of the servants returns and reckons with them, the diligent who had traded with their talents are at once admitted into the joy of their Lord. The wicked and slothful servant is immediately cast out into exterior darkness.[2] Again, the evil servant, who had grown weary of waiting and had presumed to be secure, is separated, on the arrival of his lord, and set among the hypocrites, where there is weeping and gnashing of teeth.[3] Dives and Lazarus receive at death each his due reward ; nor can either change his allotted place. " Between us and you there is fixed a great chaos, so that they who would pass from hence to you cannot, nor from thence come hither."[4] The very many warnings of Our Divine Lord to watch, " lest coming He should find us sleeping," were indeed vain, if death were not the end of our probation. " Be thou faithful unto death," says the Divine Judge, in the Apocalypse, " and I shall give thee the crown of life [5] ; but, if thou wilt not watch, I will come to thee as a thief, and thou shalt not know at what hour I shall come." [6]

To have heard these lessons of Our Divine Master would seem already to be an ample warning. His urgent pleading ought to be sufficient to preserve us from the danger of being slothful and negligent. But, in His vast mercy, Our Divine Saviour has done more : He has died Himself. From the first moment of His becoming man, He knew that death waited at the end. " A body Thou hast fitted for Me. Behold I come. At the head of the book it is written of Me that I should do Thy will, O God." [7] And the will of God for the Saviour of mankind was death on the Cross, in expiation of all sin.[8] No sooner is He born than Herod seeks to extinguish His Infant Life.[9] Simeon foretells that He will be a sign of contradiction and prepares His Mother for the piercing agony of His death.[10] From the moment that His public life opens, His enemies pursue

*Our Divine
Redeemer died*

[1]Matt. xxv, 10. [2]Matt. xxv, 21, 23, 30. [3]Matt. xxiv, 51. [4]Luke xvi, 22, 26. [5]Apoc. ii, 10. [6]Apoc. iii, 3 ; cf. xvi, 15 ; 1 Thess. v, 2–4. [7]Heb. x, 5–7. [8]Eph. iii, 9 ; Col. i, 26 ; 1 Tim. iii, 16 ; Luke xxiv, 27 ; Matt. i, 21 ; xx, 28 ; 1 Pet. ii, 24. [9]Matt. ii, 13, 20. [10]Luke ii, 34–35.

Him with implacable envy, not merely to thwart His influence but to crush Him out of life. [1]As the time drew near, He revealed His ardent wish to die that the redemption of mankind might surely be accomplished in the shedding of His blood.[2] Time after time He told the unthinking Apostles of the treachery, the outrages and the cruelty of His execution.[3] Then when His Passion had begun, in the Agony of the Garden, the Divine Redeemer took into His heart all the terror of His dread sufferings and death : the anguish of all the sin of all mankind.[4] And in His death, no pain of body was spared Him ; no class of men failed to add their tribute of insult ; no sorrow of desolation was missing from His agony on the Cross. " Father, into Thy hands I commend my spirit. It is consummated," He cried out and died.[5]

The Obedience of His Death. " Christ suffered for us," St. Peter writes, leaving us an example that we should follow His steps.[6] It is an incredible comfort that we can follow His steps into the fear and loneliness of the vale of death. By His death, Jesus Christ has expiated the disobedience of sin. By His obedience to God the Father, the Divine Saviour has, in death, which is the penalty of sin, redeemed mankind. " Therefore doth the Father love Me, because I lay down my life. This commandment have I received of My Father." [7] There is no greater test of love than that one lay down his life.[8] In complete submission to the will of God, Jesus Christ laid down His life for love of us, whom He deigned to call His friends.[9]

Our Death in Union with the Death of Jesus Christ. In the Sacrament of Baptism we become by grace the children of God.[10] From that instant we are united with Jesus Christ Who was obedient to God even to the death of the Cross.[11] The grace we share with Him is the fruit of His Sacrifice in death. Our godparents renounced for us the life of sin whose end is death, temporal and eternal.[12] We, ourselves, when we came to the age of understanding

[1]John v, 18 ; vii, 1, 20 ; viii, 37. [2]Luke xii, 50. [3]Luke ix, 22, 44 ; xvii, 25 ; Matt. xx, 17–19 ; Mark x, 32–34. [4]Matt. xxvi, 35–56 ; Mark xiv, 33–50 ; Luke xxii, 39–54. [5]Matt. xxvii, 35–56 ; Mark xv, 20–41 ; Luke xxiii, 33–49 ; John xix, 16–37 ; cf. 1 Pet. iii, 18 ; Rom. v, 9–12. [6]1 Pet. ii, 21. [7]John x, 17. [8]John xv, 13. [9]John xv, 14–15. [10]John iii, 5 ; Rom. viii, 15, 17 ; 2 Pet. i, 4. [11]Philipp. ii, 8–9. [12]Rom. vi, 3, 23.

renewed that pledge and every time that we assist at the Holy Sacrifice of the Mass, we unite with Jesus Christ, Who redeemed us from sin and broke the power of death.[1] In His dispositions of full subjection to God the Father on Calvary and in the Mass we find the answer to the fear of death. By looking at our Divine Saviour on the Cross we learn how to die like Him.

Our Death a Penalty from God.

We must die because God wills it. " It is appointed unto men once to die." [2] Death is a consequence of sin and a just chastisement. "Thou art just, O Lord. I know, O Lord, that thy judgments are equity." [3] In Our Divine Master there was found no sin, [4] yet He accepted the chastisement of sin, a death such as no mortal man ever met or can meet again. We have been born in the sin of Adam ; we have committed many personal sins. It is then just that we should die. In union with Jesus Christ, Who has won all graces for us by the death of the Cross, we humbly accept this punishment of God.

Our Death an Act of loving Obedience.

Death, which is an effect of sin, has been changed by the Divine Redeemer into a means of grace. We can accept our death in union with Him, as the act of obedience which costs us most. However closely we may follow Jesus Christ in life, by imitation of His lowliness and charity and devotion to God, there comes a moment when in death we can resemble Him most closely in total abandonment to God. Thus can our death become the most intimate union of our obedience with the sacrifice of the Cross, and thus can we finish in love the work that He has given us to do.[5]

The Final Grace of a Happy Death.

To die in grace is not within the power of man to merit. That is a gift which God can never owe to us in justice ; it is always a mercy of the secret Providence of God. The state of grace from which all merit springs is the free gift of God, and final perseverance is but the mercy which allows our death to coincide with the possession of sanctifying grace.[6] As we cannot know the moment of our death beforehand, we cannot know that the state of grace will be

---

[1]Rom. v, 8 ; 1 Pet. iii, 18 ; Tit. ii, 14 ; Col. i, 13, 22. [3]Heb. ix, 27. [2]Tob. iii, 2 ; Ps. cxviii, 175. [4]John viii, 46. [5]John xvii, 4. [6]Rom. xi, 6, 35 ; 1 Cor. iv, 7 ; Eph. ii, 5 ; John xv, 5 ; Conc. Trid. Sess. vi, cap. 6, can. 3 ; *Summa. Theol.*, Ia, IIae, q. 109, a. 5, a. 9, a. 10; q. 114, a. 9.

conserved in us by God, exactly at the instant of our death. Our fickle will is changeable throughout life, even when it is healed by sanctifying grace : it can choose the good but it cannot fix itself immovably in that perfect choice.[1] Only by the special grace of God can we persevere in good to the end. But we can obtain this final grace as an answer to our humble, trusting prayer. " All things work together unto good to them that love God," who are called according to His eternal plan.[2] But, to receive the gift of death in grace, we must love God. And it is always He " who calls us through Jesus Christ to His eternal glory." [3]

To secure the Grace of a Happy Death. It is written that " They are blessed who die in the Lord." [4] To die in Him we must have lived in Him, for again it is written of the blessed " that they rest from their labours, that their works will follow them." [5] The works of grace give us confidence that we shall obtain the grace of dying in the state of grace. Are we vigilant in avoiding mortal sin ? Are we careful to expiate the sins that we have committed ? Can we say in truth that the spirit of prayer is the guide of our daily life ? Are we humble of heart, entreating the help of grace ? Are we, especially, patient in suffering for the love of Jesus Christ, and merciful, for His sake, to all who are afflicted ? These are the qualities which can give one hope that God will be merciful at the hour of death.

Our Hope in Death. We have great need of hope, for we know our frailty and we know that, because we are so ordinary, we shall be afraid of death. We know that we shall not be spared the heart-pangs of our final loneliness nor the agony of our final dissolution. Yet the act of dying is not one in which we alone are concerned. God has a most intimate part in our death. But we do know that Jesus Christ in death has conquered death : that " to die is gain," that " our mortal life will put on immortality." [6] How many times in life have we not received Jesus Christ Himself in the pledge of immortality, the Blessed Sacrament ? Each time that we receive Him let us make a great act of hope that we shall see Him at the end. We know that He has given us a special

---

[1] Conc. Trid. Sess. vi, can. 16, 22 ; *Summa Theol.*, IIa, IIae, q. 137, a. 4. [2] Rom. viii, 28–30. [3] 1 Pet. v, 10 ; cf. 1 Cor. i, 6 ; Phil. i, 6 ; Rom. ix, 15. [4] Apoc. xiv. 13. [5] Ibid. [6] Philipp. i, 21 ; 1 Cor. xv, 53–54.

Sacrament for dying and that in the Last Anointing we shall be preserved against our natural terror and the temptations of the demon. We believe that all the traces of our sins can be effaced and our souls made ready for the immediate happiness of God.[1]

We believe that the Angels, who have assisted us through life, will guard and enlighten us especially at death. We trust in the strong protection of St. Joseph, who was helped in death by the presence of the Divine Redeemer and Our Blessed Lady. With the instinct of a child, we turn to Mary whose help we have countless times invoked for this very hour of death. She is our life, our sweetness and our hope. It cannot be that a Mother will forsake her child, in the one moment on which eternal life depends. For this moment her own Son died, on our behalf. Death is not for us the final act of one who goes out alone to enter the unknown. Death is for us a meeting and the embrace of God. It is Jesus Christ Who comes for us at death. " I shall come," He has assured us.[2]

" You now indeed have sorrow, but I will see you again and your heart shall rejoice. And your joy no man shall take from you, for I will that, where I am, you also, whom the Father has given Me, may be with Me for evermore." [3]

[1] James v, 14–16 ; Conc. Trid. Sess. xiv, cap. 1, 2 ; *Summa Theol.*, *Supplementum*, q. 29, a. 1, ad 2. [2] Apoc. xxii, 20 ; xvi, 15 ; cf. iii, 3. [3] John xvi, 22 ; xvii, 24, 11.

Chapter II

OUR JUDGEMENT

Judgement follows death.

IT is the constant and perpetual teaching of the Church that, immediately after death, each human being must render to God an account of all the deeds of his earthly life.[1] The soul, now separated from the body in which it worked for good or for evil, will at once receive from God the sentence of its reward or punishment. By the weight of its guilty aversion from God, it must fall into Hell or, by the attraction of its choice of God, it must rise to His embrace.

Throughout the Sacred Scriptures we are warned that God will judge mankind. Adam and Eve were fully aware of the command of God requiring their obedience : " Of the tree of knowledge of good and evil thou shalt not eat." [2] They understood with equal clearness the judgement that would follow at once on their disobedience : " In what day soever thou shalt eat of it, thou shalt die the death." [3] And with unfailing swiftness the sentence was executed, inwardly by the loss of sanctifying grace and other gifts, outwardly by the penalty of death : " Dust thou art and unto dust thou shalt return." [4]

The Old Testament and Judgement.

No sooner had Cain shed his brother's blood than God required that blood at the hand of the murderer : " Cursed shalt thou be upon the earth, a fugitive and a vagabond." [5] David, " despised the word of the Lord to do evil in His sight." [6] The prophet was sent to declare his sins to the king and to announce the sentence of judgement.[7] Later the contrite Psalmist would exclaim : " Whither shall I go from Thy spirit or whither shall I flee from Thy face ? " [8] " The eyes of God," says Job, " are upon the ways of men and He considereth all their steps. There is no darkness and there

[1] Clement IV and Council of Lyons ; Benedict XII, *Benedictus Deus* ; Council of Florence ; cf. Schema pro Concilio Vaticano ; Catechism of Council of Trent, Part I, art. 7, n. 3 ; *Summa Theologica, Supplementum,* q. 88, a. 1 ; q. 49, a. 2 ; Contra Gentes iv, c. xci ; De Veritate, q. 19, a. 1. [2] Gen. ii, 17. [3] Gen. ibid. [4] Gen. iii, 19. [5] Gen. iv, 11–12. [6] 2 Kings, xii, 9. [7] Ibid. 10–12. [8] Ps. cxxxviii, 7 ; cf. 2 Mach. vi, 26.

is no shadow of death, where they may be hid who work iniquity." [1] " The works all of the flesh," declares the Wise Man, " are before Him and there is nothing hid from His eyes." [2] " Woe to you," cries out Isaias, " that are deep of heart and say : 'Who seeth us and who knoweth us? My way is hid from the Lord and my judgement is passed over. This thought of yours is perverse." [3] " He is a God at hand," Jeremias warns us, " not a God afar off." [4] " The spirit of the Lord," we read in the Book of Wisdom, " hath filled the whole world. Therefore he that speaketh unjust things cannot be hid, neither shall the chastising judgement pass him by. For inquisition shall be made into the thoughts of the ungodly and the hearing of his word shall come to God, to the chastising of his iniquities." [5]

To the just, on the contrary, it is promised: "There shall be a reward for thy work, a faithful reward." [6] " They that walk in innocence shall not be deprived of good things. God will give them the requests of their heart." [7] " Fear not, my son," explains Tobias, " we lead indeed a poor life, but we shall have many good things if we fear God [8] : abundance without fear of evils, length of days and years of life and peace." [9] " They shall be my special possession," says God of His faithful people, " in the day that I do judgement." [10] " O! how great," sings the Psalmist, " is the multitude of Thy sweetness, O Lord, which Thou hast hidden from them that fear Thee." [11] " The eye hath not seen," exclaims Isaias, " what things Thou hast prepared for them that wait for Thee." [12] " Afflicted in few things," says Wisdom of the just, " in many they shall be well rewarded, because God hath tried them and found them worthy of Himself." [13] " The children of the saints," declares Tobias, " look for that life which God will give to those that never change their faith from Him." [14] Therefore the Wise Man writes : " Let nothing hinder thee from praying always and be not afraid to be justified even to death : for the reward of God continueth for ever." [15]

---

[1]Job xxxiv, 21–22. [2]Ecclus. xxxix, 24. [3]Is. xxix, 15. [4]Jer. xxxiii, 23. [5]Wisd. i, 7–8. [6]2 Par. xv, 7 ; Prov. xi, 18. [7]Ps. lxxxiii, 13 ; xxxvi, 4. [8]Tob. iv, 23 ; Prov. i, 33 ; iii, 2 ; cf. Is. i, 19. [9]Prov. i, 33 ; iii, 2. [10]Malach. iii, 17. [11]Ps. xxx, 20.. [12]Is. lxiv, 4. [13]Wisd. iii, 5. [14]Tob. xi, 18. [15]Ecclus. xviii, 22 ; cf. Eccli. i, 3.

The history of God's chosen people is one of alternate desertion of God and turning back to God. Out of all the nations of the earth they had been set apart. To them alone had been given the revelation of God's law. Theirs was the true worship prescribed by God Himself. In a certain sense, God dwelt with them. Yet they continually neglected the Commandments of God and disregarded the threat of His judgement in this life and in the next. On occasion they would amend, when the Prophets were sent to recall them from their apostasy. Yet, there must have been always in Israel very many just souls whose faith in a Redeemer to come prepared the way for the coming of Our Divine Lord Jesus Christ. When at length the promised Messias did come, many of His own people were found to be as careless of the judgement of God as had been their stiff-necked ancestors. To such as these were addressed the terrifying words : " You shall die in your sins." [1]

The Attitude of the Modern World.

We who have enjoyed the benefit of the teaching of God made man can be truly said to be more mindful in daily life of the judgement that follows death. Yet, is it not true that life as we know it, apart from the Church, is deliberately organised to fix our eyes on this world alone ? The thin soil of our Christian souls is at all times sufficient to produce the thorns that choke the seed of God's Word.[2] " The cares of this world, the wealth and the pleasures," [3] of which Our Divine Lord spoke, have been ever present to distract men from the work of their salvation. But it has been reserved for our own days to produce a civilisation that builds itself on the cold denial of the existence of God. The Communist teaching has at least the advantage of being brutal in its clearness. Much more subtly dangerous to Catholics is the society that quietly assumes that God has no part in His own creation. This is the world of which the Apostle says that " it minds earthly things." [4] It is the culture of literature, cinema and radio, of art and drama that seeks to mould the daily life of ordinary men and women. Thus, commerce, the various avocations, even the learned professions faithfully reflect the denial of the absolute rights

[1]John viii, 24 ; cf. Rom. ix, 1–5. [2]Matt. xiii, 22 ; Mark iv, 18–19 ; Luke viii, 7, 14. [3]Luke viii, 14. [4]Phil. iii, 19.

of God. Only this world matters in such a life, because only this world exists. In life there is no God except oneself, and hence, no aim worth one's effort except the power and wealth and pleasure that this world can so visibly afford. In death there is no reckoning. After death there is no survival, unless perhaps in the memory of men, who are hastening to the nothingness into which the dead have passed.

What an abyss between this way of life and the definite teaching of Jesus Christ! Our Divine Master, in speaking of the Judgement, has expressly referred in vivid terms to the General Judgement in which He Himself will sift out the wicked and the just.[1] He has not, however, left us in any doubt concerning the judgement that awaits each man immediately after death. It is thus the doctrine of our holy Faith that no soul shall remain uncertain of its lot until the final judgement but shall, immediately after death, receive its punishment or reward. Such a sentence demands a trial or judgement on the part of God.

In the Old Testament the Wise Man had written: " It is easy before God in the day of death to reward everyone according to his way." [2] Our Divine Lord, on the other hand, with sovereign power declares to the repentant thief : " *This* day thou shalt be with Me in Paradise." [3] In His own parable, the poor man died and was carried by angels into the bosom of Abraham ; the rich man died and was buried in Hell.[4] The imagery of the parables so often conveys the lesson of man being given a task by his Lord and rewarded or punished according to his fidelity or negligence. The king, who would take an account of his servants, being angry, delivers the wicked servant to the torturers.[5] The fig-tree, if after trial it bear no fruit, is condemned to be cut down.[6] The ungrateful husbandmen, to whom many messengers, even the Son of the householder, were sent, are, at the end, destroyed, for, " they who reject the Kingdom of God shall be ground to powder." [7] When the king sees the man who has come into the marriage feast not

The Teaching of The New Testament

a) Words of Our Divine Lord.

---

[1]Matt. xxiv, 27, 30–31 ; xxv, 31–46 ; John v, 28–29. [2]Ecclus. xi, 28. [3]Luke xxiii, 43. [4]Luke xvi, 22. [5]Matt. xviii, 34. [6]Luke xiii, 9. [7]Matt. xxi, 33–45 ; Mark xii, 1–12 ; Luke xx, 9–17.

having on a wedding garment, he orders the servants to
bind his hands and feet and to cast him into exterior darkness.[1] The nobleman, having received his kingdom, returns
and commands his servants to be called for trial. They who
had gained by trading are rewarded ; the wicked servant is
rebuked and punished.[2] " Blessed are those servants,"
declares Our Divine Lord, " whom the Lord, when He
cometh, shall find watching. He will gird Himself and make
them sit down to meat and will minister unto them. But the
Lord of the wicked servant will come in the day that he
hopeth not and at the hour that he knoweth not and shall
separate him and shall appoint his portion with un-
believers." [3]

These parables refer to the judgement of both the evil
and the good. But, for the just there is reserved the assurance
of eternal happiness. Is any word of Our Divine Master
more consoling than His promise of immortality to those
who receive Him in the Blessed Eucharist ? " He that
eateth this Bread shall live for ever." [4] Of the faithful who
die in the Lord He says : " My sheep hear my voice and I
know them and they follow Me. And I give them everlasting
life ; and they shall not perish for ever. And no man shall
pluck them out of My hand ; , no one can snatch them out
of the hand of my Father." [5] On the occasion of the death
of His beloved Lazarus He spoke the words that are the
unending joy of all who have to die : " I am the resurrection
and the life ; he that believeth in Me, although he be dead,
shall live ; and everyone that liveth and believeth in Me
shall not die for ever." [6] Lest any doubt assail us as to the
certainty of our eternal reward after death, Our Divine Judge
Himself assures us : " Let not your heart be troubled. You
believe in God, believe also in Me. In my Father's house
there are many mansions. If not, I would have told you :
because I go to prepare a place for you. I will come again
and I will take you to Myself : that where I am you also
may be." [7]

---

[1]Matt. xxii, 11–13. [2]Matt. xxv, 14–30. [3]Luke xii, 37, 46 ; cf. Matt.
xxiv, 44–51 ; Mark xiii, 33–37. [4]John iv, 59. [5]John x, 27–29. [6]John
xi, 25–26. [7]John xiv, 1–3.

We do not wonder then that the Apostle St. Paul should affirm that God has not destined us for wrath, but for the acquiring of salvation through Jesus Christ Who has died for us, in order that living or dead, we should live together with Him.[1] Death then for the Apostle is a gain, though in all humility he acknowledges that he must undergo the judgement of God.[2] None the less, he desires to be dissolved in death, for it is much better to be with Christ.[3] In the body we are pilgrims from God and walk in the dimness of Faith. Out of the body, after death, we are present to the Lord and in vision, see Him as He is.[4] The just Judge, he trusts, will render to him a crown of justice [5]—the reward which, haltingly, the Apostle attempts to describe : " Eye hath not seen, nor ear heard ; nor hath it entered into the heart of man, what things God hath prepared for them that love Him." [6]

St. John the Evangelist exclaims : " Blessed are the dead who die in the Lord." [7] In the Apocalypse, he sees the fulfilment of the promise of immortal life which he had himself heard from the lips of the Divine Redeemer. The souls of the martyrs who had been purchased by the Blood of the Lamb, the first fruits to God, rest, without spot, before the throne of God.[8] " Blessed and holy," he declares, are the souls of the martyrs that have part in the first resurrection, in the happiness that is already theirs before the resurrection of the body. The second death of the Day of General Judgement, when the souls and bodies of the wicked shall be condemned to Hell, shall have no power in them, for already they follow the Lamb.[9] They have been faithful unto death and He has given them the crown of life.[10]

In the teaching of Our Divine Lord Jesus Christ, there is no delay between the sentence of the Judge and its execution. The unjust steward is summoned to give an account of his stewardship. At once the sentence takes effect : " Now thou canst be steward no longer." [11] It is on this very day on which he hangs upon the cross that the penitent thief will join his

[1] Thess. v, 9–10. [2] Phil. i, 21. [3] 1 Cor. iv, 4; Phil. i, 23. [4] 2 Cor. v, 6-8. [5] 2 Tim. iv, 8; cf. 1o Cr. xiii, 9-12. [6] 1 Cor. ii, 9 ; cf. Apoc. iii, 21. [7] Apoc. xiv, 13. [8] Apoc. xiv, 5–6. [9] Apoc. xx, 6 ; xiv, 4. [10] Apoc. ii, 10. [11] Luke xvi, 2.

merciful Redeemer in Paradise.[1] Between Dives and Lazarus a great chasm is already set, immediately after each has attained his due award. [2] Of the dead who have died in grace, St. John has written : " *From henceforth now*, saith the Spirit, that they may rest from their labours. Their works follow them." [3] " The Lord of that neglectful servant shall come in a day that he hopeth not and at an hour that he knoweth not. He shall separate him and appoint his portion with hypocrites." [4] It is this night that the soul of the rich man, as he looks with fullness of pride upon his swollen wealth, will be required by God.[5] At once the ungrateful guests are rejected.[6] At once the good servants who had traded with their talents are admitted into the joy of their Lord.[7] On the foolish virgins the door is closed at the moment that the Bridegroom, surprising them in their guilty negligence, declares that He knows them not.[8] Death, indeed, is terrible ; but more terrible still, it is the end of trial. " The night cometh when no man can work." [9] For that cause Our Divine Lord warns His Apostles : " Take ye heed, watch and pray. For ye know not when the time is, lest coming on a sudden, He finds you sleeping." And He adds for our fear : " What I say to you, I say to all : watch." [10] " If thou shalt not watch, I will come to thee as a thief." [11]

Jesus Christ our Judge

To Jesus Christ has been committed by God the Father the office of judging men. " The Father hath given all judgement to the Son, that all men may honour the Son as they honour the Father." [12] It is as God that Jesus Christ will judge us. But it is fitting that He should also judge us as Man ; for is He not our Divine Redeemer and our King Who has purchased us by the shedding of His Precious Blood ? " All power is given to Him in Heaven and on earth,"[13] [12] and " He hath given Him power to do judgement, because He is the Son of Man." [14] " We must all be manifested," declares St. Paul, " before the judgement seat of Christ, that everyone may receive the proper things of the body,

---

[1]Luke xxiii, 43. [2]Luke xvi, 26. [3]Apoc. xiv, 13. [4]Matt. xxiv, 51. [5]Luke xii, 20. [6]Luke xiv, 21, 24. [7]Matt. xxv, 21, 23. [8]Matt. xxv, 10–12. [9]John ix, 4 ; cf. 2 Cor. vi, 2 ; Gal. vi, 9 ; Heb. iii, 13. [10]Mark xiii, 33–37. [11]Apoc. iii, 3. [12]John v, 22–23. [13]Matt. xxviii, 18. [14]John v, 27.

according as he hath done, whether it be good or evil." [1]
Thus will He " who hath been appointed by God to be the
judge of the living and the dead," [2] apportion to every
soul in death a due award. " Behold, I come quickly, and
my reward is with me to render to every man according to
his works." [3]

In the Sacred Scriptures, Jesus Christ is said to come to
judge us. In the Apocalypse we read that " the books were
opened, and another book was opened which is the book of
life ; and the dead were judged by those things which were
written in the books, according to their works." [4] In the
Liturgy, the Angels are summoned to offer the soul of the
departed to God. The demon is bidden to yield place at the
coming of the Judge and to flee with his angels into the
abyss of his eternal night.

The Manner of our Judgement.

But, in truth, there are no books of judgement opened.
These are but images by which the Sacred Scriptures and
the Church assist our feeble understanding and fix our
attention on the tremendous and irrevocable judgement. The
facts of our judgement are far more terrifying than the
figures of speech that aim at helping us to understand.

In the instant after death, the soul, now separated from
the body, sees at one glance, through the power of God,
its entire life, and in the same vision, its guilt or its salvation.
God is not seen at our judgement, nor even Jesus Christ.
A moment before, the soul could understand in the human
way of knowing through the senses ; it could choose this
good or that, as the intellect presented it for choice. Now the
door of bodily life has been closed for ever. The night has
fallen, wherein no man can further work in soul and body.
Now in the piercing light of God impressed upon the soul,
only the truth is seen. What a moment, in which,
for the first time, ignorance is impossible and error can have
no place ! The same divine power of Jesus Christ that
gave sight to the sightless, [5] that read the soul of the Sam-
aritan woman [6] or of Judas, [7] that revealed the unspoken

---

[1] 2 Cor. v, 10. [2] Acts x, 42. [3] Apoc. xxii, 12. [4] Apoc. xx, 12. [5] Matt. ix,
27–31 ; xx, 29–34 ; Mark x, 46–52 ; Luke xviii, 35–43 ; Mark viii, 22–26 ;
John ix, 1–7. [6] John iv, 16–18. [7] John xiii, 11, 27–28.

thoughts of Pharisees [1] and Apostles,[2] makes known to
the separated soul that it is saved or damned, according
to its works.

In the instant after death, the word of Jesus Christ
is itself the trial and the sentence. " The word that I have
spoken, the same will judge him." [3]   For the faithful soul
who has kept that word this is the moment of which it
is written : " The Lord shall be unto thee for an everlasting
light and thy God for thy glory." [4]   " If our earthly house
of this habitation be dissolved we have a building of God,
a house not made with hands, eternal in Heaven." [5]   No
longer for such a soul is there the " hope of life everlasting,"
for now at last it possesses " the inheritance, incorruptible
and undefiled and that cannot fade, reserved in Heaven." [6]

" The lamp of the wicked is sin." [7]   Of the evil it is
written that " they hearkened not nor inclined their ear :
but walked in their own will and in the perversity of their
wicked heart." [8]   Their confusion at the moment of judgment is described by God the Holy Ghost : " Why have I
hated instruction and why has my heart consented not to
reproof, and have not heard the voice of them that taught
me." [9]   There was a moment at which one could have
accepted the teaching of the infallible Church of Christ.
Now with inescapable clarity the doctrine of the Catholic
Church is seen to be the word of Jesus Christ Himself.
We could have known, and we ought to have known, the
truth of Christ. Now the Christ of Judgement is seen to be
no other than the Christ on earth. " The word that I have
spoken the same will judge him. He that despiseth Me
and receiveth not My words hath one that judgeth him." [10]
Therefore, the damned shall cry out : " Our wickedness
reproves us and our apostasy rebukes us. It is an evil and a
bitter thing to have left the Lord." [11]

*The
Preparation
for Our
Judgement
a) The
Practice of
the Presence
of God.*

The Church herself has called the judgement of each
soul " a day of fear," for it is a work of God, overwhelming,
instantaneous and irrevocable. Can we make ready for
such a single moment ? We can strive to live continually

[1]Luke vi, 8. [2]Luke ix, 46–47. [3]John xii, 48. [4]Is. lx, 19. [5]2 Cor. v, 1.
[6]Tit. i, 2 ; 1 Pet. i, 4. [7]Prov. xxi, 4. [8]Jer. vii, 23–24 ; cf. Ps. xxxv, 2 ;
xiii, 3. [9]Prov. v, 12 ; cf. Wisd. v, 1–14. [10]John xii, 48. [11]Jer. ii, 19.

in the presence of our Judge. " All the days of thy life,"
exhorts Tobias, " have God in thy mind, and take heed
never to consent to sin." [1] " Blessed is the man," says
Ecclesiasticus, " that in his mind shall think of the all-
seeing eye of God." [2] Of such a man is the word of Isaias
true : " The remembrance of God is the desire of his
soul." [3] St. John the Evangelist urges us to abide in God
and in Jesus Christ His Son. " Abide in Him that when He
shall appear in judgement, we may have confidence and
not be confounded by Him at His coming." [4] These
words are but an echo of the Divine Master's final con-
versation with the Apostles : " Abide in Me. He that
abideth in Me and I in him the same beareth much fruit,
for without Me you can do nothing." [5]

One special fruit of our living in the presence of God
is an abiding sorrow for our sins. It is not merely that we
are faithful to the practice of examining our conscience,
especially each night, in face of sleep that prefigures death.
Our sorrow is rather an effect of God the Holy Ghost
within our souls, Who enlightens, refines and urges. In
the temple of the Holy Ghost[6] the stain of sin may not
be permitted to remain. It is in His light that we see our
sins and our sinfulness. If we wander, He corrects us ;
if we are weak He is our strength ; if we are tried, He
is our consolation, in such wise that we are always lovingly
reminded of our lowliness and thus kept ready for the
coming of our Judge. " God is faithful, Who will strengthen
us and keep us from evil."[7] " He is able," says St. Jude,
" to preserve us without sin and to present us spotless
before the presence of His glory, with exceeding joy, in
the coming of Our Lord Jesus Christ."[8]

b) Abiding Sorrow for Sin.

We can prepare for our judgment by the Sacrament
of Penance. Each confession can be made before God as
if it were our last. In a moment, even after years of sin,
grace is recovered by this Sacrament. That moment must
resemble the instant in which the soul at judgement knows

c) The Sacrament of Penance

[1]Tob. iv, 6. [2]Ecclus. xiv, 22. [3]Is. xxvi, 8. [4]1 John ii, 28 ; iii, 24 ; iv,
13. [5]John xv, 4–5. [6]1 Cor. vi, 19 ; 2 Cor. vi, 16 ; cf. *Summa Theol.*,
2a, 2ae, q. 19 ; q. 141, a. 1, ad. 3. [7]2 Thess. iii, 3 ; 1 Cor. i, 9 ; x, 13.
[8]Jude 24.

that it is saved, for Our Divine Redeemer tells us that
the Angels of God rejoice exceedingly at one sinner doing
penance.[1] The Prodigal Son, a weary figure, worn by sin,
in an instant is reconciled to his father and all the emphasis
of Our Divine Lord is now upon the welcome of the father,
the rich new robe and the ring, a pledge of renewed fidelity,
set by the father on his finger.[2] They who have not sinned
grievously kneel at the feet of the Master in this Sacrament, as did formerly His faithful friends,[3] to be washed
anew in the Blood of the Lamb with increase of grace
and fervour of charity. The graces of this Sacrament
bear specially on the sins that we confess and on the vicious
inclinations from which our sins are born : weakness and
ignorance and malice. In this Sacrament we are given an
increase of Fear, the gift of God the Holy Ghost, that breaks
the hardness of conscience that is opposed to the delicacy
of God's yoke. By this disposition we are enabled " to
sweep our spirit "[4] in continual sorrow, lest we offend
by sin God Who is our loving Father. From this Sacrament, finally, comes the grace to bear our cross in penance.
In our weakness, we have offended the power of God the
Father ; in our ignorance we have made little of the wisdom
of God the Son ; in our malice we have rejected the goodness of God the Holy Ghost. Surely we have each of us
great reason for penance. We have not far to seek occasions
of making reparation. On each of us is laid a daily cross.
If we take it from the hand of God, it will keep us in the
spirit of lowly sorrow and will sanctify us in the patience
of our love.[5]

d) The Final Preparation of the Church —Last Sacraments and Prayers. There is a final preparation for our judgement, that
of the Church herself. On the last moments of the dying
the Church is wont to lavish all her Mother's care. Is
it not for this moment, in fact, that all the Sacraments,
all the graces of life have been preparing us : the first
grace of Baptism, the strength of Confirmation, the renewed forgiveness of Penance, in particular, the frequent
pledge of immortality, Jesus Christ in the Sacrament of
the Eucharist ? And now, as it groweth towards the even-

[1]Luke xv, 10. [2]Luke xv, 21-22. [3]Luke x, 39. [4]Ps. lxxvi, 7. [5]Luke ix,
22-23 ; cf. Rom. vi, 4 ; Eph. ii, 22 ; Gal. v, 25 ; 2 Tim. i, 14.

ing, the Church must hasten to gather her sheaves before the fall of night. In the presence of death, all censures are set aside. Absolution is renewed for all the sins of life, and with absolution comes the abundant calm of contrite hope. The Holy Viaticum is like a renewal of the First Communion. Then, the soul, unstained by malice, set forth on the journey of its life, in the fresh love of Jesus Christ ; now, the wounds of life all healed, made innocent once more, it faces the end, in the strength of the same Companion, the Redeemer who will be its Judge. The last vestiges of sin are effaced in Extreme Unction. [1] The anguish of our many fears is soothed. With deeper confidence and more silent resignation we accept the penalty of death, in union with Jesus Christ Who offered Himself for us in death.[2] Even then the Church, with the insistent emphasis of her prayer, repels the demon and calls on the Angels, the ministers of our redemption, to assist us in the moment on which the judgement of eternity depends. St. Joseph the Patron of a happy death, our own Patron Saints, all the Blessed are, as it were, roused to aid us. In particular, she invokes the most powerful intercession of the Blessed Virgin, who, in the measure willed by God, shared the sorrow of her Son in our redemption. With what lowliness of pleading the Church commends to God the souls of the departing. " Acknowledge Thy creature, O God, who has been made by Thee, the only God, living and true. Make glad his soul at the sight of Thee. Remember not his former sins for, though he has sinned, he has believed and never abandoned his belief in the Father and the Son and the Holy Ghost." " I have found," says God, "wherein I may be merciful to him."[3]

It may well be that God will not allow us the grace *e) The never-failing assistance of Our Lady* to be prepared for judgement by the Sacraments of the Church. If we have learned to walk in His presence and have been faithful to His love, He will have purified us in other and secret ways, in particular, by the humility

[1] James v, 14–16 ; Conc. Trid. Sess. xiv, c. 1, 2 ; *Summa Theol. Suppl.*, q. 29, a. 1, ad 2. [2] Philipp. ii, 8–9 ; Rom. v, 8 ; John viii, 28–29 ; 1 John iv, 10 ; 1 Pet. iii, 18 ; Tit. ii, 14. [3] Job xxxiii, 24.

and hope of patient suffering. We can trust His wisdom
and His love, for He Himself has died for us. In that hour
we can trust the never-failing help of His Blessed Mother.
How many thousand times in life have we not made ready
for our judgement in the humble recitation of the prayer :
" Holy Mary, Mother of God, pray for us sinners, now
and at the hour of our death, Amen." How many times
have we not pleaded : " After this our exile show unto us
the blessed fruit of thy womb, Jesus." Long ago on earth
He would not resist the intercession of His Mother.[1]
It is our firmest hope that our Redeemer and our Judge,
in whatever circumstances He may will our death, will
grant us, at her pleading, the grace of graces ; to " be
faithful unto death " and, in judgement, "to receive the
crown of life."[2]

[1]John ii, 5, 7. [2]Apoc. ii, 10.

IV—Our Blessed Mother

Chapter I

THE MOTHER OF GOD

IT is indeed remarkable that in the very grave crisis of our times the Sovereign Pontiff should have consecrated the world to the Most Holy Heart of Mary. On first reflection, we might be inclined to think that there was a greater need for recalling men to the notion even of God's existence. The claims of our Most Holy Redeemer upon our obedience and our love might well have been urged as matters of first importance. None the less, it is to the feet of Mary, Mother of God, Our Lord, that the Vicar of Christ has gently led an unthinking and rebellious world. With great fittingness, we may say in all due reverence, the Holy Father, in the agony of these fateful days, has repeated the words of Jesus Christ upon the Cross : "My sons, behold your Mother !"

At the first hour of human sin, God Himself revealed the Woman who should be victorious over Satan. " I will place enmities," said God to Satan in the moment of the demon's triumph, " between thee and the Woman, between thy seed and Her seed ; and She shall crush thy head, and thou shalt lie in wait for Her heel."[1] Satan had deceived the first woman, Eve. Through her agency, he had brought about the fall of Adam and the whole race of man, which would derive from Adam. To Adam our first Parent, God had given in trust for all mankind the noblest gifts : sanctifying grace, freedom from pain and grief and death. By his disobedience Adam had forfeited for himself and us the blessings with which the love of God had endowed his nature in its origin. It could not have been in ignorance that Adam sinned. He must have understood the dignity of his trust as fountain of

The Promise of Mary.

[1]Gen. iii, 15.

153

the human race. Therefore, his sin is, in a sense, the gravest that the mind and will of man have ever committed against God the Creator. " By one man sin entered into this world and by sin, death ; and so, death passed upon all men, in whom all have sinned."[1]

We shall never fully understand the loving mercy of the Creator, which, immediately after Adam's sin, could promise the Redeemer, Who would conquer Satan and repair the ruin wrought by sin. " As by the disobedience of one man, many were made sinners : so also by the obedience of one, many shall be made just."[2] The Woman promised by God would bring forth the Child Who " through death would destroy him, who had the empire of death, that is to say, the devil."[3] It was Eve who, urged by Satan, had induced Adam to sin. It would be the promised Woman who, as God's instrument, would crush the head of Satan. It was Adam who, by disobedience, had sinned and ushered in the reign of death. It was Jesus Christ, Son of the promised Woman, Who by His obedience would make infinite reparation for the sins of men.

This Woman, who is the sign of hope, given by God to sinful man, is none other than Mary. The Church delights from the earliest times to call her the Second Eve.[4] She is as closely associated with the Divine Redeemer and His work of grace as Eve was linked with Adam, the fount of sin, and with original sin. Rather, is it more accurate to say that she is much more intimately the source of our redemption than was Eve the occasion of our fall, for Mary is most truly the Mother of the Only Son of God, Our Lord and Saviour, Jesus Christ.

The Need of a Divine Redeemer. " The Word was made flesh and dwelt amongst us."[5] The sin of Adam was the disobedience of a man, who represented all the human race. The reparation of that sin must equally be wrought by a man in the person and the name of all mankind. But neither Adam, nor any person born from him, could satisfy the injured majesty of God. Much less could any human being undo the evil

[1]Rom. v, 12. [2]Rom. v, 19. [3]Heb. ii, 14. [4]Cf. S. Irenaeus, *Adv. Haer.* 3, 22, 4. [5]Jo. i, 14.

of original sin, in respect of human kind. For man had forfeited the grace of God, nor could he of himself even begin to attain to the supernatural love of God. Neither could any man, being a limited, poor creature, make satisfaction for his offence against an Infinite Creator. The sin of Adam, though but the sin of man, was, in a certain sense, infinite, for the reason that it outraged the infinite dignity of God. If full reparation were required by God, it was an absolute necessity for God Himself to intervene, lest the creature of His hands should be a wretched and frustrated thing. "God Who is rich in mercy, for His exceeding charity with which He loved us, even when we were dead in sin, hath quickened us together in Christ, by Whose grace you are saved."[1] We are reconciled to God in Jesus Christ, and Jesus Christ is God the Son made Man.

In taking to Himself a human nature, God found a means of reconciling human kind with the Divinity, in a manner that only Infinite Wisdom and Infinite Love could ever explain. "God first hath loved us."[2] Jesus Christ is true God, "the only-begotten of the Father, full of grace and truth."[3] He is equally true Man, the Son of Mary. The human nature which He took from her is united with the person of the Son of God. His acts as man are thus most properly divine. They have a dignity and power, which, because they are the actions of the Second Person of the Blessed Trinity, are in truth of infinite efficacy and value. "In Him dwelleth all the fulness of the Godhead corporeally."[4] "In him it hath well pleased the Father that all fulness should dwell and through Him to reconcile all things unto Himself, making peace through the blood of the Cross."[5]

Since God had willed that our peace should be effected only through the blood of the Redeemer on the Cross,[6] it was essential that God should take into personal union with Himself a human body and a human soul. The Incarnation means that God the Son, without any human intervention, by the sole power of His omnipotence, through

The Incarnation.

---

[1]Eph. ii, 4–5. [2]1 John iv, 19. [3]John i, 14. [4]Col. ii, 9. [5]Col. i, 19–20. [6]John i, 7 ; Apoc. i, 5 ; vi, 6–12 ; Hebr. ix, 14 ; xiii, 20.

Mary, assumed our human nature into the closest union of His person. " And the Angel said to her : 'Thou hast found grace with God. Behold thou shalt conceive in thy womb and shalt bring forth a Son : and thou shalt call His name Jesus. He shall be great and shall be called the Son of the Most High. And the Lord God shall give unto Him the throne of David His father : and He shall reign in the house of Jacob for ever. And of His kingdom there shall be no end.'"[1] In clearest terms the Archangel Gabriel announced the coming of the long-desired Messiah, Who was none other than the Son of God. " And Mary said to the Angel : 'How shall this be done, because I know not man ?' And the Angel answering said to her : 'The Holy Ghost shall come upon thee and the power of the Most High shall overshadow thee. And, therefore, also the Holy which shall be born of thee shall be called the Son of God.' And Mary said : 'Behold the handmaid of the Lord : be it done to me according to thy word.'"[2] The Son of God Who exists from all eternity has thus become in time the Son of Mary.

Mother of God.

" Mother of my Lord"[3] was the salutation of St. Elizabeth. The title is an apt forerunner of the solemn definition of the Church. It is an article of our holy Faith that Mary is truly the Mother of Him, who is God. The clear teaching of Sacred Scripture and the unvarying tradition of the Church were explicitly defined in the Council of Ephesus : " according to the flesh, the holy Virgin brought forth the Word of God made Flesh."[4] On this truth rests all the dignity of the Virgin Mary.

By the grace of the divine Maternity, Our Blessed Lady is drawn into the most intimate relationship, by which God made Man is in the truest sense her Son. For nine months He dwelt within her womb : in the virgin-birth She gave Him to the world. For many years, She tended Him. And to show His reverence and His love for her who had with Him the authority of a Mother, it is written that willingly He obeyed her : " He was subject," says the Evangelist.[5] In regard to the Eternal Father,

[1]Luke i, 30–33. [2]Luke i, 34–35, 38. [3]Luke i, 43. [4]Council of Ephesus, Can. i. [5]Luke ii, 51.

Mary can claim a unique position; for, as God the Son is begotten of the Father from eternity, God the Son made Man took human nature from His Mother, Mary. In regard to God the Holy Ghost, Mary is called His Spouse, for to the miraculous power of God the Holy Ghost is attributed the formation of Christ's body, inasmuch as the Incarnation of Our Divine Redeemer is a work of infinite charity and goodness.

There is then no greater union of a creature with God —except, of course, the union of human nature with the Person of God the Son—than the close relationship of nature between the Mother and her Son, the Word made Flesh. To Mary then God owed the fullest grace. Her closeness to the Most Holy God demanded that she should be equipped worthily to fulfil her office. If out of all mankind, one only was selected for the divine Maternity, no grace could possibly be spared by God in the adorning of His Mother. " And the Angel being come in, said to her : 'Hail, full of grace, the Lord is with thee.'"[1]

The most singular privilege of holiness which follows *The Immaculate Conception of Mary.* from the choice of Mary as God's Mother is her Immaculate Conception. Our Blessed Lady was a child of Adam, and in that sense she, too, had to be redeemed, according to the sentence passed by God Himself upon our First Parents. To her soul the Precious Blood of Jesus Christ had to be applied in ransom. But, in the single case of the Woman who should be His Mother, God intervened lest even the slightest taint should fall upon her soul. In the very instant of her conception, by the power of God, in virtue of the merits of the Son who would be hers, Mary was kept immune from the stain of original sin. In the beginning, God had showed to our First Parents the Woman, who, with her Child and through Him, would for ever oppose the Serpent and his followers, and destroy their rule. The word of God could not have been fulfilled, if for an instant or in any sense, Mary had fallen beneath the demon's sway. Of necessity she must have been preserved from original sin. It was a privilege which no merit

[1] Luke i, 28.

of her own could warrant. Only the power of God, foreseeing the virtue of the Sacred Passion, could protect His Mother from the stain of sin. With justice then the Angel greeted her in a manner never used to any other creature : " Hail full of grace : the Lord is with thee."[1] Truly Elizabeth declared her privilege : " Blessed art thou among women."[2] She is blessed by a privilege which in all creation is for her alone.

The Sinlessness of Mary.

We cannot think that God could love a creature with greater love than that which He kept for His Blessed Mother. Her purity, then, must be measured by God's esteem for the honour that is due to Him. For this reason the Doctors of the Church have seemed to use extravagant terms in setting forth the glory of God's Mother. " Because of the infinite Goodness which is God," writes St. Thomas, " the dignity of God's Mother is, in a sense, infinite."[3] " Her purity," he adds, " next after Christ, is said to be supreme."[4] It is the universal teaching of the Church that Mary, inasmuch as she was preserved from the infection of original sin, was saved from the disability of disordered passion. Nothing that " comes from sin or leads to sin "[5] could find a place in the holiness of God's Mother. By God's special grace, she never sinned.[6] By the singular grace of the divine Maternity, Mary was given the right to God's perpetual love. In that sense, therefore, by the protection of His Providence, she was incapable of sin. Error of mind, the weakness springing from original sin, could not have dimmed the intelligence of Mary. Her surpassing knowledge of all that touched her station as the Mother of the Word made Flesh has merited for her the marvellous title of Seat of the Eternal Wisdom.

The Ever-Virgin Mary.

There is another privilege of Mary which the Church has always loved to recognise, for the honour of the Son and the glory of His Mother. It is the unfailing teaching of the infallible Church that Mary is the Virgin Mother of the Word made Flesh. As Jesus Christ is the Only

---

[1]Luke i, 28. [2]Luke i, 42. [3]St. Thomas, Pars. i, 25, 6, ad 4. [4]St. Thomas, Pars. iii, 27, 2 ad 2. [5]Council of Trent, Sessio 5 c. 5. [6]Ib. Sessio 6, can. 23.

Begotten of the Father, so is He the Only Begotten of His Mother, Mary. It was owed to His dignity that, in the words of Isaias, " a Virgin should conceive the Son whose name should be Emmanuel, God with us, and a Virgin bring Him forth."[1] To the Angel, who had announced to her : " Thou shalt conceive in Thy womb and shalt bring forth a Son and thou shalt call His name Jesus," Mary had answered : " How shall this be done, for I know not man ? "[2] In these words the Church has seen the vow of perfect and perpetual virginity, which God had inspired His Blessed Mother to make. Again, the Angel addressing Joseph solemnly assured him that the Child which was born of her was conceived by the almighty and miraculous power of God the Holy Ghost.[3] " Who," writes St. Epiphanius, " has at any time been found, who dared to speak the name of Mary, and on being questioned, has not immediately added, the Virgin. To Holy Mary is given the name of Virgin, nor shall that name be ever changed."[4] A Virgin before the birth of Jesus Christ, a Virgin in His birth, by miracle of God, a Virgin ever after she had brought forth Our Saviour : such is the faith of all the Church from earliest times.[5] And in that declaration we love to tell not only the singular, sweet purity of Mary, but the honour due to Jesus Christ, her Son, and the reverence owed to her Spouse, the Holy Ghost.

We can now easily understand that God loved His *The* Blessed Mother more than any creature He had ever *Holiness* called from nothingness, man or Angel. Into her soul *of Mary.* then the Blessed Trinity poured, at the very instant of her conception, a measure of grace so deep and full that " only God could Himself assess it."[6] Sanctifying grace which raised her being to the level of the life of God Himself, the gifts of God the Holy Ghost, by which He could most delicately waft her to the highest sanctity, the train of all the virtues, especially charity, by which, in thought

---

[1]Is. vii, 14. [2]Luke i, 31, 34. [3]Mt. 1, 20. [4]*Adv. Haer.* 78, c. 6. [5]Cf. Apostles' Creed ; Pope St. Siricius, Ep. 9 Tenz. 91 ; Council of Ephesus, can. 1 ; Pope St. Leo I, Epist. *Lectis dilectionis,* 4; The Liturgy, passim. [6]Pius IX, Bull *Ineffabilis Deus.*

and act and feeling, she would most faithfully obey the Will of God : these are the adornments of God's Mother in her immaculate conception. For the reason that she was destined to be the Mother of the Word made Flesh, the holiness that suited her for that unique vocation was, in its beginning, already greater than the consummate perfection of all men and Angels. Though the Angel called her " full of grace," yet Mary was destined, we must believe, to advance in merit and holiness throughout her life. It could not be that the gifts of God were barren in a soul so intimately united with the Blessed Trinity. Was not her Son the self-same Person, Who is the Only-Begotten of the Father ? With God the Son, from the moment of the Incarnation, she had entered into the dearest relationship of Mother. Of God the Holy Ghost, she was the Spouse. And throughout the years when Jesus Christ would live on earth, Mary would live in daily contact with Incarnate Holiness itself. Up to the moment when in death she passed to Heaven, her soul increased in grace and merit, until that grade was reached which God in His Wisdom had decreed would be the final sanctity of His Blessed Mother. One joy we know God has kept for His elect : the vision of the holiness of Mary.

Our Lady of Dolours.

In considering the glory of the Blessed Virgin, it is perhaps easy to forget the life-long sorrow that is hers, because she is, in fact, the Mother of the suffering Redeemer. It was the loving plan of God that man, who, because of sin, had been punished by suffering and death, should in turn be ransomed by the Divine Redeemer's suffering and death. Our Blessed Lady was gifted with a vast intelligence. No sin had ever clouded her understanding of the things of God. She knew the sadness of the prophecies which foretold how the Messiah would take upon Himself the penalties of our sin. The vividness of the picture of His suffering given by Isaias must have been burnt into her perfect memory of the sacred Text.[1] Judge then the torrent of her bitterness, when from the Angel she learned that she would be the Mother of the

[1] Is. vii, 14 ; liii, 1–12.

sorrowful Redeemer. We count in our Rosaries the Annunciation as a Joyful Mystery. The joy, in truth, is ours, who have, through Mary, been given a Redeemer. The sorrow is hers who knew that He must be the Man of Sorrows. Simeon then can have but confirmed the anguish of her mother's heart, the sword had pierced her from the instant that in full submission, she had agreed to be His Mother. We can, to some extent, guess at her thoughts as she watched the beauty of her Infant and her growing Son. The Infant's face she contemplated was already stained by His Blood, and bruised for our sins.[1] "With the wicked, He would be reputed." His little hands and feet she saw as pierced with nails. And in His side, as she tended Him, she traced the brutal opening of the lance.[2] His outstretched arms were already fixed upon the Cross. How could she bear the glance of the eyes which death would veil in outrage, at the end ? The separation of the Three Years' Ministry had been long prepared. And that Separation was only the preface to the slow, long hours of His Passion when, for all her love, she could not stay beside her Son. Even the Resurrection, which for all men was to be the triumph of their peace, was sad for Mary, who knew that now His Ascension was at hand. When He had gone from earth, she lived in Faith, in the darkness of His absence from her side. It is not till the moment when, after death, her most holy body joined her soul that, after all the years of waiting, with her very eyes she looked in joy, unmixed with any sorrow we had caused her, upon the glory of her Son. The winter of her life now seemed so short ! Her springtime is eternal.[3] It was the unending moment of her Magnificat in bliss.

The closeness of Mary's union with the atonement of her Son has won for Our Lady the title which is perhaps the sweetest that a man can use in her regard : Mother of the Divine Redeemer. "There is one Mediator of God and men, the Man Christ Jesus."[4] It is only by the death of Christ upon the Cross that human kind has been

Mary's Share in the Redemption.

[1]Is. liii, 4–5 ; Zach. xi, 12 ; Ps. xxi, 17–19; Cf. Acts iii, 18 ; Luke xxiv. 25–27. [2]Zach. xii, 10 ; Exod. xii, 46. [3]Cant. ii, 10–13. [4]1 Tim. ii, 5–6.

redeemed.[1] Yet, in a very accurate sense, Our Lady by her satisfaction and her merits, under Christ and in union with the only Saviour, is called the Co-Redeemer. At the Incarnation she gave her fullest consent to be the Mother of the Crucified Redeemer, with all the martyrdom of soul that such an office could entail. In the Presentation, Mary offered to God a gift such as had never before been given Him. She it was who cared for the Saviour at every stage of His Infant and His hidden life. To suffer and to live in union with her Son summed up her life on earth. One in heart with all the thoughts and sentiments of her Son, she offered Him to God in the Sacrifice of Calvary, with an understanding and a love, which are surpassed in fulness and perfection only by the sacrificial act of the Divine Victim on the Cross. Only God made Man could offer condign satisfaction for the sins of men. Only Jesus Christ could in the most proper sense merit the graces needed for man's salvation![2] But Mary, whom the anticipation of the Passion of her Son had saved from original sin, was permitted by God so to immolate her Son, that in truth she may be said to have shared in the redemption of the human race with Jesus Christ.[3]

Queen of Heaven.

Nor was her office ended with the gloom of Calvary. It is the firm teaching of our holy Faith that Mary was not suffered by her Son to see corruption.[4] Her most holy soul on its separation from her body was borne at once to the highest Heavens. Her body had not merited the curse[5] that it should return to dust. The fulness of her sanctity and her preservation from all sin required that after death her holy body should be translated into Heaven. Above the choirs of Angels and the Blessed, the Mother of the King now reigns in queenly dignity. None other sees the vision of the Godhead with such unclouded light as does the peerless woman who remains for ever Mother of the Word made Flesh.

[1]Acts iv, 12, Rom. iii, 24–25 ; 1 Cor. i, 30 ; Eph. i, 7 ; 1 Tim. ii, 6. [2]Cf. John i, 29 ; 1 John ii, 2 ; Rom. v, 19. [3]Pius IX, *Ineffabilis Deus ;* Leo XIII, *Supremi Apostolatus ; Iucunda semper ; Fidentem ;* Pius X, *Ad diem illum ;* Benedict XV, *Inter Sodalicia ;* Pius XI, *Auspicatus profecto ; Explorata res.* [4]Cf. Ps. xv, 10. [5]Gen. iii, 19.

It cannot be thought that, with her entrance into bliss, *Our Lady Dispenses All Graces.* Our Blessed Mother could forget the sons of men upon the earth. To her with special love our dying Saviour commended human kind in the person of St. John: "Woman, behold Thy Son."[1] By the death of Jesus Christ her Son, and in the martyrdom of her own heart, we have cost her too deep a travail to permit her to forget. In the plan of God at the beginning she appeared to man as the sign of hope. In the scheme of the Redemption, she gave to us the Saviour, Source of all our grace. And now, under God, she dispenses all the grace of Christ.[2] Mother of Divine Grace, relying on the infinite satisfaction of her Son, she pleads for us with God in all our needs.

Our sweetness and our hope in this vale of tears, she is the fount for us of all the grace of Christ. We must not think that Mary intercedes for us merely to obtain those actual graces, which urge us to good and ward off evils. To her we owe, under God and Jesus Christ, even sanctifying grace, that gift of gifts by which our being is transformed and given to share in the very life of God Himself. To her we owe the gifts of God the Holy Ghost, the refinements, we may say, of the delicacy of God Who dwells within us. From her also we receive the virtues which are the supernatural power of our life. Even in the graces of the Sacraments her power intervenes, for, in a sense, she merited that the Sacraments should be given us by her Son, and now, by her intercession, she obtains not only that the Sacraments be dispensed, but also that our dispositions in receiving them be adequate and prompt.

Many times in the Litany we salute Mary as the Queen, *Mary Our Mother.* for in very fact she is the Mother of the King. Supreme in dignity and merit, she exercises over men and angels the true dominion of a Queen. But it is as Mother that we chiefly love to greet her. It is an article of the Faith that Mary is, in the spiritual sense, our Mother. Eve, the first woman, is called by God the mother of all the

---

[1]John xix, 26. [2]Cf. Benedict XIV, *Gloriosae Dominae ;* Leo XIII, *Supremi Apostolatus ; Octobri mense ; Adiutricem populi ; Diurni temporis ;* Pius X, *Ad diem illum ;* Benedict XV, *Illustriores inter ;* Pius XI, *Sollemne semper.*

living; Mary, with greater reason, in that she brought forth Christ, the source of all our grace, is Mother of all that live by Him in grace. In the spiritual sense, she brought us forth to His life of grace.[1] With motherly love, she cares for all the needs of our salvation, nor rests until she numbers us among the trophies of the Precious Blood.

He that is mighty hath done great things to Mary. For none of His creatures has He done so much. The mercy of which Mary sang in her Magnificat was not meant for her alone. She was, indeed, endowed most richly for the honour of her Son. But she was chosen, too, for the sake of all her children, the redeemed of Jesus Christ. Because she is the Mother of Our Lord and Saviour, Jesus Christ, it is to her that all the exiled children of Eve at length come back. At the feet of the Mother of the Redeemer we kneel, in the discouragement and sorrow of our daily failures. To the Seat of Wisdom we draw near, in the perplexity of our very many ignorances. To her Mother's heart we make appeal for every grace, in the prayer the Church has taught us, in childhood, through middle-age, even to our final breath: " Holy Mary, Mother of God, pray for us, sinners, now and at the hour of our death. Amen."

[1]Cf. Pius XI, *Lux veritatis.*

Chapter II

MARY, THE MOTHER OF JESUS.

(Acts, i, 14)

In the very beginning, after the Fall of Adam, God Himself reveals the Woman who should, through her Son, be victorious over Satan.[1] Later, the Prophets foretell the Virgin Mother.[2] At length, she herself appears, in the fulness of time, the Mother of Jesus Christ.[3] For some centuries of persecution, Mary seems to maintain in the Church the obscurity that she loved in Nazareth. Then, under pressure of heresy, her title of Mother of God is openly vindicated. Through the hymns of the Middle Ages, her gentle name shines as a light in a dark place,[4] bearing witness to her paramount influence, until, in the Cathedrals and the Orders dedicated to her glory, we see the widening dawn of the devotion that, under the guidance of God the Holy Ghost, has illumined the Catholic life of the last ten centuries. The Woman and her Son, of whom the Book of Genesis speaks, is none other than the Mother and her Child, whose altars and images are venerated in every Catholic Church and home throughout the universe. All generations have declared her blessed,[5] because from eternity she has been chosen to be the Mother of God made man.

We should expect to find in the Old Testament at least the hint, in prophecy and type, of so singular a person as the Mother of the Messias. Throughout the Sacred Books there runs the deep stream of prophecy concerning the Redeemer who was to save His people from their sins[6] In the faith of that Redeemer the people of God were

Prophecies in the Old Testament.

---

[1]Gen. iii, 15. [2]Is. vii, 14 ; Mich. v, 1–4. [3]Luke i, 6–7 ; Matt. i, 20–25. [4]2 Pet. i, 19. [5]Luke i, 48. [6]Matt. i, 21 ; Rom. x, 4 ; cf. Gen. ix, 26 ; xii, 3 ; xx, 17–18 ; xxii, 18 ; xxvi, 3–4 ; xxviii, 14 ; xlix, 10 ; 2 Kings vii, 14 ; Deut. xviii, 18 ; Ps. ii, 7–8 ; xv, 8–11 ; xxi ; cix, 4 ; xxxix, 7–9 ; lxxi, 11 ; Is. ii, 3–4 ; Mich. v, 1–4 ; iv, 2 ; Is. lxi, 1–2 ; liii, 3–5 ; Mal. i, 10–11 ; Zach. xii, 10 ; xi, 12–13 ; ix, 9.

sanctified. Yet, their history shows that the surrounding idolatry of heathen nations often dimmed the brightness of the revelation that God had made through the Prophets.[1] Even when He had come on earth, and had lived among men, it was necessary for Jesus Christ to open the minds of His disciples, that they might understand what had been written of Him "by Moses and all the Prophets and in the Psalms."[2] Even to-day, after centuries of Christian teaching, we need the sure guidance of God the Holy Ghost to show us, in the history of God's chosen people, the prophecies that foretell the person and the character of the Mother of the Messias. "Who shall know Thy thought, unless Thou give wisdom, and send Thy Holy Spirit from above?"[3]

The Prophecy of the Book of Genesis.

It is Pius IX who teaches that, in the Book of Genesis, God clearly and openly described the merciful Redeemer of the human race, and pointed out His Blessed Mother, the Virgin Mary. In the one eternal decree of God were linked most intimately the Incarnation of the Second Person of the Blessed Trinity and the Mother from whom that Divine Person should receive His human nature.[4] "As often," wrote Pius X, "as the grace to come is spoken of in the Prophets of the Sacred Scriptures, so often, may we say, is the Saviour of mankind found together with His most holy Mother."[5]

The Redemption by God made Man.

The plan of our Redemption is a mystery of justice and mercy hidden in the counsels of God from all eternity.[6] Adam had sinned. He had lost the gift of sanctifying grace and the friendship of God for himself and all his descendants. He had offered the Divine Majesty an offence that, in a manner, must be infinite, for God, Who had been disobeyed, is infinite in perfection. No mere creature could adequately repair the sin of Adam. Only God could give infinite honour to God. Only God, in His wisdom and mercy, could have thought of the plan of our Redemp-

---

[1]Exod. xx, 23 ; xxxii, 4, 22 ; Lev. xxvi, 1 ; Is. xliv, 10 ; Wisd. xiii, 10–19 ; xii, 23–25 ; 3, 4 Kings ; Jer. xxv, 6–12 ; Ezech. xxii, 4 ; Osee xiii, 2 ; Mal. iii, 7 ; 1 Mach. i, 55. [2]Luke xxiv, 25, 27, 44 ; i, 70 ; xviii, 31 ; John v, 46 ; Matt. xxvi, 54, 56 ; Acts iii, 18 ; xxvi, 22 ; 1 Pet. i, 10. [3]Wisd. ix, 17. [4]Bull, *Ineffabilis.* [5]*Ad diem illum :* In Scripturis sanctis . . . coniungitur. [6]Eph. iii, 9 ; 1 Tim. iii, 16 ; Col. i, 26.

tion. God Himself would become man, and the God-man would redeem us. Each human act of God made man would be the act of the Divine Person, and, in consequence, an act of infinite value. Thus would the Divine Redeemer make fullest satisfaction for the sin of man, and restore to man the life of God that had been lost through Adam's crime.[1]

To take into personal union with Himself our human nature, the Divine Redeemer must be born, in descent from Adam, of a human Mother.[2] This Mother is the Woman referred to by God when speaking to our First Parents, immediately after they had sinned. " I will put enmities between thee and the Woman, and thy seed and her seed. She shall crush thy head."[3] Between the devil and the Woman, God set an irreconcilable hostility, between the adherents of the devil and the Woman's Child a permanent enmity. Her Child would utterly overthrow Satan.

The Immaculate Conception of the Mother of God.

The words of God were addressed to Eve, but they clearly show forth the second Eve, Mary, whose Child, the second Adam, would destroy the reign of Satan and repair the ruin of the first Adam's fall. In these words of God, we have, says Pius IX, " the declaration of the stainless purity of Mary."[4] She was to be the Mother of the Divine Redeemer. It was thus altogether fitting that she should herself be perfectly redeemed. She was to crush, through the Son that would be truly hers, all the power of Satan. She could not therefore, for a single moment, herself be subject to the reign of sin. She was to be the Mother of God. God could not choose a Mother that had ever been in the slightest way defiled. We believe then, on the word of the infallible Church, that by an utterly exceptional privilege of God, Mary, the Mother of God made man, in view of the merits of Jesus Christ, the Saviour of mankind, was, in the very first instant of her existence, preserved from all stain of original sin.[5]

[1]St. Thomas, *Summa Theol.*, iii, q. 1, art. 2 ; q. 46, a. 1 ; q. xlviii ; Matt. xx, 28 ; Mark x, 45 ; Is. liii, 7 ; John x, 17–18 ; viii, 28–29 ; 1 Pet. iii, 18 ; ii, 23 ; Rom. v, 8 ; 1 John iv, 10 ; Gal. ii, 20 ; Tit. ii, 14. [2]Luke i, 32 ; Rom. i, 3 ; 2 Tim. ii, 8. Cf. *Summa Theol.*, iii, q. 35, art. 1–5. [3]Gen. iii, 15. [4]Bull, *Ineffabilis.* [5]Ibid.

Speaking of the holiness of the Blessed Virgin, Pius IX declares that " greater under God, is not understood by men." Into her soul, at the moment of her conception, was poured the fullest measure of sanctifying grace that would accord with her dignity as the Mother of God. No creature would ever reach so close a union with the Blessed Trinity. Nor would any creature ever come so close to the Author of grace as Mary to her own Son, God made man. Her dignity as God's mother is, in a manner, infinite. Her degree of holiness must then exceed the sanctity of all the Angels and Saints.[1]

The holiness of Mary that the Fathers love to celebrate[2] is not indeed infinite, like that of God. It could increase in all the stages of her life, as she merited in the Incarnation, in the days of Nazareth, and beneath the Cross. We must believe that her grace at every second of her existence was measured by the dignity of her role as the Mother of the Divine Redeemer. God, then, must have granted her the fulness of all the virtues. The gifts of God the Holy Ghost must have guided her soul with unhindered mastery. In her no evil inclination could arise, for she had in her conception been preserved from the very fount of sinful movements. She was so assisted by the grace of God that, being intensely joined in will with God, she could never choose the slightest evil. In her mind there was no error. The power of her natural intelligence was vast. A special knowledge made her adequate to the varying tasks of her unique position. From the very dawn of her existence, she had enjoyed the unclouded use of reason by which she understood the privilege of the sanctity that God had given her. She could not have been less favoured than John the Baptist, who was sanctified in his mother's womb, not less enlightened than the Prophets, who had spoken of her Son.[3]

Little wonder that the Fathers and Theologians should, in succeeding ages, vie with one another in searching

---

[1]*Summa Theol.*, i, q. 25, a. 6, ad 4 ; IIa, IIae, q. 103, ad 4. [2]*Summa Theol.*, iii, q. 7, a. 10 ; cf. SS. Justin, Irenaeus, Epiphanius, Ambrose, Jerome, Ephraem, Augustine, John Tamascene, Anselm, Bernard and Eadmar. [3]*Summa Theol.*, iii, q. 27.

the Old Testament to find figures and prophecies that might portray the holiness of the Virgin Mother of God. Where Mary is concerned, the Church's liturgy borrows from the Sacred Books all the richness of the imagery that the history of God's chosen people has evoked. She is the Morning Star,[1] and the Dawn of growing Splendour,[2] the Rainbow of Peace,[3] the Cloud of fruitful rain,[4] the Earth which shall give forth its mysterious fruit.[5] The Rod of Aaron that budded and flowered in almond blossoms.[6] Mary is the Holy City wherein God dwells,[7] the Holy of Holies all covered with gold,[8] the Ark of the Covenant,[9] which enshrines not merely the Tables of God's Law, but God Himself. Again, she is the Propitiatory that reminds us of God's favour in the past, and recalls us to penance for our sins,[10] the Golden Urn that held the holy Manna,[11] the Altar of Perfumes in the midst of the Holy Place,[12] the Table that bore the Bread that should be offered.[13]

The personages, too, of Holy Writ have furnished the image of Our Lady's role and virtues. She is the second Eve who has, through Jesus Christ, defeated the deceiving Serpent.[14] Like Sara, she gave birth to the Child of promise.[15] In the thanksgiving hymn of Mary, sister of Moses, there is found a reflection of the Magnificat of God's Mother.[16] Like Debbora, the prophetess, she has led the people of God to triumph.[17] Like Judith, she is acclaimed the glory of Jerusalem.[18] Like Esther, she has prevailed to avert disaster from her people.[19] Most frequently in the Mass and Office of the Church, the Books of Wisdom are used to declare Our Lady's glory. The words that properly apply in the sacred text to the Eternal Wisdom of God are applied in figure to the Mother of the Word made Flesh. From eternity, in the plan of God, was she linked with her Divine Son. With God's wisdom

The Types of Mary in the Old Testament.

---

[1]Eccles. L, 6. [2]Cant. of Cant., vi, 9. [3]Gen. ix, 13. [4]3 Kings xviii, 44; cf. Is. xlv, 8. [5]Deut. viii, 7–8; cf. Ps. lxxxiv, 10–14. [6]Num. xvii. 8. [7]Ps. xlv, 5–6. [8]3 Kings vi, 20. [9]Exod. xxxvii, 1–5; 3 Kings viii, 9. [10]Exod. xxv, 17; xxxvii, 6–9; Lev. xvi, 12–14. [11]Exod. xvi, 33–35. [12]Exod. xxx, 1–9. [13]Exod. xxv, 23–30. [14]Gen. iii, 15; cf. Rom. v, 14–15; 1 Cor. xv, 20–21, 46–47. [15]Gen. xvii, 16–19; cf. Rom. iv, 19; ix, 9. [16]Exod. xv, 20–21. [17]Judges iv, 5. [18]Judith xv, 10. [19]Esther xv, xvi.

shall she co-operate in the Incarnation and the Redemption. On her perfection the gaze of God will always rest with love. Her joy will be to share her secret with mankind and give to all who are united with her Son the treasure of His redemptive grace.[1]

The Prophecy of Isaias. These are but applications of Holy Writ that the later ages, enlightened by the coming of the Holy Ghost, have been able to discover in regard to the Virgin Mother of Jesus Christ. Through the very long centuries of weary expectation, the chosen people could not enjoy so clear a vision. After the first prophecy of the Book of Genesis, wherein the dawn of our redemption was clearly foreshown, in the Woman and her Child, we must wait for the Prophets, Isaias and Micheas, to shed a direct light on the Mother of the Divine Redeemer. In Isaias, we learn of Emmanuel, God with us. From His birth, He will be endowed with the gifts of God the Holy Ghost. The land of the Lord shall be His, and He shall bring final victory to His people. Holiness and peace shall mark His reign. And the sign that shall announce His coming among men is the miracle of The Virgin who shall conceive, and bring forth a Son, and shall give to Him the name, Emmanuel, God with us.[2]

The Prophecy of Micheas. The prophet Micheas is, as it were, an echo of the text of Isaias. From Bethlehem, the village that is too small to rank among the clans of Juda, shall He come forth that is to be the Ruler of Israel. His origin is from the beginning, from the days of eternity. Till she shall bring Him forth, who is to be His Mother, God shall deliver up His people, Israel. The text is an implicit reference to the virginal conception and birth. God, existing from all eternity, comes forth as man to feed His flock, in the power of the Lord, to be Himself our peace.[3]

The Preparation for Mary, Mother of God. While the world awaited the expectation of the nations, of whom Moses had spoken,[4] the invisible preparation of grace had been making ready the minds and the hearts of the chosen people. Too often we forget that all the old Dispensation, with its Law and its rites, its prophecies

[1]Prov. viii ; Eccles, xxiv ; Cant. of Cant. [2]Is. vii, 14 ; xi, 1–10 ; viii, 8 ; xiv ; ix, 1–7. [3]Mich. v, 2–4. [4]Gen. xlix, 10.

and saints, was but a prelude to the Divine Redeemer, who should be the Son of Mary.[1] In fact, we find, at the moment of His coming, a host of holy persons who are the final fruit of the grace of the Ancient Testament. Zachary and Elizabeth, the parents of Our Lady, St. Joachim and St. Anne, in the maturity of their holiness, were made worthy by God to prepare for His most holy Mother.

The Archangel Gabriel, who had announced to the Prophet Daniel the seventy weeks that were now completed,[2] and to Zachary, the miraculous conception of St. John the Baptist,[3] "was sent by God to a city of Galilee called Nazareth to a Virgin espoused to a man whose name was Joseph, of the house of David, and the Virgin's name was Mary."[4] She too was of the royal house of David.[5] Not in the splendour of the Temple did the Angel find Mary, as he had found Zachary, but in the deep obscurity of a despised village.[6] Who could have suspected the prodigy of God that the village enshrined? " Hail, full of grace, the Lord is with Thee ! " The salutation of the Archangel is profoundly reverent. No such salutation was made by Angel or Archangel in the Ancient Testament. Already then, before the Incarnation, her holiness is quite singular. God could not speak of her in terms of higher praise. She is stainless in purity. Her grace of union with the All Holy God could not be greater. But Mary, in her humility, was troubled at hearing herself thus praised.[7] And the Angel, in answer, again declared her sanctity : " Fear not, for thou hast found grace with God "—such grace that He would have her for His Mother. " Behold thou shalt conceive in thy womb, and shalt bring forth a Son, and thou shalt call His name Jesus. He shall be great, and shall be called the Son of the Most High. And the Lord God shall give unto Him the throne of David His father ; and He shall reign in the house of Jacob for ever. And of His kingdom there shall be no end." It is she who shall conceive ; she who shall bring

The Incarnation.

---

[1]Rom. x, 14. [2]Dan. ix, 24. [3]Luke i, 11–20. [4]Luke i, 26–38. [5]Rom. i, 3 ; 2 Tim. ii, 8 ; Luke i, 32. [6]John i, 46. [7]*Summa Theol.*, iii, q. 30 ; a. 3, ad 3.

forth a Son, yet her Child shall be the Son of the Most High. She would be the Mother of God made man. At that moment, Mary, with the full enlightenment of all her knowledge, must have remembered the prophecy of the Virgin Mother, and of the suffering Redeemer in Isaias.[1] Unlike Zachary, she never doubted. Mindful of the virginity that she had for ever pledged to God, she only asked what God wished from her that she might enter into His designs for the birth of the Divine Redeemer. And the Angel replied by announcing the miracle of God : " The Holy Ghost shall come upon thee, and the power of the Most High shall overshadow thee. And therefore the Holy One who shall be born of thee, shall be called the Son of God." Then, to Mary, who had never like Zachary doubted the power of God, nor ever asked for a confirming miracle, the Angel unasked reveals the miracle of the conception by the aged Elizabeth of the Precursor of the Messias. And Mary said : " Behold the handmaid of the Lord : be it done to me according to thy word." And " the Word was made flesh "[2] and dwelt in Mary.

The Visitation.

No sooner had she become the Mother of God, than Mary became the cause of blessing, the dispenser of the grace of the Redemption. She hastened in her charity to share the secret of her cousin St. Elizabeth. At the voice of her greeting, St. John the Baptist is sanctified. At her approach, St. Elizabeth is filled with the Holy Ghost and reveals the blessedness of Mary. " Blessed art thou, blessed is the fruit of thy womb. How have I merited that the Mother of my God should come to me ? " And Mary, in the joy of God the Holy Ghost, makes answer in the lowliness of the Magnificat.[3] It is a hymn of thanksgiving for the Incarnation that reveals to us the unspoken knowledge and charity and submission which overflowed her heart, as she spoke her Fiat to the Angel Gabriel.

St. Joseph, Spouse of the Virgin Mother of God.

For the sake of Mary, " who was found with child by the Holy Ghost," St. Joseph received the grace of being admitted to the secret of the Redemption. Because she was the Mother of his Saviour, he was allowed to act as

[1]Is. vii, 14 ; liii, 1–12 ; xlii, 1–4. [2]John i, 14. [3]Luke i, 39–56.

guardian of the Redeemer, beside the immaculate Virgin Mother.[1]

Then, in the fulness of God's time, Mary brought *The Nativity.* forth her Divine Son.[2] She wrapped Him in swaddling-clothes, and laid Him in a manger, because there was no room for them in the inn at Bethlehem. But if men would not welcome the Mother and Child, God's angels called the shepherds to share with them their hymn of joy that now at last God should receive the highest glory in His Son, and men on earth the peace they had sought for since the Fall. The star summoned the Wise Men from the East to pay homage to the new-born King ; and they found the Child with Mary His Mother.[3] Of Mary no word has been recorded. She kept all the words of others in her heart, pondering them in the immensity of her adoration and thanksgiving. There are some things we shall never know on earth. Among them are the thoughts of Mary. Even if we knew them we should not understand. In Heaven we hope that we shall learn a little of the depth and the beauty of her thoughts, when Jesus Christ was miraculously born of the ever-Virgin Mary.

Soon was she startled by a sudden revelation of her *The Presentation in the Temple.* secret.[4] As, in due submission to the Law, Our Lady presented the Divine Child in the Temple, Simeon, en-lightened by God the Holy Ghost, took from her arms the tiny Infant to salute in Him " the salvation of all peoples, the light of the world, the glory of His people Israel." To Simeon, as to so many others already, she had been the cause of gladness in the grace of the Redemption. To herself that grace was now declared to be such as, according to Isaias, she had always known it must be in the plan of God : a share, her Mother's share, in the sufferings of the Divine Redeemer. Between the Presentation and the Passion, there is for Mary but an interval of time ; there is not an interval of suffering. Her heart, which Simeon foretells a sword shall pierce, has been already pierced, by the knowledge she received

---

[1]Matt. i, 18–25 ; cf. Ezech. xliv, 2 ; Is. vii, 14. [2]Luke ii, 1–20. [3]Matt. i, 1–12. [4]Luke ii, 22–38.

in the moment of the Incarnation. The sword is none other than the sufferings of her Son.

The Flight into Egypt. The Three Days' Loss.

Hitherto, in the scenes of the Infancy, Our Lady has dispensed a grace of peace. The prophecy of Simeon almost at once is verified in the agony of her effort to shelter the infant Saviour from the savage hatred of Herod. Again no word is spoken by Mary. We merely learn that, at the bidding of the Angel, she carried the Child into the poverty and strangeness of heathen Egypt, and with equal obedience, journeyed back to the welcome shelter of a home in Nazareth.[1] Yet that peace is soon broken in the desolation of the Three Days' Loss.[2] Mary was not allowed by God to know all the details of the plan of the Redemption. And her Son's departure unexpectedly foreshadowed for a brief moment the final anguish for which she was always waiting. For the last time St. Luke makes note that Mary kept all these memories in her heart. During eighteen years she would guard them, in a heart that the grace of daily contact with the Incarnate God made ever more willing to receive the pain of martyrdom beneath the Cross.

The Mother of Jesus at Cana.

For a brief moment, we glimpse the presence of our Blessed Mother at Cana.[3] The last separation from the home at Nazareth has been made ; the public life which is the immediate preface to the Passion has begun. As in the Incarnation, Mary had given to men their only Saviour, so in Cana her intercession prevails with Jesus Christ, her Son, to give to men the first miracle, on which the disciples would base their faith in the Divine Redeemer. For the last time she is seen to intervene in the dispensing of the grace of Christ. When next we meet her, she is standing beneath the Cross.[4]

The Mother of Jesus on Calvary.

For this final sacrifice she had lived since the first moment of the Incarnation. In becoming then the Mother of God made man, she had become the spiritual Mother of all, who, by the grace of the Redeemer, should be made the brothers of Christ, the sons of God, the temples of the Holy Ghost.[5] Now, on Mount Calvary, Jesus Christ,

[1]Matt. ii, 13–23. [2]Luke ii, 41–52. [3]John ii, 1–11. [4]John xix, 25. [5]Gal. iv, 6 ; Tit. iii, 4–6 ; 1 Cor. iii, 16 ; 2 Pet. i, 4.

in death, declared her solemnly to be our Mother.[1] We shall never understand how fully Mary shared in the sacrifice by which alone our Redemption was accomplished. Only God made man could adequately satisfy for our sins and merit for us eternal life. But we know that all the grace of her immaculate holiness, all the grace of her complete submission to the will of God only helped to increase her union with the sacrifice of her Divine Son. And God in His mercy, we believe, was pleased to reward unspeakably the Mother's acceptance of the death of her Son, the only Saviour, Jesus Christ.[2]

In virtue of the most excellent holiness that united her with God, by reason of the close union with the Saviour, Whom she gave to the world, and offered to His eternal Father on the Cross, Mary, as by a Mother's right, dispenses the treasures of the grace of the Redemption.[3] Immediately after the Ascension of her Divine Son, we find her in the midst of the Apostles and the disciples, awaiting the advent of the Holy Ghost.[4] It is the place that she has ever kept, since God assumed her virginal body and most holy soul into the glory of the Beatific Vision. " Full of grace " in the moment of the Incarnation, she is filled in Heaven with a holiness that, in the words of Pius IX, is understood only by God. Yet all her grace was given to fit her to be the Mother of the Redeemer. No greater work of mercy on the part of God can be conceived than our Redemption by her Divine Son, Jesus Christ. So all her grace has fitted her, to be in our regard, the Mother of Mercy, " our life, our sweetness, and our hope."

The Mother of Jesus our Mother.

[1] John xix, 26–27. Cf. Leo XIII *Adiutricem Populi ; Quamquam Pluries ; Iucunda Semper.* [2] Cf. Pius X, *Ad diem illum.* [3] Cf. Leo XIII, *Iucunda Satis ; Diuturni Temporis ; Adiutricem Popul.* Pius X, *Ad diem illum.* Benedict XV, *Inter Sodalicia.* Pius XI, *Miserentissimus ; Explorata Res.* [4] Acts i, 14.

Chapter III

THE HOLY ROSARY

GOD, in His goodness, has left us many aids to our salvation. There are, for instance, the seven Sacraments, which He Himself instituted, to serve the needs of all the Faithful, until the end of time. Then, as each age has somewhat changed, from the treasury of her doctrine, the Church, which Jesus Christ in Person founded, has on occasion set forth a certain practice of devotion, to draw the minds and hearts of men towards God. Such a practice has been the devotion to the Sacred Heart of Jesus. It was a moment when dark heresy, under the pretence of greater reverence for God, was stressing the severity of God's justice and the corruption of man's inclinations. In answer, the Church set forth, in strong relief, the limitless goodness of our Divine Redeemer in His Passion and Death for our salvation and in His unceasing quest for the love of our souls. And such a devotion, while it is fostered by the anxious love of Mother Church, is but another aspect of that divine revelation confided to her care by Jesus Christ and concluded at the death of the last of His Apostles.

St. Pius V and the Breviary of the Faithful.

Side by side with the devotion to the Sacred Heart of Jesus, we can note for several centuries the widening spread of another practice : the recital of the Most Holy Rosary of the Blessed Virgin Mary. As the great Dominican Pope, St. Pius V, fixed the form of the Roman Breviary which clerics must recite each day, so too, he gave final shape to the Rosary, which his Order had, in their special love of Our Blessed Lady, for very many years preached and promoted against the increasing heresy of the times. Who can measure the effect of that single Decree,[1] by which St. Pius, the intrepid servant of Mary,

---

[1] *Consueverunt*, September 17th, 1569. Cf. *Pretiosius* of Benedict XIII, May 26th, 1727. For Indulgences of Rosary see *Preces et Pia Opera*.

established the essential form of the Holy Rosary as a
prayer of fifteen decades, with meditation on the mysteries
of the life of the Divine Redeemer and His Blessed Mother ?
St. Pius had given the universal Church a devotion which
can well be called the Breviary of all the Faithful.

Since the days of St. Pius V, succeeding Popes have *The urgent*
urged on the Faithful the devout recital of the Rosary. *desires of the*
Popes.
They have endowed it with an unusual wealth of precious
indulgences. To the intercession of Mary, invoked by
the Rosary Confraternity, St. Pius had attributed the
decisive victory of Lepanto. Again in 1716, Pope Clement
XI established a Feast of the Most Holy Rosary throughout the Church, to give thanks for the victory of Temesvar
in Hungary, which he had secured by the recitation of
the Rosary in all the Catholic world. In the following
century, at Lourdes, our Blessed Lady appeared holding
a Rosary, and herself taught St. Bernadette that form of
prayer. As the century drew to its close, and the impiety
of men and States became more open, Pope Leo XIII
in ten Encyclical Letters[1] insistently called for increased
devotion to the Holy Rosary. Benedict XV,[2] Pius XI,[3]
and the present Sovereign Pontiff, each has written to
the Faithful concerning the Rosary, calling it that form
of prayer which, in our day, is among all prayers most
needed, as a weapon against evil, a stimulus to faith,
and a ready means of acquiring Christian virtue.

In our own day, as if to confirm the message of the *The Rosary*
Popes, Our Blessed Lady, appearing at Fatima, has urged *a Prayer*
and a
us once more to prayer and penance. Calling herself Our *Meditation.*
Lady of the Rosary, she recommended chiefly the prayer
of the holy Rosary as a means of obtaining grace for sinners.
To many it may seem strange that Our Blessed Lady
should so insist upon this form of prayer. Such persons
cannot have understood the treasure of doctrine which
the Church has set within the reach of learned and unlearned, in the devotion of the Rosary. For the Rosary
is, in truth, a prayerful summary of all the story of the

---

[1]Notably *Supremi Apostolatus ; Superiore Anno ; Jucunda Semper ;
Laetitiae Sanctae ; Magnae Dei Matris.* [2]*Di Altissimo Pregio,* September
18th, 1915. [3]*Ingravescentibus Malis,* September 29th, 1937.

Divine Redeemer and His Blessed Mother. At no time would mankind appear to have been generally inclined to think about God. In these our times, we have achieved the state in which every creature of our devising is used to help us to forget the things of God. Even among the Faithful, Pope Pius XI complained that he found distaste for spiritual things and weariness at the teaching of Christ's doctrine.[1] We do not wish to pray : we have no heart to meditate. Therefore, the Church, in her gentle wisdom, has given us the Rosary : a perfect prayer and an easy meditation.

The Rosary as a Prayer. (a) The "Our Father."

Firstly as a *prayer*. It would be difficult to conceive of a more perfect prayer than is the holy Rosary. In the *Our Father*, we speak to God the Creator in the very terms which God the Son made Man once used when He said : "Thus shall ye pray."[2] Turning first to God, we admit that He is our Father ; we desire that His divinity be known and praised ; we ask that His will be done by men, as it is perfectly done by His Angels and the Saints in Heaven. Then, thinking upon ourselves, we entreat Him for all our needs of soul and body, with the pathetic reference to our *daily* bread, as creatures to whom our life is measured by God in morsels of day by day. Acknowledging that we have sinned, we beg for pardon of sin against God, and declare that we forgive the injuries of our fellowmen. Then lastly, looking to the future, and mindful of the past, we pray for help against the danger of future sin and for protection from hurt of soul or body. These vast petitions are not of merely human making. The sacred lips of Our Divine Redeemer first uttered them in prayer. To teach this prayer, He came on earth. And since that day, while countless millions have used the prayer in life and death, Saints and Doctors have admitted that no human heart can exhaust the riches of this simple prayer.[3]

(b) The "Hail Mary."

In the *Hail Mary*, so many times repeated in the Rosary, again we borrow from the words of Sacred Scripture.[4]

[1] *Ingravescentibus Malis*, September 29th, 1937. [2] Matt. vi, 9. [3] Catechism of Council of Trent, Part iv ; St. Thomas, *Summa Theol.*, Pars. IIa, IIae, q. 89, article 9. Cf. St. Teresa of Avila, *Way of Perfection*, chapters 26–42. [4] Luke i, 28, 42.

Using the salutations of the Angel Gabriel and St. Elizabeth, we renew the message of God for which the world had waited, and in which the world has ever since found peace. We greet the stainless purity of the Virgin Mother of God ; we adore her Son as Our Divine Redeemer. Then, reflecting on our need of Mary's intercession, we ask for no particular want, but in fulness of the trust that befits God's Mother, we pray just that she will remember us, now and in the hour of our death. It is the same abandonment of childlike love which caused the penitent thief to ask only that His Redeemer would remember him in death.[1]

In the " Glory to the Father and to the Son and to the Holy Ghost," we make profession of our belief in the Most Holy Trinity. In the name of the Blessed Trinity we are baptised, confirmed, forgiven sin. In that name, finally, we are sent forth to judgment. And even now on earth, we repeat the refrain of praise which the Holy Ghost has told us forms the eternal hymn of all the Angels and the Saints.[2]

(c) The " Glory be to the Father . . ."

By the form of prayers that constitute the Rosary, it can thus be seen how well the devotion fulfils the requirements of a prayer that God will bless. For it is a humble prayer.[3] In very lowly reverence, we dare to speak to God in the words which Jesus Christ Himself has taught. Bowing down with the Angel and St. Elizabeth, we adore the Incarnate God and reverence His Most Holy Mother. In a sense of utter dependence and in knowledge of our sins, we beg of God, by the intercession of Our Lady, for every need that as creatures day by day we feel. It is a constant prayer.[4] God Himself has told us that we must knock upon the door of His loving mercy. And so, insistently, without losing ourselves in detail, we repeat the simple words we learned from Himself and from His Sacred Scriptures. It is a confident prayer,[5] for we are content to leave to God the particular benefits He will surely give. Our trust is such that our demands are vast.

The Rosary a perfect Prayer.

[1]Luke xxiii, 42. [2]Apoc. iv, 8, 11 ; v, 13 ; vii, 12. Cf. Eph. i, 6. [3]Ps. ci, 18 ; Matt. xviii, 14 ; 1 Pet. v, 6–8 ; James iv, 6. [4]Luke xviii, 1 ; Matt. vii, 7–11 ; xxiv, 42 ; 1 Tim. ii, 8 ; 1 Thess. v, 17 ; Col. iv, 2. [5]Matt. vi, 5, 6, 25, 34 ; xxi, 22 ; James i, 6 ; John xiv, 14 ; xvi, 24 ; Hebr. vi, 10 ; Ps. xx, 4 ; xxxiii, 9.

Moreover this devotion of the Rosary is so open to men of every kind that it helps us to fulfil the command of God : " you must always pray nor ever faint."[1] So well within the reach of every person of good will is the recital of the Rosary that it has become the universal prayer of all the faithful. As the Mass is the unique and universal Sacrifice of the Church, so, in a sense, is the Rosary the unique and universal prayer of all the household of the Faith.

The Family Rosary. And thus is it the prayer that best unites a family round the feet of God. In the presence of the Holy Family of Nazareth, the joys and sorrows of a home are shared with God and Mary and St. Joseph. In particular, as life advances, the Rosary takes on a deeper meaning. There are vacant places in the family circle, as death and the relentless needs of life demand a separation. But, in the memory of the Rosary, no distance separates. Even the erring are kept close to God by the endless pleading for Mary's intercession. In our country, the Family Rosary has been an honoured custom. It is our most earnest wish that in our Diocese every family should renew the practice of the daily recitation of the Rosary. In the very great majority of our homes, the prayer and meditation of the Rosary will at once have fruit in solid attachment to the Christian virtues. If, however, the restlessness that has invaded some home-circles must still drive out the young to seek amusement, at least the few moments, spent in the company of Jesus and His Blessed Mother, will serve as a barrier against complete forgetfulness of God. In later years, when suffering has opened up the heart to the calls of God, the Rosary will be found to have forged strong links between the once unheeding soul and God.

The Rosary as a Meditation. Secondly, as a *meditation*, the Rosary, in addition to being an exquisite prayer, is a very easy form of meditation. Perhaps the word meditation alarms us, for reflection calls up a memory of strain. But even a child is in the habit of reflecting : he loves to recall a set of images and to rearrange them ; he remembers with ease what

[1] Luke xviii, 1.

has hurt or what has pleased. It is not different in the meditation of the Rosary. We are not asked to build a series of fine thoughts. We are given the framework of a simple prayer, and within it, we recall the actions of Our Divine Lord and His Blessed Mother, at certain moments in their life on earth. Our attitude is that of a quiet memory, made easy by the murmuring repetition of the age-old prayers. The Rosary, thus told, is a thinking with the heart. It is not the cold construction of past events in history. It is the warm recalling of a sacred event which intimately concerns us, and in which we see ourselves having some part. Each mystery of our loving Saviour and His Blessed Mother is thus made present to our mind and heart. Like Our Lady, we keep all these things, pondering them in our heart.[1] Under the influence of grace, we are drawn close to Our Divine Master, and gradually, we enter more and more into His thoughts and into the sentiments of His Mother Mary. Virtue goes out from Him, as long ago when He walked upon the earth.[2] We make our own His dispositions in the mysteries; we make too our own, at least in desire, His holy virtues in the varying phases of His suffering life.

The fruit of this prayerful meditation is beautifully set forth in the prayer of the Church on the Feast of the Most Holy Rosary: "O God, Whose only-begotten Son by his life, death and resurrection hath secured for us the precious things of our salvation, grant we beseech Thee, that we who meditate upon these mysteries of the Most Sacred Rosary of the Blessed Virgin Mary, may imitate what they contain and obtain what they promise, through the same Jesus Christ thy Son Our Lord Who with Thee, in the unity of the Holy Ghost, liveth and reigneth God for ever and ever. Amen." *The Fruit of the Rosary.*

In this prayer we are taught all that the Church has meant in giving us the devotion of the Rosary. The Only-Begotten Son of God, we learn, is by His life and death and resurrection the unique Redeemer to Whom we owe all that the life of grace can give.[3] We are bidden to pray

[1]Luke ii, 19. [2]Mark v, 30. [3]John iii, 16; xii, 31; Eph. i, 6–7; 1 Peter i, 18–19. iii, 18; Apoc. v, 9–10; Col. i, 20–22.

that God would bless our meditation on the principal mysteries of the Redeemer's life by granting us the grace to imitate the lessons which Our Lord and Master came to teach.[1] Lastly, we entreat of God that in His mercy He would give us the promise of eternal life, which we have discovered only from the life and teaching of Our Lord, and which we can now secure, only because He lived and died and rose again for us.[2] Thus are the prayer and meditation of the Rosary a summary of the story of the Redemption of mankind, the Joyful Mysteries of Our Divine Redeemer's life, the Sorrowful Mysteries of His Sacred Passion and Death upon the Cross, the Glorious Mysteries of His triumph over death and sin. It is a summary that a child can understand and learn by heart and love.

The Joyful Mysteries. The keynote of the *Joyful Mysteries* is the gladness that the presence of the Divine Redeemer brought. And yet, in each mystery, we are never permitted to forget the sorrow that marks the life of Our Divine Lord, even from His infancy.

The Annunciation is, in a certain sense, the richest of the mysteries of the Rosary, for it is the prelude to all the story of the Redemption. As we hear the Virgin Mary saluted by the Angel,[3] our thoughts go back to the beginning of mankind, where by the Original Fall, Adam and Eve lost all the life of grace. We think of the Redeemer then promised by God; we learn of the Woman who, through her Son, would crush the power of Hell.[4] This then is She for whom the weary world has waited all these ages. Immaculate Virginity, complete freedom from even a trace of sin have been her preparation to be the Mother of the Divine Redeemer. She is the dawn, from whom is sprung the light of all the world of grace. In this mystery, Mary consented to be the Mother of the Incarnate Word, but her surpassing knowledge of the work of the Messiah, even at that moment, showed her that she had become the Mother of the Man of Sorrows.[5]

[1]John xii, 26; xiii, 15; x, 9; vi, 48, 52; v, 24; iii, 13–14; xv, 4–7.
[2]John iii, 16–17, 36; iv, 14; xiv, 3; 1 Cor. xv, 20; 1 John ii, 25.
[3]Luke i, 28–38. [4]Gen. iii. [5]Is. vii, 14; liii, 1–12.

In the Visitation,[1] we see the first-fruits of the Redeemer's presence. At His bidding Our Lady makes haste to visit St. Elizabeth, not indeed without toil to herself, as her charity urges her to journey into the hill-country of Judea. Her visit earned for St. Elizabeth the grace of recognising Mary as the Mother of God. And with that greeting, the first acknowledgement of the Divine Maternity, St. John the Baptist was cleansed from original sin. The answer of Our Lady was the hymn of the Magnificat, which all the Faithful would one day repeat in perfect praise of God and thanksgiving for His Mother.

The Nativity[2] tells of the lowly entrance of God made Man upon this earth. The humble are gathered around Him : His Virgin Mother and St. Joseph, the Shepherds and the beasts. But for all the joy that made the Angels sing, we feel the harshness of the winter night. A manger of beasts to cradle Him ; a Cross to be His bed of death. We were not kind to the Saviour and His Mother.

In the Presentation,[3] we rejoice that now at last God is offered in His Temple a Gift that is worthy of Himself. Simeon and Anna were made glad by the presence of the Infant. Mary, however, was promised a sword of sorrow in her heart. Not the least of her sorrows, rather her deepest, was the knowledge that her Son would be rejected : a Child, set for the fall of many and a Sign which shall be contradicted.

The Finding in the Temple[4] is indeed a joyous happening for Mary and St. Joseph, as it ends a period of acutest pain. The mystery bears an intimate meaning for us, whose lives resemble in their distant measure the Three Days' Loss. It is not given to us to enjoy on earth the unbroken sense of the consoling presence of Our Divine Redeemer. We possess His grace. We draw near to Him in the Sacraments. We receive Him in the Blessed Eucharist. But it is not yet the time to see Him face to face.

When, in the Rosary, we next meet Our Divine Master, we have reached the period of His final days. There is no mention of His Hidden Life, nor of His preaching. *The Sorrowful Mysteries.*

[1]Luke i, 39–58. [2]Matt. i, 25 ; ii, 1 ; Luke ii, 1–20. [3]Luke ii, 22–39. [4]Luke ii, 41–52.

There is silence about His miracles. Even His Blessed Mother is not visible in the Passion. Yet when we come to follow Him in the last few hours of His life, we must remember that He, Who is suffering, is the gentle Saviour, Who for some three years had gone about doing good. He had cured every manner of bodily ailment. He had relieved the laden souls of sinful men and women.[1] Are not His sorrows, in fact, to be explained by the envy of wicked men who hated Him for His goodness, and at length secured His death ?[2] The *Sorrowful Mysteries* begin to reveal their deeper meaning, when, at the sight of our suffering Redeemer, we realise the limitless iniquity of sin.

In the Agony in the Garden [3] we assist at the unspeakable grief of God made Man. The vision of all that, in satisfaction for our sins, He would be obliged to suffer, forced the very blood in sweat from His veins. But a more fearful vision, we must believe, was the torrent of wickedness which every sin of every creature poured over the soul of God made Man. The certainty of future suffering, the loneliness of life, the treachery of trusted friends make this mystery peculiarly consoling to those whom suffering has drawn close to Jesus Christ.[4]

The Scourging at the Pillar [5] was a torture which the cowardice of Pilate had allowed : it is the expiation of the base respect for human things which prevents us from admitting the sovereign rights of God. The Scourging followed on the mockery of the sensual, brutish Herod, whom Jesus punished by His terrifying silence.[6] This agony was the expiation of man's clamorous lust.

The Crowning with Thorns [7] was the deriding of the Kingship of the Incarnate God : its agony expiated the pride which raises self above the sovereign Good.

In the Carrying of the Cross[8] we learn the willingness of the Divine Victim to bear the greatest and the least

---

[1]Matt. xiv, 35–36 ; Luke iv, 40. [2]Matt. xxiii, 37 ; xxvi, 59–66 ; Mark xv, 10–15 ; Luke xxii, 5 ; John xi, 49–53. [3]Matt. xxvi, 36–56 ; Mark xiv, 33–50 ; Luke xxii, 39–54. [4]Cf. 2 Tim. iii, 12 ; Acts xiv, 21 ; Rom. viii, 29 ; Eph. i, 5 ; Gal. iv, 19 ; ii, 19–20. [5]Luke xxiii, 16 ; John xix, 1 ; Mark xv, 15 ; Matt. xxvii, 26. [6]Luke xxiii, 9. [7]Matt. xxvii, 27–31 ; Mark xv, 16–20 ; John xix, 5. [8]Matt. xxvii, 31–32 ; Mark xv, 20–22 ; Luke xxiii, 25–32 ; John xix, 16–17.

of all the pain that satisfied for sin. In that sorrowful journey Jesus has expiated the shrinking that makes every man refuse to bear his daily cross. Following in His footsteps on that journey, we gain the courage to carry our own small cross. They who are advancing into the shadow of death draw strength and peace from the patient Saviour Who has trodden before us the way of the Cross.

At the Crucifixion[1] we are made aware of one, who in all the Passion was most closely united with the Saviour. " There stood by the Cross of Jesus, Mary His Mother." She could not be separated from her Son in death. In this mystery, Jesus Christ took into His heart and welcomed the dread penalty, which God had laid on man because of sin : the violent separation of the soul and body. In an extreme torture of His body He died : in a more terrible desolation of soul, He endured for our salvation an abandonment which we can but faintly understand. In this mystery, " it is finished " : the price of our salvation has been paid.[2]

In the *Glorious Mysteries* we can at last rejoice, without the secret sorrow that our sins are causing Jesus Christ and His Blessed Mother still to suffer. For this is the period of the Saviour's triumph. We are glad that in the sepulchre He is at rest, beyond the power of human pain.[3]

The Glorious Mysteries.

At the Resurrection[4] very quickly He arose again. We may well believe that His first visit in His glorious body was reserved for His stainless Mother. Only in Heaven shall we understand the peace of that reunion. Thereafter His time is spent in bringing peace to His loving friends, in restoring faith and confidence and love.[5] To His enemies He is invisible and very silent : yet has He triumphed. They are like moles which blindly grope about to undermine God's purposes, while all the time even their malice is being used by God for the victory of His love.[6]

In the Ascension[7] we rejoice that at length the Saviour will ascend to glory. The Resurrection had been His earthly

[1]Matt. xxvii, 35–56 ; Mark xv, 20–41 ; Luke xxiii, 33–49 ; John xix, 16–37. [2]1 Pet. iii, 18 ; Rom. v, 9–12. [3]John xix, 38–42, [4]Matt. xxvii, 1–11 ; Mark xvi, 1–13 ; Luke xxiv, 1–41 ; John xx, 1–25 ; Col. iii, 1. [5]John xx, 18–31 ; xxi. [6]Matt. xxvii, 62–66 ; xxviii, 4, 11–15. [7]Matt. xxviii, 16–20 ; Mark xvi, 19 ; Luke xxiv, 50–51 ; Acts i, 2–11 ; vii, 55.

triumph. The Ascension is the unspeakable welcome of God in Heaven to the Word made Flesh, the Saviour. The Angels adore our Divine Redeemer as their King, and with Him ascend the troops of holy ones who had waited for this day. With Him ascend into glory the marks of the Sacred Wounds : for never in Heaven shall we be able to forget that in His Wounds, the wounds inflicted by our sins, have we been saved.

The Descent of the Holy Ghost [1] consoled our Blessed Lady and the Apostles for the loss of the bodily presence of the glorious Redeemer. Jesus had promised to send the Holy Ghost to guide and console His Church, with unfailing light and strength until the end of time.[2] The Apostles were thus made strong to suffer for the Name of Jesus Christ. This grace is that which we ourselves receive in the gift of God the Holy Ghost in the Sacrament of Confirmation, which Jesus Himself has left us.[3]

In the Assumption of our Blessed Lady we are drawing to the end of the story which began with the Annunciation. The Immaculate Virgin had given the world its Saviour. Her life concluded, she was not suffered by God to see corruption.[4]   God took to Himself the virginal Mother, whose holiness, next after the sanctity of the soul of Jesus Christ, was the greatest marvel of the works of God.

In the crowning of God's Mother, we have reached the end. Fittingly she is crowned the Queen of Angels and of Men, who is in very truth the Mother of God made Man.   Mother and Queen she is enthroned beside Him ; nor can she cease to dispense [5] the graces of Redemption until the last of all God's children will have been gathered home.

And then the story of the Divine Redeemer and His Mother, told and retold in the countless Rosaries of our life, will for each of us have ended in eternal bliss.

[1]Acts ii, 1–4. [2]John xiv, 16–17 ; 25–26. [3]Cf. Acts ii, 38–39 ; iv, 33. [4]Cf. Ps. xv, 10 ; Ps. cxxxi, 8 ; Apoc. xi, 19. [5]Cf. Benedict XIV, *Gloriosae Dominae* ; Leo XIII, *Supremi Apostolatus* ; Pius X, *Ad diem illum* ; Benedict XV, *Illustriores inter* ; Pius XI, *Sollemne semper* ; *Lux Veritatis*.

PART II

Chapter I

CATHOLIC EDUCATION:
ITS FUNCTION AND SCOPE*

In this short paper, I am asked to treat of the function and scope of Catholic education. Let me first point out that independently of the systems elaborated by individual Catholics, there is an education that is always recognisable as Catholic. We shall, then, endeavour first to determine the essential feature of education as Catholic, for we shall thereby more readily understand both the activity proper to that education and the range of its endeavour. Finally, to enrich our concept of specifically Catholic education, we shall briefly set out the agreement of our traditional training with the principles of our traditional Philosophy. To put it chematically, we shall treat swiftly of :—

1. The existence of a Catholic education.
2. The essence of that specific education.
3. The activity proper to that education.
4. The range of that activity ; and,
5. The harmony of Catholic education with sane Philosophy.

I—There is a Catholic education.

When Catholic parents send their child to a School, they have set before themselves at least some aim in regard to the future of their child. There is a basic common-sense that asks for a clear return, if it were only by reason of money paid in School fees. The result desired will vary with the type and rank of parents and with the nature of the child. It is implicitly expected that a child will secure good health and proper bodily development; that is a prime consideration. A career will be chosen, especially in the later years of School life, and prepared for with greater intensity. But education

*Address given to the Catholic Truth Society Congress at Kilkenny, 1938.

is a properly human process. It aims at training the human being as a human being. It attempts to form the specifically human or higher faculties, as distinct from those which man shares with material and sensitive beings. All its instruments are used in view of those higher powers of intelligence and will. For a Catholic, however, it is not the merely higher human powers that are required to be trained. It is this child as baptised and sanctified, this child as a Catholic, that is entrusted to a Catholic School. A Catholic parent may be unable to put to you philosophically his intentions in respect of his child, but unquestionably he wants to see his child instructed and disciplined in Catholic living. Education is felt and known by him to be a training for Life. This above all he asks, by very instinct, of a School. And Catholic education, of whatever particular age, ancient or modern, in old Catholic or monastic Schools, in this or that more modern system, in this or that country, aims at one thing, as essential—Catholic living.

II—The Essence of Catholic education.   One might object that any system of education sets itself to produce a certain type of life. The later Greek and Roman philosophies strove to make their adepts recognisable by a form of living, more than by a cast of thinking. Modern non-Catholic systems equally aim at a character to be achieved in the child. That which separates Catholic education as a training for life from all other forms of instruction or training is the Catholic manner of regarding the Divine Redeemer, Jesus Christ, and in consequence, the nature of the child who is to be educated. Catholic education from first to last is based on Jesus Christ, True God and True Man, Redeemer of mankind. It firmly holds that " other foundation no man *can* lay, but that which is laid ; which is Christ Jesus." [1] Therefore, Christ is the Alpha and the Omega of our life. And Christ is specifically for Catholic education the Divine Redeemer of fallen human kind : the " Way " as He Himself declared, by which alone men can return to God. Moreover, He is " the Truth and the Life."[2] He is come "that men may have life."[3] To whom he gives that Life, He is united as intimately as the vine

[1] I Cor. iii, 11. [2] John xiv, 6. [3] John x, 10.

with its branches.[1] Whosoever does not accept Him who is the Truth cannot have Him Who is the Life.

That Life is not a figure of speech. It is a gift so real that to give it God Himself assumed our human nature, and in that nature shed His Precious Blood. What cost the Precious Blood is, then, infinitely precious; for it is none other than a created participation in the Life of God. Infused into the soul at Baptism, the Life which Christ has given men inheres to the essence of the soul, raises our inner life to the level of the Divine Life, and gives us to share by knowledge and by love in the intimate operations of the Divinity Itself. Such a life surpasses utterly man's created essence, exceeds man's nature and all that his created nature could demand for its specific functions or could by its human powers attain. To say that this real life makes us, in consequence, children of God and Temples of the Holy Spirit, is but to enumerate the riches of which in Christ we are the heirs. This life in truth is Heaven begun on earth, for the soul, while being human, already lives with God, on the plane of God's own life. Death only is required to intervene and the life commenced on earth can straightway pass into its unbroken fulness, in the vision of the Blessed Trinity.

It is a glorious gift—Sanctifying Grace, the life restored by Jesus Christ. He Himself has designated it in many lovely ways; the Pearl of great price [2] for which a man will sell all his worldly goods; the Nuptial Garment [3] that is essential to the guests at His proper Feast; most particularly the Sap [4] which vivifies the smallest branch united to the Vine, which is Himself. Catholic education, by the vision of the Faith, profoundly reverences in the smallest child this hidden but most real life. Yet, for all the glory of the child's inheritance, the Church is not blind to the nature of the child. She sees in him the fruits of the Redemption, but she knows him to be in his natural equipment fallen. The accessory gifts which once made perfect the being of our First Parents, have never been restored. When man sprang from the creative hand of God, he was free from the necessity of death; he enjoyed full happiness; and his sensitive powers perfectly obeyed his

[1]John xv, 4. [2]Matt. xiii, 46. [3]Matt. xxii, 12. [4]John xv, 4–6.

reason. The case is very different since the Fall. We are subject to death ; we are exposed to pain of soul and body ; our lower nature can anticipate the control of reason or even revolt against that control, impelling us to evil or checking us in the pursuit of good. The child, then, is not only immature ; it is impaired. For, stripped of the defending gifts of God, and exposed to discord of its powers, it finds difficulty in overcoming obstacles ; it is weakened by ignorance ; it is slack in executing the dictates of its conscience and it may even turn readily to sin from God.

The Catholic Church, then, has no illusions about the nature of the child, who is to be educated. She, who exhausts the beauty of human language in portraying the glory of Grace in the tiniest child, with pitiless clearness describes the wound and weakness of her feeble son. Therefore, she alone has held the balance between Lutheran pessimism and Rousseauist optimism. For her the child is neither totally depraved nor naturally perfect. Non-Catholics may indeed profess belief in Christ and the grace of Christ ; but either He is not the true Christ, God made man, Who has restored to us Divine Life ; or else, the grace of Christ is understood to be only a shadowy figure or an external designation. Pagans and Naturalistic teachers either ignore or deny the existence of a Divine Redeemer, and, in consequence, the Fall of Adam. Sanctifying Grace is a term as meaningless to them as Original Sin. The goal of man's existence is himself. Man, they suppose, has no need from God of inner healing.

Founders and exponents of educational systems, within the Church, may vary in the greater emphasis they put upon this or that faculty of the child, or in the type of scholar whom they attempt to train, or in the specific career they aim at. On the central doctrine of the Incarnate Son of God they may not vary. St. Robert Bellarmine, directing St. Aloysius Gonzaga, the young nobleman, and St. John Bosco, in our own day, training a child of the people, St. Dominic Savio, have each achieved a triumph of properly Catholic education, by precisely the same substantial doctrine and formation. Jesus Christ, known, loved and served, to the point of heroism, but chiefly loved in service, is equally the core and substance of their pupils' lives. It is therefore a vivid Faith in the existence and value of the grace of the Redeemer that differentiates Catholic from every other form of education, pagan or non-Catholic Christian.

In Grace we are dealing with a supernatural life and that life's power of operation. In education we are properly concerned with human training. Catholic education is never a substitute for God's action ; it is but the co-operation of man with God in the supernatural development of the child. God alone is Master of the Supernatural. Hence, God alone can directly act upon the soul so as to increase in it the life of Grace. Such an increase, the Faith teaches, is produced immediately by God alone, either through the agency of the Sacraments, when they are rightly received, or when the soul in the state of grace has disposed itself for such increase by meritorious actions. Catholic education, as such, has for activity proper to itself so to instruct and train the child that Christ, Who is the Way to God for every man, may further become, for the individual child, the Truth and the Life. *III—The Activity Proper to Catholic education.*

It is well to observe that Catholic education, for all its divine aim, is not the less a human activity conducted by human agents. It can thus help to preserve Grace, but only by preserving the child from all that would occasion the loss of the divine life. It can also assist in developing grace, but only by ensuring to the child an environment, an instruction and a discipline, thanks to which Grace can more freely operate through its own channels of activity : the Theological and Moral Virtues. Though it deals indirectly with the divine equipment of supernatural virtues, none the less, Catholic education will respect and use the natural virtues in its work, for they are the foundation and the bulwark of the supernatural virtues. Catholic education must follow the natural development of the child's faculties, marking the progressive ascent from sense-perception to reasoned judgment. It will gladly avail of every legitimate instrument of training. In other words, we shall, though engaged in a divine work, act according to the constitution of our human nature. But our activity, if it be truly inspired by the Church's teaching, can never be purely natural, nor have a purely human aim. Our proper function in Catholic education will ever be " to form Christ "[1] in the children entrusted to our care. Christian Living is our primary concern.

If Christ is to become for each individual child the Truth and the Life, there is needed an acceptance of Christ by the mind and the will. Instruction and discipline are essential portions of Catholic training, and of the two activities, discipline is, in the Catholic tradition, the more important. We shall later see that sound philosophy amply supports this conclusion of the Faith, but, turning now for a moment to the life and teaching of Our Divine Master, we can swiftly appreciate the insistent emphasis He laid on living. The point is well worthy of careful note in view of the abundant theories that now attempt to falsify the tradition of the Church.

Our Divine Master always demands an acceptance of Himself by Faith : intellect must pay its primary service. His apostles are instructed with especial care. The faith of new disciples is singled out for praise.[2] He is come " a light into the world that whosoever believeth in Him, may not remain in darkness."[3] " And, he who seeth Him, seeth also God Who sent Him."[4] " To whom then shall we go, for He has the words of eternal life ? "[5]

Thus Jesus Christ, the Truth, is the Light of the child's intelligence. For that reason Catholic education, from first to last of its processes, untiringly instructs the mind, by the truths of faith, and averts, with a care not understood at all by those outside the Church, even the shadow of erroneous doctrine. The God whom we love by Charity is indeed none other than the God Who is revealed by the truth of Faith. But the deeper emphasis of the Church is on integrity of Christian living, for she knows that she is sent " to teach all nations, to *observe* all things," [6] whatsoever her Divine Founder has commanded.

Our Divine Teacher has insisted that it is not in the things that man possesses (therefore not in his mere instruction) that a man's life chiefly consists.[7] His parables are exhortations to keeping the law of God. He Himself began to do and then to teach.[8] He has left us an example, not for speculative

---

[1]Gal: iv, 29. [2]Matth. viii, 10. [3]John xii, 46. [4]John xii, 45. [5]John vi, 69. [6]Matth. xxviii, 20. [7]Luc. xii, 15. [8]Act i, 1.

admiration, but that we may *do* as He has done.[1] And He has done always the things that please His Father.[2] The profound acceptance of Christ in Faith must, if it be genuine and integral, be translated into living. Not everyone who says, Lord, Lord, but he who does the will of His Father shall enter into the Kingdom of Heaven.[3] He that hath His commandments and keepeth them, he it is that loveth Him.[4]

Hence, Catholic education sets itself for primary task, so to train the child entrusted to it, that supernatural habits may become more firmly and more deeply rooted in the faculties of his soul. To this end, it chiefly sets before the child the truths of the Faith, knowing that conviction is the strongest buttress of the will. It insists on constant exercise of good actions, with a view to the strengthening of habits. Having learned from the Faith that " there remain in human nature the effects of original sin, the chief of which are weakness of will and disorderly inclinations," [5] Catholic education urges towards active self-denial, offers reward for right conduct, and proposes sanctions for the violations of due order. Knowing the value of example, it inceasingly keeps Jesus Christ before the eyes of the mind, that the will may follow gladly Him Who because He is known to be the Supreme Good, is the burning attraction of the heart. It reserves a quite special place for the Immaculate Mother of Jesus Christ, by reason of her unique excellence in herself and in virtue of her prerogative of Guardian of youthful Purity. It has a saint of every age and rank to bring forward as the model and the stimulus of virtue. Above all, Catholic education is unique among all systems of training, in that it alone can lead the child to the authentic fountains of divine life : the Sacraments. Morning after morning, it can bring its children to the foot of Calvary, to share in the timeless offering of Christ's perfect adoration and gratitude and reparation and impetration. And when every human instrument of mental culture and will formation has been brought into play to assist in the perfecting of the life of Grace, one final agency remains of limitless efficacy : the Blessed Eucharist. Catholic education can alone lead the child to the altar, where the Church

---

[1]John xiii, 15. [2]John viii, 29. [3]Matth. vii, 21. [4]John xiv, 21. [5]Encyc. *Divini Illius*.

dispenses no other food for mind and heart and will than Jesus Christ Himself—become the Bread of Life. " The proper and immediate end of Christian education is to co-operate with divine grace in forming the true and perfect Christian, that is, to form Christ Himself in those regenerated by Baptism, according to the emphatic expression of the Apostle : ' My little children, of whom I am in labour again, until Christ be formed in you.' [1] For the true Christian must live a supernatural life in Christ : ' Christ who is your life,' [2] and display it in all his actions : [3] ' That the life also of Jesus may be made manifest in our mortal flesh.' " [4]

IV—The Range of Activity Proper to Catholic Education.

It has been said that Catholicism is a "way of living." The description is too pragmatic. It is also a way of feeling and thinking. For it is the whole being of man that Christ has purchased by His Precious Blood and sanctified in Baptism. education, too, is concerned with a composite creature of soul and body ; its function is to assist in making perfect the whole being ; all his actions in all his relations as an individual and as a member of society. To limit Catholic education to the mere teaching of the Truths of Faith or even to the mere realm of action is gravely to mistake the integral doctrine of the Incarnation. He only is an integral Christian who in all his life-activities conforms to the teaching of Jesus Christ. It is precisely because " the proper and immediate end of Christian education is to co-operate with divine grace in forming the true and perfect Christian, that Christian education takes in the whole aggregate of human life, in order to elevate, regulate and perfect it, in accordance with the example and teaching of Christ." [5] This teaching of Pius XI is the basic reason for the insistence of the Church that in the School every agency of training should be only such as is capable of promoting the Divine Life of Grace. " Watchful care," urges Pius IX, " is to be exerted that our divine religion may be the soul of the entire academic education." [6] Professors are to have nothing more at heart than to educate the youth in " letters and sciences, according to the mind of the Church, the pillar and guarantee of Truth." [7] Leo XIII

[1]Gal. iv, 19. [2]Col. iii, 4. [3]2 Cor. iv, 11. [4]Encyc. *Divini Illius.* [5]*Ibid.* [6]Apostolic Brief *Optime Noscitis,* March 20th, 1854. [7]*Ibid.*

is not less clear. In the Encyclical " Militantis Ecclesiae," he writes: "It is necessary not only that religious instruction be given to the young at fixed times, but also that every other subject taught be permeated by Christian piety. If this be wanting, if this sacred atmosphere does not pervade and warm the hearts of masters and scholars alike, little good can be expected from any kind of learning and considerable harm will often be the consequence."

Pius XI, in our own times, is equally explicit on the universal range of Catholic activity in the field of education : " That a School be a fit place for Catholic Students, it is necessary that *all* the teaching and the whole organisation of the School, its teachers, syllabus and text books in *every branch* be regulated by the Christian spirit, under the direction and maternal supervision of the Church ; so that Religion may be in very truth, the foundation and crown of the youth's entire training." [1]

He who expresses surprise at what is sometimes called the exclusiveness of the demand of Catholic education to rule all branches of human training, has failed to grasp both the sovereignty of God, the primal Truth, and the philosophy of the composite being who is to be educated. God is Master equally of spirit and of matter. Essential Truth cannot contradict Himself in any realm of Creation. God, as known by reason and by revelation, is ineffably true in all His manifestations. And Jesus Christ, God made man, Divine Redeemer, is the chief revelation of God to human beings. When, therefore, Catholic education accepts the fact of the Incarnation, she accepts a scientific truth which all her rivals fail to reckon with. Further, by accepting the Church which Jesus Christ founded, as the pillar and the guarantee of truth, as the infallible guardian and interpreter of all morality, Catholic education is not only supremely scientific in its certitude, but is also, by that acceptance, given possession of a unique and priceless instrument of human training. For Catholic education, in the doctrine and practice of the Church, has ever ready to hand the most perfect instruments of culture—a rule of certitude in presenting Truth, a

[1] Encyc. *Divini Illius.*

criterion of the truly Beautiful, a determined goal conformable to Truth, which is the finest stimulus to the will,
and effectual discipline against human frailty and a healing
sanction, if order should be violated.

I.—CATHOLIC EDUCATION IS TRULY SCIENTIFIC

*V—The
Conformity
of Catholic
education
with Sound
Philosophy.*

Catholic education is often mocked at as being unscientific
because it is old-fashioned. We live only for Eternity and
our instruments need to be refurbished.

It is a calumny that we live only for Eternity. We train
for the next world precisely by training for this world of
everyday occurrences. Our state in Eternity is conditioned by
our life in this existence on earth. We are, then, only being
intelligent in forming to ourselves a rational clear-cut purpose,
and we are truly succeeding in life only when we are living
the full Christian life of Grace. In fact, Catholic education
alone is truly scientific for it alone is in accord with full
reality. Man's fall and his redemption are facts. Catholic
education, realising that in the actual world the perfect
human life can be attained only under the influence of
Divine Grace, resolutely sets itself to grapple with man's
nature, as in point of historical fact, it really exists. Only
Catholic education, then, can fully succeed in training man,
because alone it has the vision and the instruments : " Since
God," writes Pius XI, "has revealed Himself to us in the
Person of His Only Begotten Son, Who alone is ' the Way,
the Truth and the Life,' there can be no ideally perfect
education which is not Christian education." [1]

Our mode and instruments of education, it is said, are not
sufficiently modern. The mode of Catholic education is substantially the same the world over. It follows the nature of
man as he passes from childhood to maturity. Its purpose is
unchanging : to help to form the perfect Christian, whose life
of grace and virtue will reproduce on earth the life of Christ.
It works upon the human faculties with every legitimate
instrument and method, be they old or new. It will adapt
every new discovery, but only to use it in its proper function
of assisting in the development of supernatural life. The

[1] *Divini Illius.*

Church is very old indeed. Her memory reaches back a greater distance than that of any living institution. Even pre-Christian philosophies she has harvested, and has stored their many grains of truth in the granaries of her traditional philosophy. When eager men of the day bring home what they call new things, gently the Church looks back and sifts the age and truth of the alleged discovery. What indeed is new, she keeps with gratitude but without amazement, for her eyes are ever fixed on God, the Abyss of Being. " O the depth," she is ever exclaiming with St. Paul, " of the riches of the wisdom of the knowledge of God." [1]

Little wonder, then, that the traditional features of the education which is inspired and guided by the Church's teaching and practice, should be found on all essential points of sentiment and thought and action, to be entirely consonant with the nature of man's faculties as sound philosophy and the most modern psychology have revealed them.

2.—SCHOLASTIC PHILOSOPHY AND CATHOLIC EDUCATION

Education is now regarded by many critics as a playing field for philosophical theorists. A more compact grasp of the history of Philosophy would show these critics that the traditionally Catholic system is justified by the sane philosophy called Scholastic. Non-Catholic and the modern aberrant systems derive, as from their source, from Cartesianism. Descartes' dualism in man has of necessity resulted in spiritualist monism or materialist monism. The inevitable consequence is the spate of educational systems, more notably the Rousseauist and so-called Active types, wherein the only mistress of a very material child indeed is some form of experimental Psychology.

On the contrary, Scholasticism accepts in the child one being composed of body and soul, each part essential to the being, each part having its proper faculties. In the faculties of the composite being, there is a hierarchy of intrinsic dignity and specific function, sense under reason and reason under God. Man is not an end to himself ; he

[1] Rom. xi, 33.

is ordained to God. Man receives truth from without through the data of sense. Man's higher faculties of knowing and doing must be developed, if he is to arrive at his most complete natural or human perfection, which is rational life. Man must refrain from the irrational and bend his will to the rational, in order to achieve the purpose of a rational life. But these conclusions and principles of merely human reasoning about the being of man are exactly those which the Church has taken over and elevated by her supernatural doctrine and practice, in the traditional system of Catholic education.

To set forth very swiftly the main tenets of Scholastic philosophy, concerning intellect, aesthetic emotion and will, is to recognise the traditional formation in regard to Truth, Beauty and Goodness, availed of by all exponents of Catholic education, and, incidentally, to criticise the non-Catholic systems, which, having lost the guidance of Faith, have now lost the assistance of the sound Philosophy elaborated under its aegis.

3.—WHICH IS THE MORE IMPORTANT FACULTY ?

The intellect, in dignity of nature, is our prior faculty. Its function is to enlighten, and through the will, to rule the lower powers, which execute only orders from above.

By reason, intellect perceives truth ; then by the reasoning process it compares its concepts and sets them in order. It applies its reflexions to concrete things to use them ; judges and presents its judgment to the faculty of action. The Will freely chooses means apt to its end, and then commands the lower powers. But in view of obtaining the end of education, which is perfection of the moral being here on earth, the will is more important. For the will is the faculty of action. It is related to the intellect from which it receives orders and to the lower powers which it commands. It is the master faculty whose object is the universal good, and this it pursues, not as the intellect pursues its own proper end, universal truth—but rather in view of the demands of each faculty and in view of the whole being of man.

Each faculty, then, must be fully developed to attain the complete perfection of the moral being ; but intellect is wise to no purpose, unless the will directs it to the good of the whole being—and in this point many educational systems fail. On the other hand, the will remains inactive unless it receives a direction from the intellect, which because it is conformed to Truth, is accepted by the will as Good.

This primacy of the will over the intelligence in view of living is the reason why Catholic education while it most carefully instructs the mind in the truths of Faith, yet will never rest in knowledge for its own sake, but will ever push onward to the practical application of knowledge in daily human conduct. Faith must be operative in deeds of charity. Human perfection consists in Charity.

4.—THE FORMATION OF THE INTELLECT

(a)—The Presentation of Truth

Intellect is formed by the presentation of truth. Now among all objects of knowledge the highest is God. God is the master-notion of all education. Speaking in merely human fashion, to deprive a child of the idea of God is to take from it the concept of the highest in the order of being and the one notion that is capable of explaining the universe. It is practically to set the child adrift on a voyage of purpose-less existence. Catholic education, therefore, at the earliest moment presents the idea of God. As the Child develops, that notion is not left for the wayward caprice of sense to smother it, but is carefully elaborated. The poorest parent teaching an infant to lisp the names of Jesus and Mary is thus, did he but know it, a consummate philosopher.

In respect of reality the intellect is trained only when it can form a reasoned judgment ; it must hold universal principles from which it will draw particular conclusions.

From external objects presented by the senses to the active intellect, the intellect abstracts the nature of things visible ; from such concepts proceed first principles. Education then must choose external objects which are best capable of assist-ing the intellect to formulate the most essential principles.

Many mechanical processes, such as memory work, are indispensable, but the traditional teacher will aim at the general ideas which are to be found in literature and the sciences. He neither gives the principles ready-made and unrelated to things, nor pours into the intellect objects unrelated to their governing principles.

As the child develops, his intellect applies principles to particular things and reasons concerning them. This operation in our traditional system is of capital importance for life. That teacher alone has truly instructed his pupil who has so trained the intellect by presenting truth that now in conduct the youth can maturely judge.

It needs but little reflexion to see in this assisted progress of the child from sense-perception to reasoned judgment, the explanation of the care that Catholic education ever takes to avoid error and present only truth, in respect of every subject of the curriculum.

In violent contrast with our system and with sane philosophy, stand those types of the so-called New or Active School (such as the materialist system of the authentic Madam Montessori and the experiments of Decroly, Ferrière and Laparede), wherein, because the child is supposed to be his own end or to be physiogically predetermined or make his own truth, the task of the educator is practically reduced to observing the spontaneous activities or the general and individual needs of the children.

(b)—Aesthetic Emotion

The intellect is not fully formed unless it has attained to a reasoned esteem of beauty.

Beauty is a certain splendour of Truth and attraction of Goodness, which supposes in the multiple parts of an object an integrity and a proportion. It is this proportion which, grasped by the intellect, reacts upon our being, for the intellect perceives a relation of order between the parts and that higher type which the object represents. Such a relation pleases the intellect and sets up a series of relations that harmonise and join again in oneness. Such a harmony in the midst of multiplicity evokes the sentiment of aesthetic emotion. This emotion is indeed fundamental in our nature for our intellect is ever perceiving harmonious relations of being.

It is the function of education to bring back this emotion to God, its final goal, in Whom Beauty and Truth are met in consummate unity and of Whom all earthly Truth is only a created participation. In concrete things, Beauty and Truth are diverse according to the diversity of beings, but education must train to recognise true Beauty, lest sensual emotion be substituted for intellectual emotion, lest the immature pupil stop short at the creature and fail to reach the one ideal summit of Being, God. Only the ordered can be both true and beautiful.

I should like to make a special plea for the swifter restoration in our land of that portion of traditional Catholic formation of the intellect which is the reasoned esteem of the Beautiful. It is not difficult to train native good taste to see the beauty of the Creator in natural beauty, and the lurking radiance of God in objects of artistic value. It were surely easy to surround the impressionable child, after the manner of so many Catholic educationalists, with genuinely lovely pictures. Into that cultivation of the intellect can be pressed Poetry and Music and Painting and Architecture, for in all these departments Catholic genius has supremely flourished. " Truth seen through Beauty of external forms " is a phrase that might well explain the educational value of Catholic Liturgy.

Beauty elevates the intellect, but it also attracts the will. The moral beauty of the life of Christ, and of His Blessed Mother and the Saints is an unending spring of admiration and of love. In them Truth and Beauty meet in one synthesis of divine perfection, the harmony of which is capable of drawing the child to reproduce in himself, by living, that splendour of truth, which is the Christian Life.

5.—THE FORMATION OF THE WILL

(a)—Exercise of Will-Activity

The will, we have seen, is the master-faculty, in that it is the faculty of action. It must be trained by exercise in the

deliberate choice of right action. Now, the object of the will
is the Universal Good. In relation to that Good, the will can
receive its impulse only from its initial mover, the Creator.
To that good the will tends of its own movement. It has no
need of external impulse towards particular goods. God is
not comprehended on earth, and hence in its tendency to the
Complete Good, the will must tend to particular goods. But
because the finite cannot absorb the full activity of that
which has for object the Infinite, there ever remains in the
faculty the power of bearing towards another and even a
contrary good. Further, at times, to choose this or that, is a
duty imposed by an authority external to our being. On such
an occasion the will has power to choose indifferently, but it
must answer for the choice.

Hence the grave need of education so to form the will that
it may act easily and habitually, according to right order.

Now, the will is educated by exercise. The will is the
dynamo of human activity, but only God can act on it
directly. Human influence is always indirect ; through the
action of the intellect. To exercise the will, it is first necessary
for the intellect to propose an object of action which is conformed to truth ; then the will finding an object ordered in
itself and in its relation to the being which is to seize it,   and
conformed to its own activity, will tend to that object. The
intellect is therefore indispensable to a voluntary act. And
herein that insistence of Catholic education upon the truth
and only the truth, in every subject of the curriculum, finds
its completest justification. *In all its studies, the child must
be shown the truth as true in itself, and as desirable or good.*
Throughout the school-work, the teacher will see to it that
the expanding intellect exercises the will-activity, by the true
good that it will propose. From such exercise alone can
come the permanence of judgment that we call conviction.
To help the child to order its life by the light of truth is to
help most effectively to support the will, both in its normal
activity and in times of stress.

There is no higher truth, no greater good than God. When
Catholic education from the early days of life proposes in
graded knowledge the teachings of the Faith, it is thus seen
to be utilising at once the strongest stimulus and most con-

stant support that can be conceived in relation to the will. And when the teacher, supervising the judgment of the intellect, constantly urges to the practice of supernatural virtues, supplies occasions for that practice, and rewards good deeds, he is not merely doing that to which his Catholic instinct impels him, but he is calling into play the most scientific stimulus to will-activity ; a clear-cut, noble ideal conformable to truth, and therefore good.

(b)—The Right Use of Pleasure

Catholic education does not fear the name or use of pleasure, for that accessory of training has a rightful place in will-activity. Pleasure is but the complement of well-ordered activity, and, as such, strengthens both the act and the faculty of action. Since we aim at fully developing the will, we should aim at assisting it to produce its fullest activity. We cannot, as we have shown, act directly on the will, but only on the will through the object proposed to it. The good, as the object of the will, to be complete, must possess not only truth but beauty. The supreme attraction of the good, and thus the greatest source of pleasure in the activity of the will, is this radiance of beauty.

Education, then, will early urge that action is good not only because it is conformable to truth, but also because, being beautiful in itself and its effects, it gives a true and proportionate pleasure to our rational nature. The child, by such training, will be prevented from resting, while yet its reason is dormant, in the objects of sensible beauty. As the child advances, he will slowly be trained by long research, to the pleasure of spiritual beauty.

In the light of these philosophical principles, one very quickly understands the insistence of Catholic education that art and literature and science should be not only negatively free from error, but should positively, by their content, prove capable of attracting towards the perfect Christian life. Hence, at the time of adolescence, when passion and the power of reasoning are coming into their early maturity, Catholic education seizes the chance of setting anew before the young the true beauty of nature and supernature in science and in literature, in art and in life. But Catholic education never rests content with the mere perception of visible loveliness nor with aesthetic emotions, nor even with intellectual pleasure ; it holds that these pleasures are but grades of ascent to the supreme happiness which is the enraptured contemplation and all-sufficing love of supernatural Beauty, God Himself, in the revelation of His inner life. *Gaudium de veritate* will be our Heaven ; but Heaven is begun already here on earth, by the grace of Christ which is the germ of Vision and of Bliss.

(c)—*The Discipline of the School Regulation and Sanctions*

The human will must be not only drawn to do good, but also prevented from turning away, in whole or in part, from the end. Discipline, therefore, becomes necessary, prescribing a barrier and imposing a penalty. A school regulation, of itself, is insufficient ; and a sanction, of itself, is a violence. The will endowed as it is with liberty, can choose that which is good or that which, being but an apparent good, is really evil. When the good commanded is left undone, or when the opposite act is chosen, the man is guilty of a moral failure. Now, a school regulation is meant to be both a salutary barrier against the possible abuse of liberty, and a guide to the deliberate choice of right moral action. When the child is young, its dormant reason has need of more detailed and explicit guidance. But as the pupil advances to the fuller exercise of rational choice, the school regulation is wisely left more wide, for the rational barrier aims at checking the will, only when evil is in question.

Hence, in the traditional Catholic system the child is neither left completely in the hands of his own counsel, nor cramped within a network of minute prescriptions. The Church knows that his nature is not upright, and that his will more than any other faculty has suffered from the wounds of original sin. It is, then, inconceivable that a traditionally Catholic School should fail to establish *a firm regulation which, while is prevents abuse, yet leaves liberty intact, and which, by invoking the concept of moral obligation, urges to right activity.* The fragmentary vision of naturalistic systems of formation can permit the child to liberate, according to need or interest, his spontaneous activity, but it cannot explain the moral instability of choice which is often too apparent in its adepts. Nor can such systems achieve the constancy of true character.

If a child should violate the law, a reparative sanction proportionate to the fault is demanded. Unquestionably, penalties are required, for in fact the animal portion of man does frequently revolt against order ; but all such penalties are only indirect instruments of will-formation. The child is free, and if his conscience be rightly formed, is himself the first judge of his own fault. The external authority in that case must be careful to proportion his sanction to the interior verdict of the child. If the conscience fail to judge aright concerning the moral fault, a due sanction helps to arouse the child to the consciousness of his failure.

What, however, may never be omitted is the instruction which may form the intellect and stimulate the will to give interior assent.

In the Catholic system, sanctions have their acknowledged right of place. But the Church has for Divine Founder Him Who said : " Suffer little children to come unto me." [1] He "Who had compassion on the multitude" [2] asked all "who laboured and were burdened to come to Him " [3] that He might give true rest of soul. One may not then crush that for which He even died. The traditionally Catholic system is, then, fatherly, both in the firmness with which it apportions penalties and in the delicacy with which it judges individual frailty.

The education that we have considered deals properly with *Conclusion.* the young, but it does not end with the adolescent. The perfection of our moral being is consummated only in Heaven. Catholic education, for all the beauty of its human reasonableness, and supernatural purpose, will have miserably failed, if the child has not firmly grasped true principles, and bent himself, by daily exercise, constantly to live according to these principles of Christian action.

[1]Matth. xix, 14. [2]Matth. ix, 36. [3]Matth. xi, 28.

To have prepared the child to live this full life of supernatural grace is to have achieved the specific purpose of
Catholic education, and to have done what only Catholic
education can do ; it is to have " formed Christ " [1] in the
child. It remains for the youth, " doing the truth in Charity"[2],
to press forward to the goal ; " unto the perfect man, unto
the measure of the age of the fulness of Christ." [3]

[1]Gal. iv, 19. [2]Eph. iv, 15. [3]*Ib.* iv, 13.

Chapter II

CATHOLIC UNIVERSITY OF IRELAND
CENTENARY CELEBRATIONS
JULY 8TH—23RD 1955. *

" When Herod was dead, behold an angel of the
Lord appeared in sleep to Joseph in Egypt, saying :
Arise and take the child and his mother and go
into the land of Israel. For they are dead that sought
the life of the child."

IT is surely strange that, when God became man to redeem
His own creatures, at once it was sought to destroy the
Divine Saviour. For a long time God had revealed His
divine will through Prophets. At length, He spoke through
His own divine Son. The goodness and kindliness of God
appeared in human form on earth. Without delay, the
Incarnate God had to take refuge in the heathen land of
Egypt. When at last they were dead that sought the life of
the Child, Jesus Christ returned unto His own, the chosen
land of Israel. He would live in peace with His Blessed
Mother and St. Joseph only until He should begin to teach
the Way of God to men. At once, men would again, track
Him down with envy and hatred, until their will should have
been consummated in the cruelty of Calvary. And, in the
moment of their success, God made Man would rise immortal, glorious and triumphant over sin and death. That
which had seemed to be the victory of pride would prove,
in the designs of God, to be but the fulfilment of His
loving providence towards all mankind. " How incomprehensible are His judgments and how unsearchable His

*Sermon preached in St. Andrew's, Westland Row, on the occasion
of the Opening Votive Mass.

ways ! " And the life of Jesus Christ is the compendium of the history of His Church.

When the visible presence of Jesus Christ had been withdrawn from earth in the Ascension, His place was taken by God the Holy Ghost, Who, since that time, has brought to our minds the truth of Jesus Christ and sanctified us in the observance of the Faith. Jesus Christ lives in our midst, because, through the grace of the Holy Ghost, we possess Him in our mind and heart by Faith and Charity. And, since the Ascension, the persecution of Jesus Christ unto death has been pursued in the person of His disciples, who hold and cherish Him in Faith. How many times have not these disciples gone down into Egypt, returned to Israel and ended their suffering on a Calvary ! How many times has not the Resurrection been manifested in the invisible resurgence of the Faith !

If, today, we are permitted to celebrate the Centenary of the Catholic University of Ireland, we do but commemorate another mercy of God's providence towards His Church. As with the Holy Family, in the Hidden Life at Nazareth, we were allowed in Ireland a comparatively long period in which to savour the peace of Christian life and grow to the fulness of the stature of the Faith. Then followed the three centuries of searing persecution. Confiscation, imprisonment, exile and death had all but achieved the extinction of Jesus Christ in our midst, when, as gradually as the dawn of His own Resurrection, the Faith was led from the tomb, and again, with gentle radiance, shone upon our land.

The Catholic University of Ireland was one of the first achievements of the resurgent Faith. With unerring insight of pastoral zeal, the Hierarchy at once fixed its attention on that which is the core of Catholic life, the education of the young. For long, we had been obliged to seek in foreign Universities the learning that was nurtured in the bosom of the Church. Now we could give ourselves, by the fostering care of the successor of St. Peter, such an Institute of universal learning, dedicated to Our Lady, Seat of Wisdom, as would link us openly with the culture of the Faith.

The instruments of that achievement bear all the marks of the virtues and defects of which God is wont to make use in the history of the Church : Paul Cullen, Apostolic Delegate, Archbishop of Dublin, and John Henry Newman, scholar-convert, recently ordained a priest. Of Cardinal Cullen I dare to say before this venerable assembly, with the knowledge I possess as his successor, that no writer has done adequate justice to his character or stature. To his cultured appreciation of Newman's work, we owe the deliberate choice of Newman, as Founder and first Rector of the Catholic University. Silent, magnanimous, farseeing, Cardinal Cullen would seem to be as heedless of self-justification after death, as he was intrepid in administration during life. Not his the multitude of letters and scrupulous autobiography that help a later age to re-construct the picture of the unspeaking dead. How strange in the plan of God that this prelate trained at the heart of Christianity should have chosen for guide of the higher education of our youth, as it emerged from persecution, one who had been reared in heresy, an alien, of the race that had striven to destroy in us the Faith of Jesus Christ. But within that Faith, " deep calleth unto deep." Not the mere patristic learning, nor the subtle eloquence, nor the personal charm of Newman, nor, indeed, his inheritance of classical and European culture, as the Oxford of his day haltingly endeavoured to interpret it, had captured Cullen's admiration. It is the candid acceptance of the Faith of Jesus Christ by this great and gentle scholar that explains the presence in our midst of Newman, Rector of the Catholic University of Ireland.

This is not the moment to detail the history of our vast debt to Cardinal Newman. Brief indeed his sojourn in Ireland, but his saintly presence lingers in his lovely church, in the rooms in which he spoke with such sensitive persuasiveness, most of all in the treasured heritage of his noble thoughts. That which he came to found and rule, his College, was destined to find a development other than he had dreamed. For sixty years, the flame that he had kindled and helped to fan was tended by the devotion of laymen, priests and Bishops. The patronage of the Civil powers disregarded the existence of the University. Parallel institutions with a counter-purpose reaped the rich benefit of influence, financial and political and always alien. But, all the while, the University of Pius IX and the Catholic

Hierarchy and Cardinal Newman persisted in the Faith of loyal Catholics. Today that University has issued in the Dublin College of the National University. A lurking hatred of the Faith of Jesus Christ refused to Catholics the juridical form that is their right, and must ever be their aim, in the foundation of a genuine universal school of learning. But " when they were dead that had sought the life of the Child," the Faith again had its silent triumph. Today we can salute in University College, Dublin, successor of the Newman College, an assembly of learned Professors, a throng of eager students, loyal in thought and living to the Faith of Jesus Christ.

I shall be pardoned if, in the limits set for me, I evoke the names of only two protagonists in the history of our struggle for Catholic and University education. But may I make amends by asking you today to recall with veneration the unnumbered multitude of the dead, our hidden saints and scholars. Their eyes have longed to see what we have seen In the dimness of persecution, in the loneliness of exile, in the agony of torture, they kept the vision of the Faith. For centuries they sojourned in the land of Egypt that we their children might be at length brought back by God into the land of Israel. On this day we are enabled to rejoice, but we shall remember that we are indeed the harvest of their sorrow.

Through all the dark centuries God has guided the uncertain counsels and faltering steps of our faithful people. On this day we humbly give thanks to God for the mercies of His providence. " How incomprehensible are His judgments and how unsearchable His ways !" Our human eyes may not pierce the mists of future centuries. Our knowledge, however, of the past must teach us that the sanctification of our people will always follow the pattern of the suffering life of Jesus Christ. But our Faith can firmly rest in the omnipotence of God, Who is our Father. Our hope can trust in Him Who has foreknown us and elected us to share the Faith of Jesus Christ. Our heart's affection can cling, despite our many failings, to God Who died for us and rose again that we may live to Him in Faith and at the last, in vision, " The God of all grace, Who hath

called us unto His eternal glory, in Christ Jesus, after we
shall have suffered a little, will Himself perfect us and
confirm us and establish us. To Him be glory for ever and
ever. Amen."

SPEECH OF HIS GRACE, THE ARCHBISHOP, AT CLOSE OF THE
CEREMONY OF THE PRESENTATION OF ADDRESSES

In concluding this session, I wish to express my gratitude
to His Excellency, the Apostolic Nuncio, the Chancellor
of the National University, and the President of University
College, Dublin, to whom we are indebted for the honour
of their addresses.

I thank, too, all those personages who, by the courtesy
of their attendance, have enhanced the dignity of an occasion
that is for us historic.

For the presence of Delegates from so many Universities
has rendered this Centenary a truly notable event. The
seats of learning, ancient and modern, that they worthily
represent, have eagerly seized the opportunity to greet
fraternally the Catholic University of Ireland and University
College, Dublin, which now inherits its position. We, who
seem to be of yesterday, have been generously welcomed
in the assembly of the sages.

A century is indeed a brief span in the life of Universities.
But may I invite you to see in the Catholic University of
Ireland of one hundred years ago, and now in University
College, Dublin, not so much a new institution and its
continuing successor, but rather the renascence and the
growth of an unbroken tradition of age-old scholarship in
this little land. Thus viewed, our institution holds venerable
place of honour in a commonwealth of learning that includes
the early Sophists, the monastic teachers, the medieval
philosophers, and the scholars of our time.

One hundred years ago, when Newman strove to assert
the balance between the culture of intelligence and the
acquisition of technical or professional knowledge, he
dedicated his University to Our Lady, Seat of Wisdom.
' he truth made known in Jesus Christ, the Eternal Wisdom,

born of the Virgin Mary, would guide our steps in the pursuit of learning, human and divine.

To-day, University College, Dublin, bears on its crest the lapidary motto, *Ad Astra*. The maxim, I take it, would express the strain to grasp and to assert in life the value of the spiritual. Such a motto might well appear too natural in the purely human purpose that it proclaims. But the ambiguity, if such existed, has long since been resolved in the supernatural Faith and life of Professors and of students. Thus the aim of either College has, in fact, remained unchanged.

For that reason, I am enabled, as Rector of the Catholic University of Ireland, to return the greetings of the Delegates in the spirit of the Founder and first Rector, Cardinal Newman. *Cor ad cor loquitur*, heart speaketh to heart, was his chosen motto. Let, then, the heart of the Catholic people, whom I represent, speak to you in the genuine accents of the Faith, and, wishing grace to all men without exception, pray that God may guide you, by the intercession of Our Lady, in all the varied paths of scholarship, to the attainment of the Truth, which is Himself.

Chapter III

THE INFLUENCE OF EUROPE ON AUSTRALIA

SYMPOSIUM IN THE GREAT HALL, UNIVERSITY
OF SYDNEY, 20TH APRIL, 1953

I owe it to the gracious kindness of his Eminence of Sydney
and to the Authorities of the University of Sydney that I
have the privilege of addressing this very distinguished
audience in your University.

It is with a sense of deep appreciation that I wish to
express my gratitude for the honour that is thus done to the
Irish Hierarchy and to Ireland.

The invitation to speak on the influences that Europe has
exercised on Australia offers one a vast canvas. If I feel
obliged, in the very short time at my disposal, to set aside
the consideration of many relevant aspects of my subject—
economic and political—I feel that I shall be given a ready
indulgence. I trust that this learned audience will be satisfied,
if I confine myself to the attempt to sketch in outline
the philosophy of the chief cultural influences of Europe
on Australia. Being a stranger to your country, I must
approach the treatment with a conviction of my inability
to enumerate all the factors and to assess their comparative
value. At least I will endeavour not only to pass a just
judgment but also to speak with the understanding of
charity.

Australia produces in a stranger the feeling that he is
dealing not with a country, but with a continent. That
continent pulsates with the vigour of its relative youth.
The horizon of your opportunity seems to be illimitable,
the wealth of natural resources in your good earth still
unassessed. You have the capacity to absorb many more
millions of human beings.

Yet one cannot fail to note the marks on your country
of a very ancient culture. For the most part, the influence

that has moulded you has been European, chiefly English-speaking in origin.

There is first of all the Faith of your early settlers : the Protestant Faith of the rulers and the Catholic Faith, in most part, of the subjects. That historical fact seems to me to explain very much of your civilisation, for, at basis, culture is founded on religion and is expressed in education. Your culture and your education derive, then, from a double source.

May I be allowed to point out that the culture and education that have formed Europe, and in consequence, Australia, is, first of all, Catholic. It is the Graeco-Roman culture conserved by the Catholic Church and purified by vast numbers of unknown scholars. Boethius and St. Basil the Great, Cassiodorus and Martianus Capella are but eminent examples of a common education that began with the Sophists of the 5th century before Christ and was continued in the early Schools of Greek philosophy. The system was preserved through Rome of the Republic and the early Empire. It was renewed by such men as Boethius and passed to the Benedictine and Celtic Schools. The palace and cathedral schools slowly carried it forward through centuries that, by the misunderstanding of Renascence scholars, have been called the Dark Ages, until, in the seven Liberal Arts, it gave to Europe an unsurpassed instrument of Christian formation. In the mental and moral discipline of the Scholastic philosophers that tradition had, in unbroken fashion, moulded Europe into a civilised unit of social, juridical and religious culture. This is the Europe of the Cathedral and of St. Thomas Aquinas.

The Italian Renascence of classical learning is rightly regarded as a return to Graeco-Roman culture. Very soon, however, one finds, at the core of the movement, evidences of a philosophy that, in spirit and in fact, aimed at effecting a rupture with the authentic European development of that culture. For two centuries, Italy was the leader and teacher of civilised Europe, until she succumbed to the military power of Spain and ceded to France the hegemony of Culture. Despite the very many monuments of literature and art produced in those centuries, one notes an emphasis on language for the sake of rhetoric to the disregard of the content of the classical writers, especially of Cicero. One remarks, too, a grave decline in the pursuit of genuine philosophy, in the nominalism of Ockham, who more than any other single writer, broke up the synthesis of St. Thomas and of European culture. Man and Nature, each an end in itself, tend to become the aim of human investigation, not Man and Nature, as components of a universe, of which God is the ultimate explanation.

The disruption of the Renascence was sadly reinforced by the Religious Revolt of the sixteenth century. Henceforth, European culture (and this, I think, is a point of cardinal importance for the understanding of your culture) divides itself into two streams of parallel importance. They flow strongly still through our contemporary world of Europe. On the one side, there is the culture that stems off from the Protestant revolution. One is not always too conscious of the division, because, I think, at the head of the current stands for English-speaking students one figure, who unites in himself the old perfection of the Greek dramatists and the moral outlook of Catholic, mediaeval Europe. Shakespeare, perhaps more than any other writer, conceals the break in European culture and unites the English-speaking world with an age with which it has largely lost conscious contact. The logic, however, of human thought, gradually and of necessity, found its proper outcome. The discoveries of the physical sciences and of mathematics, made possible, be it noted, by the scientific method of the Scholastics, could not offset the strong trend towards a mistrust of human reason and even a disrespect for human will. The angelism of Descartes was succeeded by the rationalism of the French philosophers, only to be followed, in turn, by the sensism of Hobbes and Locke, Berkeley and Hume, and lastly by the materialism that lost the true concept not only of God, but of man and of Nature, for so long the chosen objects of philosophical investigation. And to understand the line of descent from Ockham, it must be remembered that Descartes and Locke were strongly nominalist. Descartes and Spinoza, Kant and Hegel are names of very great intelligence. They are equally figures of solitary grandeur who speak and write as if the previous conquests of the centuries were of nothing worth. And the fruit of their thinking has been, in the social and juridical world, tyranny and revolution. For Marx, the disciple of Hegel and Feuerbach, there is, at the heart of human things, an innate contradiction. That contradiction must be solved by man evolving towards an earthly paradise that will be found in the conquest of the universe by internecine revolution. As a result, there are very many persons in Europe today who believe that they are moving somehow towards a goal of indefinite human progress. They cannot tell you how they are developing, nor even whither they are travelling. For all their literary and technical perfection, they have surely succeeded in making for themselves a Dark Age of human culture. There are equally very many others whose happiness consists in the effort to wipe out their fellow-men so that, by means of class-revolution, the survivors may enter a heaven of material power and prosperity.

The Rationalists and Liberals and Materialists who have their proximate origin in the Italian Renascence and the Religious Revolution of the 16th century, have produced similar fruit in other orders of human life.

In aesthetics, we have lived to see in Europe the rise of dadaist, cubist and surrealist schools of painting and sculpture. Let us allow at once that Picasso can draw with a purity of line that rivals the perfection of the old Greek vases. Let us admit the sincerity of these artists, their desire to express again the simplicity that they claim is to be found in Nature. Yet, it is surely not necessary to return to the bib and pinafore stage of life to show that we desire to follow a cult of child-like naturalness. One cannot thus recapture the golden simplicity of Giotto and Fra Angelico. The modern artists have given themselves for aim not to portray Nature as it is in itself and as it is seen by all men. They desire to body forth the chaos of the very universe that the nominalist philosophy of recent centuries has created. They have, we must conclude, lost the very purpose of art ; the portrayal of being as it is beautiful. They have missed the intelligible and the universal as it reflects the uncreated beauty of God.

In the order of the drama, we have reached through

Kant and Nietzsche the existentialism of Sartre. At least, one may say, the existentialists are concerned with being rather than with mere matter. But Descartes and Kant had given to the mind as object of study its own states, thus making it impossible to grasp the reality of the universe. Existentialism now takes its revenge by teaching that one can reach the reality that is incapable of being understood by living in that reality. It is a concept of being that destroys itself by its innate contradiction and its rejection of valid human reasoning. It is a philosophy of nihilism and, in consequence, of despair.

In the order of pedagogy, the last few centuries have tended to set themselves the merely psychological task of training the human subject. The normative sciences of ethics and theology have been gradually set aside in education in favour of a psychology that is less and less rational and more exclusively experimental. The psyche, regarded as a function of matter or a condition of consciousness, has given us, in analysis, the so-called new knowledge of the depths of human instinct and motivation. And, infallibly, the strong instinct of sex has taken a paramount place in the study of the human animal. Fear, in its aggressive or its shrinking aspects, is now striving for prime consideration in the field of depth-psychology. Yet man as he is, animal and spirit, by a strange but inevitable logic, contrary to the data and requisites of strict science, remains unstudied by very many modern psychologists.

In the curricula of schools and universities, the philosophers have, with varying emphasis, turned to the utilitarianism of the early London University and the philology of the German scholars. Languages, as languages, apart from their value as literature, have been made the basis of a gentleman's, that is, a cultured person's education. To that barrenness has succeeded the modern cult of history. History, as it is now understood, is an attempt, and to that extent a praiseworthy attempt, to return to something more like the older humanism. Too often it is, in the French sense, *la petite histoire*, or else a chronicling of events and character. History, in itself, is a science properly so-called only in so far as it uses scientific method and bases itself on allied sciences. History, as the record of human trends or character, itself requires the aid of many sciences to explain the data that it has for its proper purpose to accumulate. History, in the modern sense, is incapable of filling the intellectual soul of man when it is divorced from a philosophy that can truly interpret events and character.

We remark, too, on all sides, an inclination to develop strongly the study of mathematics and the physical sciences. Technical, mechanical progress can in part explain this necessity felt by modern universities. A reaction is seen in the work of Hutchinson, who has given such a stern swing towards the humanities in Chicago. But the humanities are not of themselves sufficient to satisfy the intellect : much less are mathematics and the physical sciences, by the admission of very honest masters and pupils. Each science is, doubtless, queen in her own domain and her conquests must receive full reverence. But the moderns have not yet understood that they have lost, not only the humanism that would have given food to the intellect, but also the cosmology that would have integrated their sciences into the unity of a complete philosophy.

Such, in briefest outline, are some of the European trends that have their proximate origin in the recent centuries. But there is, as I have already suggested, another vast current of European and Catholic culture that sweeps unbroken through the same centuries. The Italian Renascence had stimulated interest in education ; it had not created that interest. The monastic schools, the Cathedral schools, the feudal castle schools, the parochial schools and the colleges of the Friars within the universities, testify to a well-established cultural system created and preserved by the Church. And be it noted that these schools were genuinely and remarkably democratic. The effect of the Protestant revolt, particularly in Germany, was to destroy the school-foundations of the Church and, in increasing measure, to call for State intervention both in the establishment of schools and the ordering of curricula. Prussia may be thanked for the first, the exemplar system of State schools. France followed suit, but two hundred years later. England copied Germany and France much later still. The Prussians had

held that the school existed to teach religion—the Protestant
religion—and in this aim were faithfully copied by England.
Republican France, when it broke with the Church, under
the influence of the iniquitous Declaration of the Rights of
Man, with extreme violence of logic decreed that religion
had no part at all in education. In varying degrees, Europe
still undergoes the influence of these governmental trends.
The measure of excessive State intervention or the measure
of respect for religion in school-systems is to be explained,
at any given period, by the current swing of the contemporary
philosophy from Rationalism to Materialism and to academic
liberalism.

The European and Catholic culture, to which I have
referred, has maintained a firm existence, side by side with the
disintegrating culture that is now ending logically in chaos.
Certain names stand out in history as the standard-bearers—
indeed, the saviours, of the culture that links us up with all
the past. I shall not be misunderstood if, in the time allotted
me, I choose but a few of those glorious names. The Jesuits
have done for recent centuries what the Benedictines had
achieved from the days of St. Benedict and Alcuin to the
age of St. Louis IX of France. To associate them with a mere
Ratio Studiorum is to minimise gravely their undaunted
mastery of every branch of human learning, and their
incredible success in founding schools for every type of
pupil. In that vast array of teachers, we are indebted not
only to the organising foresight of a Spanish founder, but
to the rich variety of priest-teachers who represent the
Catholic culture of every country in Europe.

With another name, that of St. Jean Baptiste de la Salle,
we declare our very great and often unsuspected debt to
France, the nation that has been the norm of European
culture. In the days of St. Louis IX, France had shed over
Europe the radiance of her intellectual conquests. To the
intellect of the saintly Jean Baptiste de la Salle, not Europe
only, but the whole civilised world owes very much of what
is now accepted as commonplace in primary and secondary
education. The Brothers of the Christian Schools have
become the symbol of the many teaching Congregations
that owe their inspiration to this educational genius, who

was at once a conservative traditionalist and an unexampled pioneer.

To France again we owe St. Madeleine Sophie Barat, foundress of the *Dames du Sacré Coeur*. Let her single name stand for the many brave and holy women who answered the Revolution by founding in secret schools for both poor and rich. Their work now openly flourishes in the five continents of the world. St. Madeleine Sophie was herself trained in the best Catholic and classical tradition. She is but one of a long line : Paula, St. Lioba, St. Mechtilde, Blessed Alix Le Clerc, St. Angela Merici, Madame Acarie and Madame de Maintenon. Her " Plan of Studies " is an exemplar of the Catholic education that, using to the full the mother tongue as well as Latin, aims at a balance of scholarship and graciousness. Most significant, I venture to think, of her ideas is her insistence on the need for women of a solid grounding in the elements of philosophy.

There is another name which I have learned is deeply reverenced in Australia. John Henry Newman strove manfully, just one century ago, to maintain the humanism of European culture as it still existed in the magnificent classical tradition of his Oxford. The enemy that he opposed was the utilitarian and technical learning of the new London University. Newman aimed also at the restoration of the cultural position of the old University by the revival of the collegiate system of mediaeval Catholic colleges, in which students could be tutored in knowledge and disciplined in morals. By his writings Newman has succeeded in drawing attention to aspects of our culture that had been neglected in England and elsewhere for centuries.

There is yet another influence on which I may be permitted to dwell for a moment : I mean the Irish influence. Our monks assisted the Continent of Europe to know the Faith ; they also helped to preserve the Graeco-Roman culture. At no too distant date from our own lives, the hedge-schools of Ireland fostered the very same culture in the students who later passed to the schools and universities of Europe. These were the men, priests and brothers, and layfolk, who transmitted to your land our unbroken tradition of European Catholic culture. Do they think of it, I wonder, the sisters in the lonely bush-schools, the brothers in the city or the country schools ? They are each a link in the unending chain that reaches back, through all the ages, dark or bright, to the Colleges of the mediaeval University, to the monastic and guild schools, even to the schools of ancient Greece and Rome.

From Ireland, too, has come to you the most remarkable modern instrument of the apostolate, both individual and social. The Legion of Mary, by its spiritual basis, its personal approach, its firm and flexible organisation, its constancy of aim, has succeeded in carrying the gentleness and strength of the charity of Christ into every country of the world.

Lastly, may I mention the paramount influence of the Dominicans. At times it is so hidden that it reminds me of the man in Homer who, in an upland farm, jealously guards in the ashes the living seed of flame. The Friars Preachers have throughout the centuries most faithfully kept and developed the philosophy of St. Thomas. Aquinas, a son of Italy and France, stands at the head of the double current that I have endeavoured to explain. His merit is not merely, as one so often hears, that he christianised Aristotle. His achievement is much more fundamental in relation to the ages that should succeed : he made a synthesis of the whole order of the universe, natural and supernatural. It is as if God in His providence had given us a teacher who, in later ages, would unfold from his almost limitless treasure-house, the old and new in knowledge, human and divine.

If you should ask me wherein lies the answer to the perplexity of mind and disarray of conduct that Europe now betrays to you in its inner life, I should reply at once : a return to the Faith that moulded Europe and to the perennial philosophy of St. Thomas that links us with our cultural origins. Let it not be thought that such an answer is a flight of fancy. I should be surprised if I did not learn that, in your continent, as in that continent which Australia in so many ways resembles, North America, one did not find the same thirst for lasting truth. In a young country where the naturalism of Dewey and the activism of Blondel could rightly be expected to find immediate allegiance, one finds on the contrary, the warmest welcome being given to the philosophy of St. Thomas. And in University College, Dublin, heir to the Catholic University of Newman, not only students of the Faculty of Arts, but also and especially students of the Faculties of Engineering and Architecture, Law and Medicine are more and more urgently asking for the assistance of courses in Scholastic Philosophy.

That movement of the spirit is no accident. One sees the guidance of the Church in the last will of Pope Nicholas V, who determined to seize and utilise the learning of the Renascence. One sees the same guidance in the Social Encyclicals of Leo XIII, who revived the study of Scholastic Philosophy. May I, with respect, remind my audience of the indwelling in the Church of God the Holy Ghost, by Whose vivifying action the grace of the Redemption ultimately triumphs. To His creating spirit is due the uprise and continuance of the mighty forces that I have been privileged to describe in part today. He guides, He sanctifies. And may I, in the charity of our common Faith, express the prayer that, by the unfailing advocacy of Our Blessed Lady, Seat of Wisdom, this land of Australia, so young in vigour, so old in the heritage of its civilisation, may be so guided by God the Holy Ghost, in its proper path of material and spiritual development, that we in Europe, looking towards the South, may see mirrored for us once more the radiance and beauty of the culture of the Church.

Chapter IV

ADDRESS OF WELCOME TO THE DELEGATES AT THE OPENING SESSION OF THE SIXTH INTERNATIONAL CONGRESS OF CATHOLIC DOCTORS*

I have the privilege, as Patron of this Congress, to welcome to this City and Capital the Delegates who have graciously accepted our invitation to meet in Dublin.

We, in Ireland, are indeed conscious of the honour and advantage that we shall enjoy by the deliberations of the Congress.

We trust that our visitors, in the unity of our Faith and the kindly hospitality of our people, will feel the warmth of the welcome that is proper to the household of the Church.

The union of so many brilliant minds in the effort to discover and set forth the truth, under the guidance of God the Holy Ghost, must greatly help to free us from the strain of problems that vex our times. " The Truth shall make you free," because, being genuine scientists, you will acknowledge that you do not create, but rather discover and submit to Truth : you will admit that God is the Author of our nature and Sovereign Master of the science and the art that should collaborate with the Creator in the healing of mankind.

May I be allowed to say that your profession has great need in every country to close its ranks in face of theories and practices that are but a cancellation of human nature. In the history of Europe, the University and the Judiciary, by dint of hard combat, have achieved a lawful independence in the body politic. Only in recent times has your profession encountered the open or subtle violence that would destroy the liberty of free men to fulfil the personal and social responsibility of their vocation.

* July, 1954.

For us in Ireland—a land so poor in natural resources, so tiny in extent but, under God, so rich in the intelligence of the Faith—it would be a vast consolation if this International Congress held in Dublin, under the protecting intercession of Our Lady, Health of the Sick, should so strengthen your convictions and arm your energies that, above every other aim, you would henceforth maintain an unflinching personal responsibility to God, in the pursuit of your noble science and most human art.

Chapter V

ADDRESS TO THE INTERNATIONAL CONGRESS OF THE CINEMA, JULY 1955

I am happy to welcome the delegates of this International Catholic Cinema Congress to this City.

We rightly look to your Congress for instruction and support on the question of the moral classification of films. And by moral I mean doctrinal classification, for morality is based on the doctrine that is the deposit of Faith, entrusted by her Divine Founder to the Church.

It is a grim fact of modern life that films must be subjected to a moral classification, for the simple reason that even the notion of an absolute moral law of nature is dishonoured by some of the fractional commercial group that manufactures films.

One can understand that scenario writers have never undergone the discipline of being taught the theory of dramatic structure and the differences between the main types of literature. In consequence, films are but too often a massing of numbers, a display of costumes, and an unrelated juxtaposition of incidents. One misses the strong subordination of many actors to one or two major characters, the choice of action that, in its deliberateness, reveals the inner springs of character, the selection of relevant incidents that bear forward the stream of interest that we call plot. One could pardon the omission of these vital elements, for the reason that the manufacturers have been denied the culture of a balanced education. One may never pardon the base theme and the unhealthy emotionalism that have issue in an immoral film. It is to be expected from all men that the natural law imprinted on their being by God should guide them to a respect for the mind and emotions and actions of other men. No perfection of technique, no facile explanation of art for art's sake, can excuse the human activity of film making from subjection to the divine law of morality.

We note a tendency to abandon to the State the responsibility for classifying films. By reason of its duty to pursue the common good, the public authority has the right and the duty to take cognisance of the moral character of the cinema, for the common good is not, as so many seem to think, a merely economic good. The common good is the spiritual good calling for the creation and the preservation of all those circumstances that make it possible for men to live a good life.

Subsidiary groups have the right and the duty to assist the civil authority in maintaining public morality. In fact it is only with the aid of such men of good will that the State can properly fulfil its function of safeguarding the common good.

In this little country, happily we have a system of State censorship that, in general, satisfies the demands of the common good. But fortunately we have also the National Film Institute, a voluntary body that by its rightness of outlook and its courage, has already in a few years made a firm contribution to solving the problems of the modern cinema in a positive manner.

It is well, I think, to point out to the foreign delegates that in this Catholic country we do not entertain two moralities, one for aesthetics and one for living. Because we have retained, at great cost, a system of Catholic voluntary education, that is fully respected by the State, we are enabled to hold firm to the traditional concepts of natural law and divine law. Therefore you must expect to find here a definite outlook that derives from the acceptance of the Catholic Faith. We have scant respect for the system that calls itself liberal, though, in fact, it is the intolerance that will allow every liberty except that of choosing objective truth.

Hence, if your deliberations are to assist us, you must respect our outlook. We think that in the judgment of films one must purge one's soul of the decadence caused by the writing of novelists called Catholic, however loud be the world wide noise of undiscriminating praise. We willingly allow every just freedom to differ in judgments that concern mere aesthetics, but we hold to the norms of a conduct that is none other than the moral law : the law of nature and the law of God, as they are interpreted by the Catholic Church. Only to the one authority of the Catholic Church has her Divine Founder guaranteed the gift of infallible certainty in proclaiming and interpreting the moral law. It is our task in this Congress humbly to ascertain the findings of that law, and with courage to apply those findings to the modern products of the cinema.

On the crest of our National Film Institute one reads the motto : " In lumine tuo, videbimus lumen "—" In Thy light we shall see light." And the crest itself bears the image of Mary, the Mother of God, showing Her Divine Son to the world of men. May She obtain for us in the deliberations of this Congress the grace to understand with clearness the teaching of the Church, and the greater grace firmly to use that teaching to solve the problems of the modern cinema.

Chapter VI

CLOSING SERMON OF EUCHARISTIC CONGRESS
ST. MARY'S CATHEDRAL, SYDNEY.*

" THEN He opened their understanding, that they might understand the Scriptures. And He said to them : Thus it is written and thus it behoved Christ to suffer and to rise again from the dead, the third day ; and that penance and remission of sins should be preached in His name, unto all nations, beginning at Jerusalem. And you are witnesses of these things. And I send the promise of My Father upon you. " (St. Luke, XXIV, 45–49).

In the days that followed the Resurrection of our Divine Redeemer, we are made aware of a great contrast in the attitude of the Apostles. To terror and cowardice, peace and courage have succeeded. There is no change in the Risen Jesus. We note the same majestic patience, the same gentleness of instruction, in particular, the same insistence on the doctrine that He had, so often and so vainly, set forth, even to His chosen Apostles and disciples. Shortly before His death, He had openly made known the sorrow and the outrage of His Passion. " Lay up in your hearts these words, for it shall come to pass that the Son of Man shall be delivered into the hands of men." The Apostles had not only failed to understand, but St. Peter had rejected the idea that His Master could be betrayed and crucified. Again, immediately before the Agony in the Garden, our Divine Saviour had taken His farewell of the Apostles in a long discourse, that, in the retrospect, must have been for them a heartbreaking memory, but that, at the moment of His speaking, was veiled in the darkest mystery. A few moments later, at the approach of danger, they all had fled. And God made Man was left to tread the wine-press of His Passion alone.

* 19th April, 1953.

228

The first words spoken by the Risen Jesus after the Resurrection were a salute of peace : " Peace be to you." And at once He set Himself to convince the Apostles that truly He was risen from the dead. Then He opened the eyes of their soul that they might understand the mystery of His Passion and Death. To the days and nights of agonising fear now follows the old security that His presence had always given in the years of their company with Him. The night-mare of failure had passed : He was with them again. But that which had seemed a failure to men must be understood to be a triumph of God. Only He could open their very human minds, that they might understand the Scriptures concerning the Divine Redeemer and His work. " And He said to them : ' Thus it is written and thus it behoved Christ to suffer and to rise again from the dead the third day.' " Then at length they remembered that it had been written of the Messias : " Behold I come. In the head of the book it is written of Me that I should do Thy will, O God." They remembered too that the Messias had said of Himself : " Therefore doth the Father love Me, because I lay down My life ... This commandment have I received of My Father." Now they could understand the decree of God concerning our salvation : the will of God required that Jesus Christ should die for our redemption. And in delivering Himself up to the Justice of God in death, Jesus Christ had satisfied for the sins of men.

Now too they could understand that, in the decree of God, the work of the Redemption was to be continued by them, the Apostles : the world, beginning with Jerusalem, should be converted by the penance that would obtain remission of sin. In the name of Jesus alone should penance be preached. In the name of Jesus alone should sin be forgiven. " And that penance and remission of sin should be preached in His name, unto all nations, beginning with Jerusalem." The prophecy of the *Benedictus* and the *Nunc Dimittis* are at last made clear in these final words of Jesus Christ.

" And you are witnesses of these things." For their task, Our Divine Redeemer had chosen and formed His Apostles. Now He sends them to bear witness to the ful-filment of all that had been written of Him and of His work. To all nations they will announce that Jesus Christ is God made Man, the Saviour of the world.

"And I send the promise of My Father upon you." To aid them in their task of bearing witness to Himself, Jesus Christ assures them that He will send the Holy Ghost, Whom the Father has promised to give. That gift will transform them. Even now, we read, although their Master was departing in the Ascension, they returned to the hostile Jerusalem, from which their preaching should begin, " with great joy." After the Holy Ghost had come upon them, they were clothed with power from on high. Their dullness gives place to the clear understanding of the revelation they had been given. Their fear yields to a radiant courage that inspires them to suffer and to preach in face of persecution, even to accept for His name's sake, the martyrdom of the Master's death.

"Ought not Christ to have suffered these things and so to enter into His glory ? " My brethren, " the servant is not greater than his lord ; neither is the apostle greater than He that sent him." We shall not, therefore, wonder that the path of the Christian life for individuals and for peoples should resemble closely the way of our Divine Redeemer : we too must suffer to enter into our glory. " Christ has suffered for us," says St. Peter, " leaving you an example that you should walk in His footsteps." Your land and mine have known great sorrow for the sake of Jesus Christ. Like Him you have been spied upon and driven into hiding. You have been forbidden to worship God as God Himself requires that He be worshipped. The Holy Sacrifice has been banned. Instruction in the Faith of Jesus Christ has been made difficult for your children. You have been set apart and looked upon with a suspicion that is hatred. And they who so acted knew not that they were renewing in the disciples the Passion of the Master.

To those days of grief has succeeded a period of great joy. Your vine has been purged by God the Husbandman that it might bring forth great fruit. In the darkness of the Passion, you have received the light to understand the Cross. And through the Cross, your Church has risen to its resurrection, serene, majestic and triumphant.

As representative of the Irish Hierarchy and of the Ireland to which you look with eyes of loving gratitude today I am privileged to bring a message of affectionate congratulations to this Church, which our faithful priests and people, in pain of body and sorrow of heart, have so largely helped to found.

Today your lovely land is filled with churches in which the Real Presence finds Its home. In the remotest corners of your Continent, Catholic Schools—core of the Faith— not only maintain the message of God's revelation but also foster the age-old culture of the Church. The works of mercy have inspired the building of havens of refuge for every shape of human suffering. The call of the counsels of perfection has peopled your territory with houses of Religious. On all sides one hears the sacred name of Mary invoked in Church and School and Hospital. And, chief glory of the grace of the Blessed Eucharist, hundreds of thousands in your land today are living habitually in the grace of God.

For the past week your eyes have seen what many have desired to see and have not seen : the triumph of the open adoration of the Sacred Host. Today, my brethren, our thoughts go back, in poignant reverence, to the poor man who guarded the Blessed Sacrament through the months that must have seemed to him an age until a priest should come to celebrate again the Mass, or to that other Irishman who, longing for the Mass, would climb the hill each Sunday and look in prayer towards the distant place where the Holy Sacrifice was being offered. May we not believe that in this congregation, presided over by His Eminence of Sydney, the Cardinal Legate, and graced by the presence of two other Cardinals, of many Archbishops and Bishops, Priests, Religious and faithful lay-folk, there is present another host of silent worshippers : the countless number of your saintly forebears, the assembly of the Priests and Prelates who have shepherded your people to the triumph of this hour.

"And you are witnesses of these things." Like the Apostles who descended from Mount Olivet after the departure of their Master in the Ascension, you will return to your houses, "with great joy." A certain sorrow creeps into the accents of our rejoicing on this final day, when His presence is withdrawn. But your mind has been opened to the grace of Faith. You have received the Promise of the Father in the outpouring of the graces of this Congress. Your hearts will be glad because in this land and City, which once knew the darkness and misery of the Passion, Jesus Christ has triumphed, to the eyes of Faith, in the hidden glory of the Blessed Eucharist.

Let us not forget, particularly in this hour, the real motive of our Divine Redeemer in instituting the Blessed Eucharist : " Do this in commemoration of Me." The Blessed Eucharist was to be a memorial of Jesus Christ, in that it should represent His death for us. " As often as you shall do this, you shall show forth the death of the Lord." " The Son of God," exclaims the Apostle, " loved me and delivered Himself for me." To be the Victim of God's Justice, to immolate Himself for the sins of men was the single purpose of the life and death of Jesus Christ, our Divine Redeemer.

" And you are witnesses of these things." In virtue of your Baptism and your Confirmation, in virtue of the Precious Blood which has cleansed you from your sins, in virtue of the Body of Jesus Christ received so often as the pledge of a glorious resurrection, like the Apostles, you are each the witness of the death and resurrection of Jesus Christ. " Thus it is written and thus it behoved Christ to suffer and to rise again from the dead." This, then, is the grace of the Eucharistic Congress : that in your life of sacrifice you witness faithfully to the sacrifice of Jesus Christ.

" If any man will come after Me, let him take up his cross daily and follow Me." It is the decree of God that we cannot reach the fulness of the grace of Christ, unless we become like to the image of the Crucified. " The servant is not greater than his lord." In the pain of penance we must follow the Man of Sorrows, for we have sinned and it is our sins that He has borne in His body on the Cross. In the measure in which we shall have crucified the flesh and its lusts, we shall merit the serenity of His resurrection from the dead. To our Divine Lord alone we owe the description of our daily life as a carrying of the cross. But the same Lord has said : " Come to Me all you who labour and are burdened and I will refresh you."

And what refreshment He has given us ! " Lord, to whom shall we go," asked the Apostle, " for Thou hast the words of eternal life." He has given us more than the words of eternal life. He Who is " the Resurrection and the Life " has given us Himself in the Blessed Eucharist to be our life. This is that grace of transformation into Christ of which the Apostle speaks : " And Christ died for all, that they who live, may not live unto themselves, but unto Him, Who died for them and rose again."

By the unfailing intercession of Our Blessed Lady, Mediatrix of the grace of Christ, by the merits of your saintly forebears, who have preserved for you the grace of Faith, may God, in His gentle mercy, multiply upon your land, as a reward for your profound devotion to the Blessed Eucharist, the grace of sanctity among the Faithful and the Pastors, that, taking up your cross in daily life, " you may henceforth grow in Him, Who is the Head, even Christ, unto the measure of the age of the fulness of Christ."